JOSEPHINE BAKER'S CINEMATIC PRISM

JOSEPHINE BAKER'S
CINEMATIC PRISM

JOSEPHINE BAKER'S CINEMATIC PRISM

TERRI SIMONE FRANCIS

INDIANA UNIVERSITY PRESS

This book is a publication of

Indiana University Press
Office of Scholarly Publishing
Herman B Wells Library 350
1320 East 10th Street
Bloomington, Indiana 47405 USA

iupress.org

Manufactured in the United States of America

First printing 2021

Library of Congress Cataloging-in-Publication Data

Names: Francis, Terri Simone, author.
Title: Josephine Baker's cinematic prism / Terri Simone Francis.
Description: Bloomington : Indiana University Press, 2021. | Includes
   bibliographical references and index.
Identifiers: LCCN 2020035857 (print) | LCCN 2020035858 (ebook) | ISBN
   9780253356536 (hardback) | ISBN 9780253223388 (paperback) | ISBN
   9780253017598 (ebook)
Subjects: LCSH: Baker, Josephine, 1906-1975—Criticism and interpretation. |
   African American women dancers—France. | African American motion
   picture actors and actresses—France. | African Americans in motion
   pictures—France | African American entertainers—France.
Classification: LCC GV1785.B3 F73 2021 (print) | LCC GV1785.B3 (ebook) |
   DDC 792.8092 [B]—dc23
LC record available at https://lccn.loc.gov/2020035857
LC ebook record available at https://lccn.loc.gov/2020035858

For my parents

CONTENTS

ACKNOWLEDGMENTS

I WOULD SAY IT TOOK a village to publish this book, but the writing and rewriting process has taken a city—many cities of readers, listeners, and institutions. First, I thank my present employer, the Media School at Indiana University Bloomington, for research funds and my cinema and media studies colleagues and students for their support in completing this book. My years in the Department of African American Studies and the Film and Media Studies Program at Yale University were transformative; every autumn I think fondly of the changing leaves on the trees along Wall Street. I am particularly grateful to Katie Trumpener and Glenda Gilmore, who provided excellent feedback, which I tried to follow.

As a graduate student at the University of Chicago, my research was supported by the Marcia Tillotson Travel Award, the Georges Lurcy Dissertation Research Fellowship for Study in France, the François Furet Travel Grant, a Humanities Division Overseas Travel Grant, and the Rosenthal Dissertation-Year Fellowship.

Priceless assistance in accessing rare primary sources was provided by the staff at the Beinecke Rare Book and Manuscript Library, at the Schomburg Center for Research in Black Culture at the New York Public Library, at La Bibliothèque nationale, and at the Black Film Center/Archive at Indiana University. I am especially grateful to Eric Lange and Sylvie Georgianne of Lobster Films, Muriel Charpentier of Forum des Images, and Julia Gibbs at the Film Study Center at the University of Chicago for sharing their expertise and archival treasures with me at crucial turning points in my work.

I thank my mentors for their dedication and guidance, particularly Lauren Berlant, James Lastra, and Jacqueline Stewart. And I must acknowledge Kenneth Warren's advice in the formative stages of my graduate studies. To the members of the Department of English Association of Students of Color at the University of Chicago, especially my homegirl Yolanda Padilla, thank you for your fellowship and camaraderie.

When I think of the people who engaged my work or provided respite at various stages during a nomadic writing process, I picture the places where we talked, whether it was on a panel, out for a walk, or over coffee: Deb Willis at the Sorbonne; Allyson Field and TreaAndrea Russworm in Ghent; Manthia Diawara in a café (probably) near the Luxembourg Gardens; Jacqueline Stewart in Hyde Park, Paris, Florence, and Soweto; the late Michel Fabre in Parc Montsouris; Ja'Tovia Gary in the Brooklyn Botanical Gardens; Christopher Harris in Chicago and Orlando; Elizabeth Alexander in Chicago and New Haven; and Numa Perrier in Bloomington and Memphis.

I am deeply grateful to the anonymous peer reviewers and the incredible staff at Indiana University Press who brought this manuscript to life.

Finally, I thought this book was finished when, in June 2019, I found myself at Middlebury College again, this time not for French language study but for a two-week workshop on scholarship in sound and image. Through our assignments, I created several video essays where I explore Baker's career; making my videos among the generative and brilliant community of video camp rekindled my faith in Josephine Baker, and I was once again able to delight in her paradoxes.

Glimpses of my initial efforts at formulating Josephine Baker's cinematic prism can be found in earlier publications:

"Josephine Baker's French African American Films." InMediaRes.com. August 28, 2014.

"Sighting the 'Real' Josephine Baker: Methods and Issues of Black Star Studies." In *Black Venus 2010: They Called Her "Hottentot,"* edited by Deborah Willis, 199–209. Philadelphia: Temple University Press, 2011.

"The Audacious Josephine Baker: Stardom, Cinema, and Paris." In *Black Europe and the African Diaspora*, edited by Darlene Clarke Hine, Trica Keaton, and Steven Small, 238–59. Champaign: University of Illinois Press, 2009.

"What Does Beyoncé See in Josephine Baker? A Brief Film History of Sampling La Diva, La Bakaire." In "Josephine Baker: A Century in the Spotlight," edited by Kaiama L. Glover, special issue, *Scholar and Feminist Online* 6, nos. 1–2 (Fall 2007–Spring 2008). http://sfonline .barnard.edu/baker/francis_01.htm.

"Embodied Fictions, Melancholy Migrations: Josephine Baker's Cinematic Celebrity." *Modern Fiction Studies* 51, no. 4 (2005): 824–45.

JOSEPHINE BAKER'S CINEMATIC PRISM

JOSEPHINE BAKER'S
CINEMATIC PRISM

PROLOGUE

What Might Be Josephine Baker's Film History

AT FIRST, ACTOR LYNN WHITFIELD was reluctant about the partial nudity required to play the role of Josephine Baker in the 1991 HBO historical drama *The Josephine Baker Story*.[1] She said, "When we shot it I thought 'OMG! I'm from Louisiana and I'm going to be topless and half naked. I hope my parents don't judge me.' And then in between takes I didn't want to put my robe on. It felt so good to be living through her experience. She wasn't like in the strip club! She was more like Eve, she didn't even know she was naked . . . like a beautiful tease. At the time she had to find the beauty."[2] Whitfield, a winner of multiple NAACP Image Awards, reflected further on what it meant for her to embody Baker: "I think people think of me as the older Josephine because she was seemingly so touching near the end of the movie. I wish they would remember more of the banana dance."[3] For Black women, public visibility, especially with sexual references, carries risk with harsh consequences, and this led Whitfield to approach playing Baker with understandable caution.

Was Baker herself initially hesitant to adapt to the Parisians' ease with performing bare-breasted in music hall performances? Jean-Claude Baker, biographer (and restauranteur who created Chez Josephine in homage to the Parisian sensation), quotes Jacques Charles, one of the producers of *La revue nègre*, as saying, "I had already noticed her beautiful body, but to be honest, Josephine rejected my suggestion that she dance almost nude." Yet this story is contradicted on the same page by fellow dancer Lydia Jones, who said of Josephine, "You know, she was always naked at the hotel, laughing and posing in front of the mirrors."[4] Such divergent accounts speak to the complexity of Baker's story.

As Whitfield reflected on her experiences starring as Baker, she grappled with how her dancing expressed Baker's (and her own) unique talent and

1

exuberance, while it was, at the same time, haunted by what cultural critic bell hooks, in her classic essay "Selling Hot Pussy," termed "the white European fascination with the bodies of black people, particularly black female bodies."[5] Whitfield's concern about what her parents might think perhaps suggests her fear of the broad social consequences of broaching "the traditional black pornographic imagination" for Black women.[6] However, poet and essayist Audre Lorde, in her conception of "the erotic as power," offers a spiritual, even liberating, view of nudity and, by association, sexualized representation generally. Lorde writes, "When I speak of the erotic, ... I speak of it as an assertion of the lifeforce of women; of that creative energy empowered, the knowledge and use of which we are now reclaiming in our language, our history, our dancing, our work, our lives."[7] Lorde goes on to unpack the ways that women's sexuality has been co-opted by the pornographic, which, in her formulation, is the opposite of the erotic. From different vantage points, then, Lorde and hooks both grapple with the long-standing concern that representations of sexuality are themselves oppressive tools, particularly with regard to Black women's images.

Professor of feminist studies Mireille Miller-Young delves into the tension Black women sex workers experience between their agency and the derisive commentary and unfair practices they face within the porn industry, using her frameworks of "illicit eroticism" and the "illicit erotic economy."[8] In her research, Miller-Young implicitly challenges the protective notions of respectable Black womanhood articulated by hooks (and others) as she shines empowering light on the persistence of women's subjectivity under hostile conditions. The so-called strip club Whitfield referred to above can, in Miller-Young's view, at times, serve women "in their attempts at survival, mobility, self-authorship, and self-care."[9] The following question arises: "Where are black women workers *not* exploited by advanced capitalism?"[10] What Whitfield fears when she evokes her parents' disapproval is the social death that can come in the form of banishment, scorn, or ridicule as well as the particular misogynistic name-calling that occurs when one traverses the razor-like boundaries of what is considered normal and dignified behavior for Black women.

The process of writing about Baker brought me face-to-face with my own vulnerability within the academy, as my body and my work is linked to Baker's banana dancing and what others thought of that—or, more precisely, what they thought about me when they thought of that. I found myself immobilized under the weight of what theorist of Black feminism Patricia Hill Collins terms "controlling images" about Black women.[11] I did not want to be Jezebel, the beguiling and exotic other useful only as a representational face of diversity within the institution, nor the mammy consigned to the endless servitude of

Fig. P.1. A portrait of Josephine Baker.
Photo by Mondadori/Getty Images.

managing white feelings. Communications scholar Cerise L. Glenn explains
that in the workplace, "African American women learn that we will have to deal
with stereotypes formulated by members of dominant social groups."[12] And it
is these stereotypes that oppress us from the outside and repress us from within,
undermining the full expression of our ideas, feelings, and, ultimately, our intellectual authority, on the very matters in which we are experts—where we are
most powerful and, therefore, most threatening to the status quo.

Over time, I have realized that although Baker operated in a very different era and professional sphere than mine, I would have to claim, define, and
defend my own agency, as I believe she did, largely within my own quietude and
through insisting on driving the narrative of my own story. On my own, even

when in community, I would have to figure out how to see myself clearly, how to right myself with the "crooked room" of race and gender misrepresentations.[13]

Among the insidious effects of having been brought up in America is that, as sociologist and author Crystal Fleming put it, "like most people in the US, I was not socialized to take Black women's knowledge seriously—which of course means that I was not socialized to take my own knowledge seriously."[14] Reading her words, I gasped in recognition and had to nod in agreement. As Baker would unsettle Whitfield, so too did she disturb me as a young professional academic finding my way. But in our quietude together, Josephine and me, I decided to guide my research and writing with a simple but profound ethic: treat Baker with care and seriousness as a producer of knowledge rather than as merely the subject of my analysis. Scene by scene, gesture by gesture, I worked on providing the attention and context Baker's career deserves. Baker's own words, her actions, gestures, and presence, provided the direction for my work; her knowledge grounded my own.

I hear over and over again that Baker had to go to Paris. No, Baker *wanted* to go to Paris. There is a difference of agency and of self-visioning between the two. In a video apparently recorded October 3, 1950, and labeled "not for broadcast" but now uploaded to YouTube, reporter Jack Mangan interviews Baker as she is boarding the SS *Liberté*. After flattering her as "the toast of the continent," Mangan asks Baker what had prompted her to go "out on a limb" to Paris, France, all those years ago in 1925. Baker replies, "I thought by going to Paris—and then of course because everybody loves Paris and knows about it. It's the city of art. And I thought that I would probably get the possibility of doing something in my [inaudible; Mangan interrupts]."[15] Baker wanted to go. In her first coauthored memoir, published when she was just twenty years old, she writes, "Before meeting Mrs. [Caroline Dudley] Reagan, I already wanted to go to Europe."[16] About leaving St. Louis, Baker writes, succinctly, "I cut my hair. I left my family."[17] Baker's migration to Paris was an experiment, a venture "out on a limb" as that reporter put it. She took off on her own "directionless search for a free territory," not knowing how it would turn out.[18] Although she became the toast of Paris and, indeed, admired around the world, I imagine Baker as a young woman among the early twentieth-century Black American women of the 1920s, known and unknown, whom Saidiya Hartman lauds as "wayward" and "radical thinkers who tirelessly imagined other ways to live and never failed to consider how the world might be otherwise."[19] Baker was an adventuress and an artist who took major risks—and in doing so opened up possibilities for thinking through performance in film history, which I will explore in this book.

Baker's preparation to go on stage, or before the cameras, was thorough and meticulous, but she took big leaps of faith as well. Rather than avoiding the perils of racial-sexual representation, she danced in to them, laughing as she drifted between respectability and "waywardness"—in Hartman's usage of the word, a yearning, "the avid longing for a world not ruled by master, man or police . . . not the master's tools, but the ex-slave's fugitive gestures, her traveling shoes."[20] I look at Baker's career as wayward in this sense, with her few but sparkling exploratory films containing shadow and light but also embodying on the whole, gestures of her own "practice(s) of possibility" and her own "ongoing exploration of *what might be*."[21] I have hoped that my writing about her would feel like a duet, a collaboration between Baker and me; as an author of her film history, we frame one another, waywardly, faithfully, and tenderly while, naturally, retaining our pleasures in opacity.[22]

NOTES

1. Gibson, *Josephine Baker Story*.
2. Burke, "Lynn Whitfield Celebrates."
3. Ibid.
4. Jean-Claude Baker, *Josephine: The Hungry Heart*, 111.
5. hooks, "Selling Hot Pussy," 63.
6. Ibid.
7. Lorde, "Uses of the Erotic," 53, 55.
8. Miller-Young, "Putting Hypersexuality to Work," 224.
9. Ibid., 222.
10. Ibid., 226.
11. Collins, "Mammies, Matriarchs," 86.
12. Glenn, "Stepping In," 138.
13. Harris-Perry, *Sister Citizen*, 29.
14. Fleming, *How to Be Less Stupid about Race*, 55.
15. Jeffsabu [pseud.], "Ship's Reporter Interview: Josephine Baker," uploaded March 15, 2020, YouTube video, 4:24, https://www.youtube.com/watch?v=zKO1YLXqxTU.
16. Josephine Baker, *Les mémoires de Josephine Baker avec Marcel Sauvage*, 72.
17. Ibid., 61.
18. Hartman, *Wayward Lives, Beautiful Experiments*, 227.
19. Ibid., xv.
20. Hartman, *Wayward Lives, Beautiful Experiments*, 227.
21. Ibid.
22. Glissant, *L'intention poétique (Poetic Intention)*.

INTRODUCTION

Hey! Ha! Shimmy My Bananas!
Refracting Baker's Image

AT THE HEART OF AN American film historiography that might have been lies Josephine Baker's film history—one that includes Black directors, crew, writers, actors, and audiences as central to the vision of creating and thinking about what cinema is. Baker should have been recognized long ago as a film pioneer. She starred in *La sirène des tropiques* (Henri Étiévant, 1927 France; 1929 United States), *Zouzou* (Marc Allégret, 1934), *Princesse Tam-Tam* (Edmond T. Gréville, 1935), and *The French Way/Fausse alerte* (Jacques de Baroncelli, 1945). And she features in the short erotic fantasy film *Le pompier de Folies Bergère* (1928) and the promotional compilation film *Josephine Baker, Star of the Folies-Bergère and the Casino de Paris* (1926), which I will discuss in this chapter. More of Baker's work is collected in *La revue des revues* (1927; now accessible on DVD). Directed by Joe Francis, this collection features two scenes from her 1927 Folies Bergère works, "Plantation" and "Baker '27." Though Baker, an African American entertainer, lived in France and worked there exclusively with a white film company, white costars, white writers, and white directors, she holds monumental significance in African American cinema as the first truly global Black woman film star.

In the 1926 recording of her Folies Bergère performance of *la danse des bananes*, or the banana dance, Baker plays Fatou, a dancer dressed mainly in a skirt of bananas. She enters the mise-en-scène high above the music hall stage "through a dense electric twilight, walking backwards on hands and feet, legs and arms stiff, down a huge jungle tree."[1] Large, tropical-looking leaves resembling those of a banana tree, or its plant cousin, the bird of paradise, complete the framing. Cut to a scene that shows a tent on the stage. In a medium close-up shot, a white man wearing a pith helmet represents a colonialist figure and plantation boss.

Fig. I.1. Josephine Baker reading the newspaper seated at her office desk in her own bar. © Bettmann/CORBIS.

He is costumed in a white shirt and pants, and he lies on his side with his head propped up by one hand, in repose, watching the scene in which he is a central animating character unfold. Cut to a wide shot of the stage. Fatou, seen among the trees, suddenly whirls across the platform like a daydream banshee over the boss's head. Cut to Fatou twirling along the lower edge of the frame before she lands with one leg stretched behind her and the other tucked underneath, with her arms stretched out so that her body forms a horizontal curve nearly parallel to the stage. She holds that shape for a moment before unfolding like the blooming of a giant bird of paradise. The next shot shows Fatou rising to face the boss while an ensemble of dark-skinned shirtless men sit watching her, posing as the onstage audience, before standing to play drums as her onstage accompaniment. Through the film's editing and the suggestion of the bananas costume that Baker wears, the boss appears to have imagined that a bunch of bananas has ripened into a fantasy dancer, that Josephine Baker is simultaneously a living bird of paradise and a ripe hand of bananas that has fallen at his feet ready to eat.

Pause. What might be going on here? What is this film, and where does it come from? Where might it be going? Where might it be taking Baker? How

Fig. I.2. The mise-en-scène of *la danse des bananes* features Fatou (Baker) performing for a lounging banana plantation boss.

Fig. I.3. Fatou (Baker) extends her arms upward with hands together in the form of the stem atop a bunch of bananas.

Fig. I.4. The plantation boss fantasizes about Fatou as he lounges.

does one think about this material? Whose story is this—what is the story? Why bananas? Who made this?

This 16 mm footage of the banana dance is one of the rare documentations of Baker's work at the Folies Bergère, or in any other venue, in the mid-1920s. Filmed in black and white without sound, the roughly three-minute banana dance material is included within a longer compilation titled *Josephine Baker, Star of the Folies-Bergère and the Casino de Paris*, the purpose of which was promotional.[2] Continuing to circulate as a publicity tool and historical footage today, this Folies Bergère footage introduces Baker to new audiences, whether through clips of it used in documentaries or through videos on You-Tube. The late Jean-Claude Baker credits Mario Nalpas with filming the Folies Bergère material, noting that the extant version is the American one, "in which she had to wear a bra. Lost for sixty years, the footage was found in a box in Rochester."[3] Though this film is precious for the ways in which it allows historians and fans to see Baker in motion, Professor Phyllis Rose cautions as follows:

> You'd think that [film] would allow us to see what people saw in
> 1925, but it does not. The film shows that heinie moving as fast as a

hummingbird. It shows a dancer who is energetic and contagiously happy, but not particularly sexy. The conventions of her moves being more familiar to us, we cross no boundary in watching her. She can delight us but not shock. Perhaps the best way to imagine how sexy she looked to people brought up on the waltz is to remember how and why Elvis Presley once seemed obscene. It was equally a matter of violating white conventions of movement.[4]

Bracketing the question of whether Baker was sexy and to whom, I want to focus on how this footage and contemporaneous descriptions of it show Baker's improvisational solo comedy dancing being reframed as an American Afro-Atlantic aesthetic revelation in Paris: French dance critic André Levinson thoughtfully assessed her work, writing, "Ballet measures music by a tacit recognition of accents and rhythm where the Negro step marks them out, assigning each accent its own sound and movement. The eye not the ear perceives the unity of time, and vision and sound are separated. But in Negro steps the body appears to be a visualization of sound."[5] Leading *Candide* journalist Pierre de Régnier concurs, writing in his 1925 review of *La revue nègre*, "She seems like a moving saxophone and the sounds of the orchestra appear to come from [her body]."[6] The film *Josephine Baker, Star of the Folies-Bergère and the Casino de Paris* captured her practice, and it shows that though she might have "exploit[ed] white eroticization of black bodies," Baker was a transformative innovator of Africanist dance and was recognized as such by general audiences, fellow artists, and career critics.[7] Lest her strategic thinking get lost in a narrative of instinctiveness, Jean-Claude Baker writes of Baker, "She had made it look so easy, effortless, so spontaneous that some observers were fooled into thinking the performance they had just seen was an expression of her nature, not a product of her art. They were mistaken. Josephine was not a natural child, she was a complicated, driven nineteen-year-old. She herself had created that 'magnificent dark body,' out of will and her need to be noticed."[8] And noticed she was, both in Europe and back home in the United States: biographer Lynne Haney cites a screening in a Columbia, South Carolina, theater where a patron "sprang to his feet and yelled louder and louder, 'Do Jesus! Do Jesus! I've never seen a woman dance so good in my life.'"[9] What's more, Baker's good dancing and its legacies consist of a number of interconnected prismatic concepts that, rather than breaking down Baker's image into illegible pieces, actually constitutes a refracted image or a prismatic image that can hold paradoxes, making the figure of Baker a particularly potent form of colonialist figuring and creative expression.

THE AFRICANIST PRISMATIC

Art historian Robert Farris Thompson writes, "The founders of African civilization, the Yoruba maintain, created the first styles of bodily address and dance. Many traditional people in Africa believe that when they dance or strike an honorific pose they are standing in the image of their ancient divine fathers."[10] True to this concept, Baker danced in the image of her divine fathers and mothers of the vaudeville stage, of the nightclub, and in so doing brought remnants of African dance to a wide audience. Baker's dancing solo as Fatou resembled a single-person dance revue, with multiple poses, gestures, facial expressions, and full body movements drawing on many traditions while appearing distinctly Black, deeply ancient.

Baker's work is "Africanist," as dance historian Brenda Dixon Gottschild defined it, in that she draws on "forms that have roots/origins in Africa and the African diaspora."[11] Africanist influences are evident when she bends at the hips and knees. Polyrhythmic and polycentric movements feature prominently in Baker's dance as well, which too is characteristic of Black motion: movements within movements. Baker used her face and hands expressively, crossing her eyes, arms, and legs, all at different speeds. She smiled constantly, dancing with her entire body, conveying the impression of unlimited energy. The seasoned performer created a visual montage of varied and constantly changing effects with her body by dancing very quickly, emphasizing abrupt improvisational turns, jumps, bends, stretches, kicks, struts, and glides.

Baker's banana dance film demonstrates her devotion to her craft; she was a student of dance and of her own personality, continually shaping and projecting herself to her audiences. Baker's French biographer Ean Wood writes, "During the six weeks of rehearsal she was a torrent of enthusiasm, involving herself in all aspects of production. She took an interest in the sets, the lighting, the costumes and the stage machinery."[12] Knowing she would be dancing without Joe Alex, her partner in *La revue nègre*, Baker prepared an elaborate solo. She studied various dance movements and traditions, including those of her fellow dancers with international backgrounds, then she combined them with her own well-established repertoire that she had developed in St. Louis and during her tours on the American vaudeville circuit, where African cultural retentions were present in dances such as the staircase dances, frenzied high-speed Charleston, knee rocks with rubbery legs, and the camel walk.

Baker's version of an eclectic Black dance language was itself drawn from American, Caribbean, and African-style movements and is present throughout her choreography. In *Josephine Baker, Star of the Folies-Bergère*, once Baker as

Fatou lands at center stage, she rises slowly and begins an exuberant perform-ance, communicating the Africanist principles of vitality and youthfulness through flexibility in the joints and the ability to make quick changes.[13] In a gesture to Black American adaptations of African dance that Baker brought to Paris, Fatou thrusts her hips from left to right while throwing her arms in the opposite direction, repeating this motion facing one side of the stage, then the other. She stands upright, proud and strong. Pauses. And change: Fatou bends at the waist, with her arms stretching toward the ground and her knees bent—a posture that raises and isolates Baker's famous derriere. But it is her work with the legs that is most significant here, as Thompson explains: "The Kongo sense of flexibility in the dance is stark: dance with bended knees lest you be taken for a corpse."[14] Fatou, with bended knees, then pivots in a circle while shaking her hips very quickly, the impression of speed enhanced by the shaking bananas.

The absence of sound here acts as an inadvertent extratextual element, at once bringing contemporary viewers into the imagination of this scenario but alienating them somewhat; the drummers move around Fatou, creating the illusion of musical flow from the drums to her body and back again. In Baker's dance, emphasis is placed on the lower torso rather than the chest and arms, which are positioned akimbo or stretched outward from the sides of the body. She might hold one outstretched arm still while the other hits her hip or makes a circling motion. Baker's dance, characteristic of Africanist and Afro-Americanist dance, is energetic and polyrhythmic, and it also tends to pull the body downward—even a leap pushes toward the earth through the form of bent knees and squared feet. Baker's work is thus grounded in African-ist dance traditions and connected to the earth.

In another sequence, Fatou dances in the center foreground. As writer Nancy Cunard observes, "the dancing could be compared to the purest African plastic in motion—it was free, perfect and exact, it centered admirably in the spare gold banana fronds round the dynamic hips."[15] Characteristic of her mode of dance expression, Baker combines a series of postures and movements, going through them in a disjunctive fashion with quick, clipped phrasing and only brief dance poses. Her dance goes beyond the mere sensation of movement; she communicates an attitude of readiness for change and power. She extends her arms upward with her hands together in the form of the stem atop a bunch of bananas. She pauses briefly and then twirls and separates her hands slowly, shakes her head, smiles, and circles her hips quickly while moving her stomach slowly. The bananas jiggle at her hips in yet another sphere of rhythm as they independently knock against one another and against Fatou's legs, illustrating once again the polyrhythm principle of Africanist dance. In contrast to Baker's exuberant choreography, the camera is relatively static, and the editing follows her movements.[16]

Significantly, in the banana dance section of *Josephine Baker, Star of the Folies-Bergère and the Casino de Paris*, Baker's feet are not a focal point. The focus is, instead, on her face, torso, and upper legs. For contrast, *Josephine Baker visits Volendam—Outtakes*, a Fox 35 mm newsreel shot by illustrator Mac-Djorski on her visit to Volendam, North Holland,[17] shows Baker performing or attempting to perform the Charleston while wearing clogs. Attention is focused on her full body with the camera pointed downward at times to focus on her feet. The framing in her sections of *La revue des revues* does include her footwork, at one point even catching the edge of the stage in the shot, as it is filmed partly from within the audience. But in *Josephine Baker, Star of the Folies-Bergère*, Baker's face (rather than her feet) constitutes the site of intricate expression and spectacle, along with her hips and bent knees as she performs variations on the Charleston. The spectacle comes from Baker's jangling jewelry, funny faces, and kinetic costumes, each contributing to the overall spectacle of motion.

Given the offbeat rhythm of the dance, Baker's repetitious motions such as the circling rump and the rocking tummy or shimmy provides a structure, a kind of physical chorus whose lyrics are sung by the body. In Baker's Africanist phrasing, the offbeat effect arises when she suspends the continuity of her gesture to make a change and then returns to the original movement.[18] Such compelling Africanisms and Baker's overall fabulosity make it easy to perhaps mentally edit out the wider colonialist scenario in which she performs, but as my guiding metaphor of the cinematic prism suggests, Baker's context is multifaceted.

For twenty-year-old Baker, the reception of the banana dance in 1926 was part of a greater wave of success following the 1925 *danse sauvage* in *La revue nègre* in Paris. According to *Josephine*, a memoir assembled posthumously from her notes by her estranged husband Jo Bouillon, Baker's producers gave her the best possible treatment, writing, "Monsieur [Paul] Derval couldn't do enough for his star. He told me to buy anything I wanted and charge it to him. I spent hours at the dressmaker's and hair dresser's. I was manicured, pedicured, pampered, perfumed. . . . What a wonderful revenge for an ugly duckling! I now lived in two large rooms in a boardinghouse near the elegant Parc Monceau."[19] Although she did not have top billing (a middle-aged overweight white male comedian known as Dorville was the actual lead performer), Baker became the best-known member of the show, was featured on the program cover, and was the inspiration behind this major showcase of her work.[20] Like all Derval's shows at the Folies Bergère, *La folie du jour* had exactly thirteen letters in the title, per his superstition. The cast included seventeen British "John Tiller Girls," along with a chorus of Russian dancers, all fair-skinned with blonde or red hair to accentuate Baker's darker skin.[21] There was a full orchestra and even fireworks as the perfect setting for Baker's "hard athletic body, radiating kinetic energy, [and] sheer blazoning vitality."[22] The music hall was at its zenith, and Baker could not have been a more ideal star and inspiration. She had been a smash hit in a previous show, *La revue nègre* at the Théàtre des Champs-Elysées, and was thus a known attraction, and she was part of the growing interest in and presence of African and African American cultural events, products, and people among Parisian tastemakers. Baker's moment was the moment of "negrophilia," when she, Ada "Bricktop" Smith, and other musicians and entertainers found that "white interest in the Charleston, lindy hop, black bottom and shimmy dances could earn them a significant income."[23] This phenomenon, known as *Le tumulte noir* or "Black craze," was an enthusiastic curiosity, a fandom, at times a fetishistic one, for Black Americans, based largely on stereotypes, that swept the Parisian artistic avant-garde as well as theatrical entertainment.[24]

To give a sense of the genre in which Baker worked, the music hall program generally included a variety show or revue that featured magic acts, slapstick comedy, and "current events in an often pornographic and satirical format"; the Black-cast *La revue nègre* iteration had been a controversial and ultimately high-return gamble at being risqué artistically, politically, and racially.[25] Folies Bergère brought Baker into their programming and upped the ante with use of prominent songwriters and musicians as well as designers in a range of disciplines. Wood explains, "Among the impressive list of names who designed the décor and costumes were Brunelleschi, José de Zamora, Georges Barbier and Erté, the great exponent of art deco."[26] The sets in show were designed by Louis Lemarchand and featured both modernist and primitivist elements.[27] Yet none of them is officially credited with designing the show's most famous costume: the banana skirt.

Baker performed multiple pieces in *La folie du jour* but, as she writes, "the thing that caused the most comment opening night and for fifty years to come was my banana waistband. Sixteen bananas pointing comically toward the ceiling were attached to a belt slung low around my hips to accentuate my forward and backward movements."[28] Jean-Claude Baker further quotes Josephine as saying, "In this revue, they had the idea to dress me with a belt of bananas. Oh! How ridiculous people have been with this idea! And how many drawings and caricatures came out of it. Only the devil, supposedly, could have invented such a thing."[29] Josephine even cited French poet and filmmaker Jean Cocteau as the costume's designer.[30] Wood speculates that illustrator Paul Colin designed it "as a fanciful drawing that Paul Derval saw and liked."[31] It was a storied, absurd, and cute costume that was wildly popular, perhaps all the more so for its mysterious origins. Rose linked Baker's performance to *La revue nègre* to make a larger point about its colonialist and exoticist framework: "The Folies-Bergère would make the colonialist fantasy even more explicit with Josephine Baker as Fatou, the native girl, clad in a skirt of fake bananas, who climbs down the limb of a tree and into the life of the white explorer as he lies dreaming under his mosquito net. Like the picture postcards of veiled but bare-breasted Algerian women that were popular in France in the early twenties, the Revue Nègre excited its audiences by reminding them of a world that was both mysterious and sexually available, alien yet subject."[32] Baker's performance tapped into colonialist culture as she helped to generate a new iteration of it.

Clever and in constant motion, the banana skirt defines Baker's cultural significance as well as her cultural framing in France as an exotic jezebel and a serious challenge to the status quo in terms of her dance aesthetic. The actual formation of the costume varied: reporter Leo Guild recalls, "Once she danced with just three bananas decorating, or hiding, three of her most vulnerable female spots. The performance made headlines. Josephine Baker, it seemed, could get away with anything—in Paris, that is."[33] Baker's costume did recur throughout the late 1920s and 1930s in various formations with fewer or more bananas, or with stiffer materials, than the original. In *Josephine Baker, Star of the Folies-Bergère*, the costume appears to consist of dozens of false bananas sewn together somehow, but Guild's sensationalist description demonstrates the type of rumors that attended Baker and the sexual references a writer might employ.

The way the bananas bounce between Baker's specific star persona, which was in the process of being defined in France, and the colonialist character she played made it instantly iconic and ironic, particularly given her later accomplishments on behalf of the French Resistance and her later activism against segregation in the United States, when she often wore a military uniform. This 1926 costume still defines Baker in many ways, not the haute couture gowns and the French military uniform that the "Jazz Cleopatra" wore in later years.[34] Her combination of sensual allure and comedic physicality resonated within a racial-sexual schema, as it does now. Toward the end of her career, Baker wryly observed, "Where are my bananas? When I had my bananas, I didn't have any complications."[35] It might have appeared simple and gimmicky, but this belt of bouncing phalluses worn early in her Parisian career certainly portended a Black woman entertainer who could take a joke, make it her trademark, and launch herself as a cultural phenomenon.

THE IMPERIALIST BANANA PRISMATIC

The banana costume may have nebulous origins, but as a choice for Baker to wear it, it holds significance. As historian John Soluri explains in *Banana Cultures*, "prior to the nineteenth century, few residents of the United States had tasted a banana and fewer still ate them on a regular basis."[36] During the early twentieth century, the banana underwent a cultural process by which it was transformed from an exotic item to a commonplace snack and breakfast food in the United States. In the early 1920s in the United States, Central American bananas were nearly as common as apples, with wide resonance in popular culture, as heard in phrases that are still with us today such as "I'm going bananas" and "That's bananas," capturing the fruit's association with eccentricity and wackiness. Examples of musical references to bananas include composer George Gershwin's silly lyric "Havana, Havana, banana, banana" in "Let's Call the Whole Thing Off" and the 1923 tune "Yes! We Have No Bananas," published by the Skidmore Music Company. Soluri explains, "By the end of the year the company was selling thousands of copies of the sheet music and dance-hall bands were performing the tune throughout the U.S. and in many parts of Europe. One of the song's composers, drummer Frank Silver, organized a ten-piece 'banana band' that toured the U.S. with a set that included real bunches of bananas."[37] In the mid-1920s, when Baker performed her banana dance in France, the fruit was on its way from being relatively rare to widely available in the United States, while retaining its tropical association. As Soluri observes, "Yankee writers tended to view the tropics as a world apart, filled with dark, sensual, slothful people who survived largely due to the natural fecundity of the sun- and rain-drenched landscapes that they inhabited."[38] As bananas became all the rage, they became an everyday way of consuming ideas about the tropics without even needing to explicitly acknowledge that specific geography. Bananas crossed over from novelty to mainstream staple because of their success at being different and, specifically, because they were tropical.

France's role in the evolution of banana cultivation in the Caribbean found representation in Baker's banana dance in *La folie du jour*. The first banana to reach the New World in 1516, possibly the Cavendish, came from the Canary Islands, carried by a friar, Padre Berlanga. Bananas subsequently recrossed the Atlantic to France and other European ports en route from Caribbean plantations.[39] Legend has it that in 1837, a single Gros Michel rhizome was carried from Martinique to Jamaica, where the variety prospered. From Jamaica, the fruit traveled to Panama in the mid-nineteenth century.[40] After the opening of the Panama Canal in 1915—which was built by West Indian laborers like those represented in the banana dance footage—bananas spread throughout Central America, where they were cultivated for export to North America. As it was organized at the turn of the twentieth century, banana cultivation in the Caribbean was different from the Latin American situation in that it was a decentralized industry run by small farmers and individual cultivators or bosses. This small-farm scenario is evoked in *La folie du jour*.

France imported bananas from multiple sources and in various quantities according to economic and meteorological events; most exports from the French colonies in the Caribbean and Africa to France consisted of coffee and cacao.[41] Bananas reached Europe, Germany in particular, by ship from Colombia, Honduras, or the Canary Islands, but the value of those imports "was small in 1921 and negligible in 1922 and 1923 . . . improved economic conditions in 1924 resulted in a resumption of imports on a large scale," according to a July 1929 issue of the *Commerce Reports*. This activity might have impacted the availability and appeal of the fruit in France.[42] Prior to the 1920s, in Guadeloupe, writes economics scholar Don Hoy, bananas were merely a cover crop for the more valuable cacao and coffee, but after two storms devastated those crops, bananas were cultivated instead. In the mid-1920s, "the speculators, more closely associated with the vagaries of export trade, knowledgeable of the French market and its needs, initiated the export of bananas, and within the space of a few years bananas outranked both coffee and cacao both by volume and value as an export commodity."[43] Still, until 1928, the vast majority of bananas imported to France came from non-French-controlled areas, particularly the Canary Islands. Baker's bananas were thus likely imported by the British, as banana cultivation in the Canaries was run by Fyffe, a British company. In 1928, however, the French government increased import duties, and during the 1930s, various laws were passed that effectively eliminated the foreign importation of bananas.[44] But banana production in the French possession of Guadeloupe increased.[45]

Bananas were also connected to racist commercial images of Africans and others of African descent, such as in an advertisement for the French breakfast product Banania, which is made from chocolate, bananas, honey, and cereal. Boxes of the product in the 1920s displayed a smiling African soldier and the slogan "Y'abon," a supposed representation of a Senegalese dialect of French. The image featured a cartoonish figure with a smiling facial expression rendered through American blackface minstrelsy coding.[46] As in the American context cited earlier and described by Soluri, the tropics and the bananas had negative connotations. The banana was not even a valuable crop until coffee and cacao had been destroyed; before it was cultivated as a product for wide, profitable consumption, it was merely a subsistence crop for indigenous people and Black laborers.[47] In designing the banana skirt, Baker and her collaborators, intentionally or not, drew from symbolic objects in Paris and on the world stage that were available yet coveted, comical, problematic, and associated with Black people.

Baker's whimsical bit of banana footage is historically weighted with the imperialist prismatic intersecting with the colonial imagination, reflected in the Africanist and literary prismatics. The Folies footage is a document of Baker's performance, certainly, but as mediated imagery, it captures, reflects, and, to some extent, creates two key aspects of Baker's larger cinematic prism, those being the long-standing exoticisms of indigenous and nonwhite women residing in lands taken by colonial conquest. The plantation context is actively present here, working on and working over Baker's image. The arrangement of gazes that structure the footage reveal the power relations at work around Fatou and around Baker. In the film, Fatou represents a fantastical creature, a bunch of bananas animated as a beautiful dancing girl, transformed by colonialist fantasy. The lounging plantation boss dreams her up, and the images are presented as though they are actually coming from his subconscious, floating from his mind onto the stage. The banana dance footage shows how Baker was at once a figment of the colonial imagination, as Fatou, and an innovative choreographer in her own right. Those moments when she is the center of the frame as well as when she is center stage and the plantation boss and other characters are nowhere to be seen are crucial, in my view, if contingent, moments when Baker's autonomy might be imagined. As such, Baker epitomizes the struggle between the life force of the creative self and the often oppressive artifice of the entertainment industry, which persists to this day.

THE POP CULTURE PRISMATIC

Baker's early twentieth-century banana dance found new life when it was restaged in 2006 by Black woman entertainer Beyoncé, an innovative and pioneering celebrity in her own right. As seen in the concert performance of the song "Déjà Vu" live at Fashion Rocks, Beyoncé captures Baker's style and ambition without attempting a literal imitation.[48] Beyoncé's lush hairstyle is the opposite of Baker's short, lacquered bob with the distinctive flat curl on the sides and forehead. Beyoncé's hairstyle is composed of long, curly, brown and blonde waves that bounce along with her movements, which blend selected Baker moves with Beyoncé's hip-hop-inspired repertoire. Beyoncé incorporates a few flirtatious winks into her routine the way Baker did, but she does not imitate all of Baker's moves. There is neither Baker's signature eye-crossing nor the classic Charleston within a series of quickly changing kicks, turns, bends, and slides. Instead, Beyoncé strategically samples Baker's famous costume and dance practice of speed and Africanisms and combines them with American dance gestures. She remixes the original diva's 1920s aesthetics for contemporary audiences. Beyoncé's dancing controls the show. And Beyoncé frames the dance with an Afrocentric aesthetic, represented by drumming heard early in the video.

Beyoncé, like Baker, is herself an ever-unfolding prism of self-citation and reflexivity. She, too, is a cinematic prism, and she likely recognizes herself in her muse, underscoring that insight when she lends her own body to the expression and revitalization of Baker's ideas. Beyoncé's evocation of the uncanny banana dance charts the history of pop music from classical through African drumming to jazz and foregrounds her muse's role in galvanizing that trajectory.[49] Beyoncé all but announces that she is Baker already seen and returned. Beyoncé's "Déjà Vu" *is* a déjà vu. Meanwhile, Baker is reanimated, as though one of Paul Colin's drawings had come to life from history's pages. (An illustration of Baker's face provides a glowing backdrop to Beyoncé's performance.) Yet Beyoncé incorporates her own authorship into the performance through this historical allusion to the dance in ways that are less apparent in Baker's work. When Beyoncé's husband, Jay-Z, appears—a parallel to the male presence in the original banana dance—his presence reads as an intrusion, as an unnecessary break from her performance, and, ultimately, as superfluous. Beyoncé calls for hi hat and functions as a band director throughout her dance, which is vastly more agentive than Baker's role as the figment of the plantation boss's imagination. Beyoncé was able to see the glimmers of Baker's power, however, and magnify them to advance her own creative authorship.

The year Beyoncé performed her song "Déjà Vu" at the 2006 Fashion Rocks program was auspicious: Beyoncé celebrated her twenty-fifth birthday that year, she released the album *B'Day*, and it was Baker's centennial. Baker inspired the production of *B'Day*, especially Beyoncé's autonomy, in significant ways. First, Beyoncé recorded it on her own, without, she said, the knowledge of or input from her usual management crew. In a *Good Morning America* interview on September 7, 2006, she told Diane Sawyer what qualities in Baker inspired her: "I wanted to be more like Josephine Baker, because she didn't, she seemed like she was just possessed and it seemed like she just danced from her, her heart, and everything was so free. . . . This record sounds like a woman possessed. It sounds like a woman that is kind of desperate, and I wanted it to come from the soul. I just did whatever happened there."[50] Beyoncé's word choice—"possessed"—acknowledges her power while also disavowing it. She indicates that she did not make the music, but that it came to her, and she does not fully control it. But she *did* make it. She experienced desire as a creator. She worked through the medium of Baker's total movement, sense of abandonment, music possession, and unpredictability. As a Black woman entertainer aiming for a global reach, Beyoncé chose to pay tribute to Baker's multiplicity and oppositionality—the illusions and strategic revelations that characterize the latter's career and spectacular prismatic performance style.[51]

Beyoncé joins Diana Ross as a Black woman entertainer who considers Baker to be a trailblazer worthy of embodying on the stage. Ross played Billie Holiday in the film *Lady Sings the Blues* (1972) and went on to pay tribute to Ethel Waters, Bessie Smith, and Josephine Baker in a live theatrical performance at the Palace Theatre on Broadway (1976) and in a television special and live album (1977), both titled *An Evening with Diana Ross*. Recalling what inspired her, Ross described Baker as "hot":

> She was a hot lady. But deep in her thinking. Intelligent woman. I'm fascinated because Josephine, to me, is me, in this time. I think there's a lot of the same kind of survival. I also admire Josephine for her generosity, and her caring about putting together a family of 12 adopted children of different races from all over the world. And she was a very courageous, a very strong woman, to be admired. And that she could come from America, and come into France and become the toast of Paris, and be respected by all the top French society and artists and creative people, then she must have something that I would like to know about.

Baker was "a star bigger than life," and Ross had two remarkable encounters with her hero. The first took place when Ross received a César Award for her work in *Lady Sings the Blues*, and the second took place when she attended a concert of Baker's. According to Ross, Baker approached her, put her hands in the younger woman's hair, and stared into her eyes for several moments before walking on toward the stage, saying nothing.[52] Unfortunately, Ross has not yet realized her dream of making a Baker film.

Decades beyond her death in 1975, the fabulous Baker remains an icon for a new generation as seen through citations of the banana dance and of Baker's style in the popular press and social media—particularly in beauty and culture blogs such as Afrobella.com, BlackPast.org, and ForHarriet.com.[53] The now-defunct website Coloures.com, which celebrated beauty "in all shapes and shades," referenced a circa 1920s photograph of Baker in its description of the fantastically pearl-studded Calvin Klein gown that Lupita Nyong'o wore to the 2015 Academy Awards.[54] The young editors of *Rookie*, an online magazine for teenagers, bestow "hero status" on Baker for her humanitarianism, internationalism, and self-invention.[55] *Bitch*, a feminist pop culture magazine, formulates Baker's and Beyoncé's shared "bootylicious feminism," observing, "Both Beyoncé and Josephine Baker's careers are inevitably tied to race and therein lies the Catch-22 of their sexuality. Why is a woman's appreciation for her body and her astronomical levels of self-confidence painted as indecency and immorality? We want to simultaneously frown upon and marvel at the exhibitionism of pop stars."[56] The venerable African American publication *Ebony* further parsed the conundrums of what it called Baker's "scandalous joy."[57] The tension between pleasure and controversy in Baker's work made her a compelling muse for many artists, particularly because of her willingness to disregard conventions and offer a path beyond them.

Baker's boldness, wayward and multifaceted as it was, continues to inspire an eclectic group of admirers today, especially artists working to find a place beyond or through "the exotic" at the nexus of art and entertainment. Soprano Julia Bullock writes in the program notes to *Perle Noire: Meditations for Joséphine*,[58] "Sparked by complex feelings and questions around identity, I began to study the life, performances, and music of the entertainer, who, at that time, I identified as 'the woman who danced in the banana skirt.'" Bullock's program does include a brief, striking dance sequence, but it focuses largely on songs, and a screen above the stage emphasizes the lyrics, inviting the audience to study them. Bullock writes, "I shared songs that touched on themes that seemed to pervade her life—exploitation and objectification, issues of identity, and the difficulties in maintaining intimate relationships—and the roles that she played—an exotic identity in a foreign place, a charmer, activist, and nurturer." The show draws on a range of musical forms, including jazz, blues, spirituals, and the ballads featured in Baker's films. By including songs that Baker performed as well as those that formed the aesthetic milieu of her African American culture, Bullock is able to speak to Baker's full range of musical possibilities. At times, Bullock sounds like Baker—not as an imitation of Baker but as if in unison with her—bringing her tone and timbre into the room but somehow clearing the distractions and distortions to which Baker would have been more vulnerable. Not that the static and pops of a 1930s record are not delightful, but Bullock conveys the strength, clarity, and creativity to which Baker aspired when she performed. Poet Claudia Rankine's text and composer Tyshawn Sorey's music performed (and commissioned) by the International Contemporary Ensemble brings Baker into conversation with the contemporary Black Lives Matter movement. The project is "not so much about her, but for her." As if echoing Bullock, author and performer Cush Jumbo writes of her one-woman play *Josephine Baker and I* that she "idolize[s] Baker for her bravery, her willingness to reinvent herself, her flouting of restrictions."[59] Both Jumbo and Bullock, like Beyoncé, and Lynn Whitfield, embody Baker's movements, words, and ideas with their own bodies. In a sense, they give themselves over to Baker as engaging with her helps them to come into their own practice as artists.

Baker's likeness—particularly reproductions of the banana skirt, her camera-ready face, and various illustrations—constitute a commodity to this day. Etsy features several pages of Baker-inspired merchandise, including handmade jewelry, hats, and household accessories. A cosmetic company even named an eye shadow after Baker; the description of the color read, "How do you fit a bad ass story of rags to riches to espionage to fighting Nazis and racism into a single colour of awesomeness? We're still working on it. In the meantime, this shimmering color does its best to live up to the super spy's 'Black Pearl' nickname. The dark shades of cocoa swirl with iridescent green for a deadly color you don't want to mess with."[60] Speaking of bad ass, Barbadian singer, actor, and businesswoman Rihanna hinted that she might play Baker in a biopic. In summer 2014, Rihanna cited Baker in a tweet to contextualize her transparent head-to-toe dress.[61] The Parisian lingerie brand Princesse tam.tam appropriates the title of Baker's 1935 musical comedy. And there is a swimming pool in Paris named La Piscine Joséphine Baker. Built on a barge in the Seine River, this remarkable monument to Baker is further distinguished by its glass roof and its location next to La Bibliothèque François Mitterrand.

Baker's performances—her self-possession, her creative imagination, and her life's explorations—have inspired a range of movie moments and characters. In multiple cinematic references, Baker evokes a very specific time and place, such as interwar Paris, as when she comes up in conversation in Jim Jarmusch's 2003 film *Coffee and Cigarettes*. Two old-timers in a bar toast Josephine Baker, the elegant people, and the joie de vivre of 1920s Paris and late 1970s New York City—both important sites of artistic experimentation. But Baker can also signify a wistful feeling or a way of being that is beyond time and place. Akira Kurosawa's film *Ikiru* (1977), the tale of a bureaucrat contemplating his mortality, features Baker's recorded songs, and her associations with Paris, luxury, and sensuality represent the joie de vivre he seeks. Not the object of desire, Baker's persona evokes desire itself. Baker here represents a celebration of life, connection to life. The films *Touki Bouki* (Djibril Diop Mambéty, 1972) and *Alma's Rainbow* (Ayoka Chenzira, 1994) both cite Baker, explicitly in the former and indirectly in the latter, as a muse for self-actualization, play, and ambition. Baker is about living beyond survival. She means Paris—a sweeter, sparkling life, but one not without the darker aspects and the cultural realities of that effervescence.

In *Madame Sata* (Karim Ainouz, 2002), Baker evokes passion, vulnerability, and theatricality, citing the drag cabaret and cinema as dream spaces of agency. For the film's protagonist, Baker's character-within-a-character in the 1935 *Princesse Tam-Tam* serves as an apt medium of their own self-reflection and reinvention as it is at once a migration story and a rags-to-riches story. The role of an African American in a French production edited into a Brazilian and French coproduction raises questions about the links between the Global South and the Global North, tropical cinema, and Hollywood that needs investigation beyond this brief catalog of Baker's revival as muse and guiding figure. It suffices to say here that in *Madame Sata*, Baker, in many ways located far from Hollywood, stars in and makes this motion picture into a reflexive commentary on the film industry. Its film-within-a-film structure reanimates and exalts Baker's film career at the same time.[62] It reimagines Baker's work circulating in Brazil and among international Black audiences more broadly. At least in *Madame Sata* there is a glimpse of the idea that, despite the colonialist typing in Baker's persona, a figure of the Black diaspora can look at her and see themselves in a positive, inspiring relationship to her.

The way Baker could be cited by suggestion in these films and through a fragment cameo is prismatic, showing that she was both so expansive and yet so specific that merely the mention of her name evokes a whole world of emotion and meaning. Such embodiments and homages as well as items of commerce demonstrate Baker's current relevance. More than just a burlesque star from a bygone era, the figure of Baker is a clutter of citations across time and mediums. There is enough material to replicate and more to recuperate, for artists and scholars alike.

THE ACADEMIC PRISMATIC

Baker's memory lives on not only in popular culture but also in a substantial body of Baker scholarship that stands as testament to her complexity and breadth as a subject. Yet unlike the previously discussed enthusiasms of celebrities and media makers, the academic fascination with Baker tends to operate within a polarized discourse.[63] This tracks with the ways that Baker was "decried by some as an agent of minstrelsy and a toady to whites" while she was also celebrated "as a black heroine and the first modern, international star," according to film scholar Fatima Tobing Rony.[64] Baker's inherent hybridity, Rony suggests, lends itself to a particularly unyielding dichotomy. While many scholars do acknowledge Baker's success and its significance in vindicating African American talent, others express reservations.

Feminist French literature scholar Tracy Denean Sharpley-Whiting contends that Baker found "personal and financial validation in her constructed primitivity. Yet she was simultaneously locked into a derogatory and objectified essence of black femaleness."[65] Sharpley-Whiting writes that Baker's dual associations in France as either cute or savage elided her artistic potential—a framing the author underscores with her formulation of the "Black Venus narrative" drawn from nineteenth-century examples and early twentieth-century cinema. Sharpley-Whiting's analysis traces a pattern of objectification of the Black female form in French literature, art, and performance, where she rightly sees Baker's "imported" body, like nineteenth-century imaginary bodies in literature and painting, as representing "the colonized black female body, that is, a body trapped in an image of itself, whose primitivity, exemplified in a childlike comedic posture, sexual deviancy, degradation, and colonization, is intimately linked with sexual difference."[66] Her work critiques "the monolithic, homogenizing constructions of black femaleness,"[67] shedding light on how the pattern of exploitation of racial and sexual difference was a primary way that Black culture was understood in France, guided by and reflected in ideological binaries of sexually liberated/deviant, joyful/childlike, and modern/primitive, which were themselves sustained in cinema, literature, and beyond.

A number of Baker scholars have sought to delineate and recuperate what American historian Matthew Pratt Guterl calls Baker's "pastiche." He characterizes Baker as "a comedic critic of empire [who] stitched together the whole messy universe of colonialism into one vast backdrop."[68] In another example, dance scholar Ramsay Burt addresses Baker's "fictionalism" as it applies to film recordings of her dancing: "What can be seen on this film are neither the Charleston itself nor an authentic African dance but a wonderfully inauthentic misleading and mischievous performance."[69] Both Guterl and Burt reframe Baker's prismatic ambivalence as comic, whereas Sharpley-Whiting views it as tragically absent the complex characterizations and explorations that would counter stereotyping. What comes through in Guterl and Burt is a sense of Baker's improvisational use of multiple sources and the creative potential of this approach.

The early and foundational era in Baker's career of the 1920s is largely dismissed in Bennetta Jules-Rosette's crucial monograph *Josephine Baker in Art and Life* in favor of a focus on Baker's films of the 1930s and her activism of the '40s and '50s. In the foreword, Simon Njami writes, "Baker must be seen beyond the banana skirt syndrome."[70] Jules-Rosette uses "semiography" to "excavate the narratives, images, and representations that constitute the public and private lives of [Baker]. It traces the story of [her] life through signs,

Fig. I.5. A double exposure from the banana dance video
transfer illustrates Baker's cinematic prism.

symbols and images."[71] Going beyond the so-called syndrome to which Njami
referred, Jules-Rosette's attention to structure carries over to Baker's films,
where the author makes the important case, fundamental to my own thinking, that Baker created her image through everything she did, whether it was
directly related to film, television, or other media. Although Jules-Rosette does
not foreground the concept of prism explicitly, as I do, her references to Baker's
"multiple back-and-forth reflections" and the ways Baker "appropriated others'
images of her and added new and unanticipated facets to them" speak to how
I feel it is important to reconceptualize the entertainer's mediation beyond a
simple photo and its singular meaning.[72]

Some approaches to Baker seem similarly aimed at shifting the discussion
away from Baker's exploited racial and gendered difference and its implications
to focus more on her role as a leading sign of her era's cultural discourses. In
Second Skin: Josephine Baker and the Modern Surface, Anne Cheng resists reading Baker as a mere ethnographic subject: "When we move Baker outside of
[this] well-rehearsed framework and juxtapose her celebrated naked skin . . .

next to other surfaces and other techniques of display in the first quarter of the twentieth century, what we find is a radically different account of what constitutes the Baker phenomenon."[73] For Cheng, Baker exemplifies "the modern skin and its distractions." Baker here is an abstraction and an aesthetic symbol.

Such a discussion of surfaces shares conceptual sensibilities with media scholar Katherine Groo's focus on Baker as a modernist cinematic subject, referring to Baker's films as "subversive shadow lives" with "a logic of repetition."[74] Part of what is operating here, and has always operated in Baker scholarship, is a tension between Baker as a person whose biography, context, and intentions need to be more fully understood and Baker as a persona whose spectacular structures and effects call for greater illumination. Yet for many scholars of race, African American history, women, gender and sexuality, and related fields (including me), this tension between abstraction and identity, form and content, persona and personhood does not shake the desire to restore, or at least evoke, Baker's voice and agency through research and theory, where it has been perceived as compromised.

Mae Gwendolyn Henderson, scholar of Black women's writing and performance, considers Baker's agency, writing that she was "not only a product of the French colonial imaginary but also the producer of an image that contributed toward shaping that imaginary." While establishing "Baker's agency as a self-authorizing text and self-constituting subject," Henderson acknowledges that the performer is "liable to diverse and sometimes contradictory and paradoxical readings." Underscoring that Baker performed within an entertainment marketplace, Henderson argues that she maintained "a degree of agency."[75] It is the location of this "degree" that inspires continued scholarly discussion on Baker from a variety of viewpoints.

The structure of Baker's agency is a central problem in assessing her legacy. Dance historian Anthea Kraut argues, "A parsing of choreographic influence, authority, and attribution vis-à-vis Baker's dancing . . . problematizes conventional models of authorship and helps flesh out the contours of her struggle for self-determination. In particular, Baker herself points to the idea of 'bodily intelligence' as a way of confronting questions about the nature and locus of her agency."[76] Artists who work in the medium of "bodily intelligence" uniquely adapt and appreciate Baker's expressions and what she did with the instrument of her body.[77] So much of the most compelling work on Baker is done by artists and scholars who reimagine and pay critical homage to Baker's image in a variety of media, creating her "afterlife" in contemporary popular culture. As I have written elsewhere, Baker citations are rich instances that "foreground the interplay of subjectivities that constitute Baker."[78]

Fig. I.6. Josephine Baker promenades with her pet cheetah, Chiquita, surrounded by onlookers. © Bettmann/CORBIS.

Henderson and Regester's 2017 *The Josephine Baker Critical Reader* shares many of the concerns I raise and aspirations I hold. At this point in Baker scholarship, after many biographies and dichotomous assessments, I agree that it is time to render Baker as a "prime exemplar of the multiplicity and fluidity of postmodernist identity during an age shaped and defined by modernist aesthetics."[79] Baker was before her time in the 1920s and 1930s, and now in the early twenty-first century, we have caught up with her and we need her. Similar to Henderson and Regester's collection, I hope the chapters of my book function as "performances of memory and imagination, scholarship and speculation, reconstruction and critique."[80] With a specific focus on the filmic nature of Baker's work, mine is not a conventional and single-minded work of scholarship. Film is multidimensional. I have written the book with the aim of being prismatic, to better reflect and engage with Baker's own "ambivalences, inconsistences and redundancies" and celebrate as we analyze her "richly malleable afterlife" and many-splendored fabulosity.[81]

Chapter 1, "Traveling Shoes: Baker's Migrations and the Conundrums of Sweet Paris" is a historical narrative in which I make the case that Baker's early career in the United States is instrumental to understanding her later international success and prismatic image. This early work might not have given her complete satisfaction, but I explore how the rickety stages of American vaudeville provided the platforms on which Baker made her mark as the so-called comedy end girl—a minor role she turned into the main attraction. I sketch Baker's unique American context—the Black backdrop of the Great Migration in the Midwest, blues women, and the impact of the 1920s musical *Shuffle Along* as well as African American journalists' documentation of her move to Paris—in bringing together a transatlantic perspective that connects her early US years to her Paris years.

The second chapter, "Shouting at Shadows: The Black American Press, French Colonial Culture, and *La sirène des tropiques*," centers on how film critics in the Black press sought to reimagine Black film through Baker's stardom. It documents their anticipation, criticism, and disappointment. Through conflicting stories of her marriage to her manager, Pepito Abatino, I illustrate Baker's ability to manipulate the press by confusing the truth and thus creating her success out of what others wanted to see in her. The African American press provides a crucial alternative perspective to that of the Parisian press, through which I explore the complex reception of *La sirène des tropiques*, the most heavily promoted of Baker's films, especially in the United States.

Chapter 3, "Unintended Exposures: Baker's Prismatic Ethnological Performance in *Zouzou*," highlights the ethnographic gaze of Baker's first sound film through a comparative analysis with Saartjie Baartman, known as the Hottentot Venus. I analyze Baker's screen image in dialogue with her off-screen performances in the press as well as peripheral events, cultural figures, and texts that informed the creation and interpretation of her work. Taking up the question of Baker's agency within her cinematic prism, I explore specifically how Baker took advantage of the ways she was situated in both American post-minstrelsy and French exoticism. Further, the documentation of Baartman's experiences is examined both for the historical information it reveals and the affective context it provides for thinking through Baker's work.

The fourth chapter, "Seeing Double: Parody and Desire in *Le pompier de Folies Bergère* and *Princesse Tam-Tam*," foregrounds Baker's mastery of, if not total authority over, her own image making, examining in detail the feature-length *Princesse Tam-Tam* and the short *Le pompier de Folies Bergère*.[82] Similar to the earlier discussion of the banana dance, I view Baker here through a prism of gazes. A shot-by-shot analysis of Baker's work engages her image as a text with connections to the genre of colonial cinema and those early ethnographic displays that took place in Paris.

Finally, the epilogue, "Long Live Josephine Baker!," engages with the citationality of Baker's iconicity, exploring some contemporary reworkings of Baker's image and text, including an unpublished short story that is attributed to her, "The Fairytale of Wisdom" (1973). I begin with a discussion of Stew Rodewald's rock chorus "Josephine Baker Says It's Alright" in *Passing Strange* (2009) and move on to readings of Carrie Mae Weems's *From Here I Saw What Happened and I Cried* (1995–96), in which Baker is accused of being "an accomplice," and Haitian artist Jean-Ulrick Désert's *The Goddess Project* (2009–), in which Baker is hailed as a goddess. The epilogue also includes a treatment of Baker's rarely discussed 1945 film *The French Way*. Filmed during wartime and released after World War II, the film features Baker as Zazu, a cabaret owner, and the character of Zazu is built around Baker's singing rather than dancing. Rather than thinking of her character in this film as totally unrelated to those of the films of the 1930s, I see Zazu as a reworking, a citation of Baker's star persona of the 1930s.

NOTES

1. E. E. Cummings, quoted in Hammond and O'Connor, *Josephine Baker*, 41.

2. Mario Nalpas, *Josephine Baker, Star of the Folies-Bergère and the Casino de Paris*, D1507, 16 mm, Film Studies Center, University of Chicago, Chicago, IL.

3. Baker and Bouillon, *Josephine*, 135.

4. Rose, *Jazz Cleopatra*, 29.

5. Levinson, *La danse d'aujourd'hui*, 272.

6. de Régnier, "La revue nègre," 6.

7. hooks, "Selling Hot Pussy," 63.

8. Jean-Claude Baker, *Josephine: The Hungry Heart*, 7.

9. Haney, *Naked at the Feast*, 99.

10. Thompson, *African Art in Motion*, 47.

11. Gottschild, *The Dancing Body*, xii.

12. Wood, *The Josephine Baker Story*, 105–6.

13. Thompson, *African Art in Motion*, 10.

14. Ibid., 9–10.

15. Quoted in Hammond and O'Connor, *Josephine Baker*, 57.

16. Today fans can view Baker's banana dance on YouTube or in GIF formats, which pointedly tend to highlight the dancing rather than the story surrounding it.

17. Mack van Lier and Debels George, *Josephine Baker visits Volendam—Outtakes*, August 24, 1928, Fox News Story C8059, Moving Image Research Collections,

Digital Video Repository, University of South Carolina Columbia, SC, https://mirc
.sc.edu/islandora/object/usc%3A1750.

18. Thompson, *African Art in Motion*, 11.

19. Baker and Bouillon, *Josephine*, 63.

20. Wood, *The Josephine Baker Story*, 105.

21. Ibid.

22. Haney, *Naked at the Feast*, 97.

23. Archer-Straw, *Negrophilia*, 20.

24. *Le tumulte noir* is a portfolio of forty-five hand-colored lithographs by Paul
Colin, published in 1927 by Edition d'Art "Succès" in Paris. An achievement of
art deco graphic design, the project captured both the craze for black culture and
the roar around Josephine Baker. See Colin, *Josephine Baker and La revue nègre*,
1–63.

25. Archer-Straw, *Negrophilia*, 114.

26. Wood, *The Josephine Baker Story*, 104.

27. Ibid., 107.

28. Baker and Bouillon, *Josephine*, 63.

29. Jean-Claude Baker, *Josephine: The Hungry Heart*, 135.

30. Ibid.

31. Wood, *The Josephine Baker Story*, 105.

32. Rose, *Jazz Cleopatra*, 23.

33. Guild, *Josephine Baker*, 43.

34. Rose, *Jazz Cleopatra*, xi. The nickname "Jazz Cleopatra" connotes timeless
beauty and personal strength combined with the cultural transformations
brought to Europe by black culture, jazz, and Josephine Baker as she conquered
Paris.

35. *The Josephine Baker Show*, presented by Jacques Rutman, 1964, 90 min. "Où
sont mes bananes? Quand j'avais mes bananes, je n'avais pas de complication."

36. Soluri, *Banana Cultures*, 1.

37. Ibid., 58.

38. Ibid., 2.

39. Mintz, *Tasting Food*, 39.

40. Soluri, *Banana Cultures*, 6.

41. See Hoy, "Banana Industry of Guadeloupe."

42. *Commerce Reports: A Weekly Survey of Foreign Trade* 3, no. 30 (July
1929): 275.

43. Hoy, "Banana Industry of Guadeloupe," 262.

44. Ibid.

45. Ibid.

46. Likosky, *With a Weapon and a Grin*, 50.

47. Hoy, "Banana Industry of Guadeloupe," 262.

48. For a recording of the performance, see Beyonce Knowles [pseud.], "Beyonce feat Jay Z Deja Vu Live @t Fashion Rocks," uploaded September 9, 2016, YouTube, 4:18, https://www.youtube.com/watch?v=PQ1khee8vCA. For a broader discussion of Baker's citations in a range of independent and foreign film, see Francis, "What Does Beyoncé See"; Brooks, "Suga Mama"; Durham, "Check on It"; Brooks, "All That You Can't Leave Behind"; Valenti, "Beyonce's 'Run the World'"; Allred, "'Schoolin' Life.'"

49. Coffman, "Uncanny Performance."

50. "Beyonce Hits Milestone," ABC News, September 7, 2006, https://abcnews.go.com/GMA/SummerConcert/story?id=2404367&page=1.

51. Francis, "What Does Beyoncé See."

52. Footage from *An Evening with Diana Ross* was found on YouTube; see Cliporama [pseud.], "Diana Ross on Josephine Baker—Diva on Diva," uploaded June 18, 2018, YouTube video, 12:28, https://www.youtube.com/watch?v=n4NZu9LCUFk. For an image of Ross in her Baker-inspired costume of bananas, see "Diana Ross Goes to Broadway in Show That Sizzles," *Jet*, June 10, 1976.

53. See Yursik, "28 Moments in Black Beauty."

54. "Lupita Nyong'o Rocks a Gorgeous Pearl-Covered Calvin Klein Dress to the Oscars," accessed March 10, 2015, http://www.mycoloures.com/2015/02/lupita-nyongo-rocks-gorgeous-pearl.html. Page no longer available.

55. See Valentino, "Hero Status."

56. Willoughby, "Applauding the Bootylicious Feminism."

57. Pickens, "The Scandalous Joy."

58. *Perle Noire: Meditations for Joséphine*, performed by Julia Bullock, composition, drums, percussion, and piano by Tyshawn Sorey, spoken texts by Claudia Rankine with quotes by Joséphine Baker, conceived by Peter Sellars and Julia Bullock, commissioned and performed by International Contemporary Ensemble, Oberon, Harvard University, Cambridge, MA, May 3, 2019.

59. Soloski, "Cush Jumbo."

60. "Josephine Baker Mineral Eyeshadow," Beauty Bohemia, accessed March 10, 2015, http://www.beautybohemia.com/products/josephine-baker-mineral-eyeshadow. Page no longer available.

61. Lauren Smith, "Rihanna Responds."

62. Francis, "What Does Beyoncé See," 4.

63. Baker's centennial in 2006 was an important year for Baker scholarship, highlighted by the group of artists and scholars who gathered for a conference titled Josephine Baker: A Century in the Spotlight. For essays from the conference, see the special issue of the same name in *Scholar and Feminist Online*, edited by Kaiama Glover. See also Sowinska, "Dialectics of the Banana Skirt"; Dayal, "Blackness as Symptom."

64. Rony, *The Third Eye*, 199.

65. Sharpley-Whiting, *Black Venus*, 107.

66. Ibid., 10.

67. Ibid., 121.

68. Guterl, "Josephine Baker's Colonial Pastiche," 26.

69. Burt, "'Savage' Dancer," 68.

70. Njami, Foreword, xii.

71. Jules-Rosette, *Baker in Art and Life*, 5.

72. Jules-Rosette, "Inventing the Image," 4.

73. Cheng, *Second Skin*, 6–7.

74. Groo, "Shadow Lives," 9.

75. Henderson, "Colonial, Postcolonial, and Diasporic Readings," 1.

76. Kraut, "Whose Choreography?," 1.

77. Baker's metacritical positioning as both an object and subject of the sexualizing and racializing gaze broadens her appeal to the point where even the two metalhead dudes of "Wayne's World" put her at number eight on a list of hottest babes: "Okay . . . . You see, Josephine Baker was a babe in the twenties, who, although she was a victim of the prevailing racial morays [*sic*] of her native United States, become the toast of Paree, known primarily for her exotic Banana Dance." See King, "Wayne's World." The opening sequence of the French animated film *The Triplets of Belleville* (directed by Sylvain Chomet) literalizes the cartoonlike physicality of Baker's live dancing, celebrating as it reanimates her humorous and erotic jiggling bananas of the 1920s.

78. Francis, "What Does Beyoncé See," 8.

79. Henderson and Regester, *Josephine Baker Critical Reader*, 1.

80. Ibid., 2.

81. Ibid., 7.

82. *Le pompier de Folies Bergère* is also known as *Les hallucinations d'un pompier* and *Un pompier qui prend feu*; I use the first name per the catalog of Lobster Films.

ONE

—⚍—

TRAVELING SHOES

Baker's Migrations and the Conundrums of Sweet Paris

JOSEPHINE BAKER'S LIFE HAS BEEN the subject of several documentaries and biographies; thus, the broad outlines of her story are fairly well known. She is often cited in popular culture as a notable African American figure whose fame abroad cast into stark relief the limitations that were placed on Black success in the United States. On June 3, 2017, Baker's 111th birthday, Lydia Nichols's Google Doodle honored Baker, who Ernest Hemingway called "the most sensational woman any one ever saw or will,"[1] with a series of interactive slides that highlighted Baker's life and career milestones: Baker's childhood in St. Louis, her upbringing during the early twentieth century, and her journey to Paris.[2] Several scenes that show the music hall star dressed in fabulous and leg-revealing costumes, including the famous banana skirt, capture the fantastical aesthetic of Baker's 1920s music hall performances at the Théâtre des Champs-Élysées and the Folies Bergère. In contrasting the bright colors of the music hall with the dull tones of St. Louis, the Google Doodle effectively communicates the political stakes and hopes of Baker's relocation to Paris, where she seemed to be free of the racial barriers found in US society. This book focuses less on Baker's life and more on her cinematic prismatic life: her artistic development and her contributions to film.

One illustrative slide in the Google Doodle shows Baker in character with a clapperboard, hinting at the French feature films in which she starred: *La sirène des tropiques*, directed by Henri Étiévant (released in 1927 in France and 1929 in the United States), *Zouzou* (directed by Marc Allégret, 1934), and *Princesse Tam-Tam* (directed by Edmond T. Gréville, 1935) as well as her short film *Le pompier de Folies Bergère* and the performance footage compiled in *La revue des revues* and *Josephine Baker, Star of the Folies-Bergère and the Casino de Paris,* particularly the famous banana dance. Also included is *The French Way*, by Jacques Baroncelli (1945).

Nichols's Google Doodle traces Baker's transitions from St. Louis to Paris and from dancing onstage to film acting to humanitarianism. As Guterl writes, "[Baker] defined herself by relentless movement, dislocation, and self-transformation" in an itinerancy whose power she learned early in her career traveling with Clara Smith and *Shuffle Along*.[3] Professional evolutions were certainly part of her strength. Following her service as a French Resistance spy during World War II, Baker launched a visionary initiative in which her home would serve as a multicultural haven for discussions of racial harmony. To that end, she adopted many children of different races, and she was an activist who pushed to desegregate many of the American venues where she appeared, such as the Copacabana in Miami Beach, Florida, in 1952. Baker's bananas at times eclipsed her political work as well as her contributions to the cinema, but that performance was a gateway. The figure of Baker is a cultural phenomenon generated by her environment, to be sure, but she was an agentive craftsperson as well. Because her films constitute the most visible but, in many ways, ironically, least truly seen aspect of her legacy, they require further examination—particularly now that the film landscape has changed so radically to include a wide variety of Black women filmmakers and screenwriters in the early twenty-first century.

Josephine Baker was born Freda Josephine MacDonald in St. Louis, Missouri, in 1906. In her 1927 memoir, Baker described St. Louis in straightforward terms: "It was full of railways, factories that blew smoke over all the houses, and cold."[4] St. Louis expanded into a major industrial city in the early twentieth century, and the city became one of many significant destinations for African Americans leaving the rural South. From 1915 to 1970, "some six million Black southerners left the land of their forefathers and fanned out across the country" in a series of movements that became known as the Great Migration.[5] When African Americans from the South reached their destinations, they often found competition, hostility, and further deprivation. Conflict arose as "negroes organized campaigns to challenge not only the concept of white supremacy but also the discriminatory practices resulting from it."[6] St. Louis might have been a city of promise for many, but physical violence worked in tandem with white-supremacy campaigns to systematically disfranchise Black citizens and destroy their communities.

Baker's posthumously published autobiography, *Josephine*, begins with a vivid account of her "worst memory": the East St. Louis Riot of 1917, which took place across the Mississippi River in East St. Louis, Illinois. Racial tensions between whites and Blacks in East St. Louis had been heated long before the riot started. White unions sought to prevent African Americans from joining them, reducing African Americans' chances of getting and keeping jobs and discouraging more Blacks from moving to the area. Unsubstantiated and malicious rumors that Black men were harassing white women circulated, enraging whites and endangering the lives of Black men and their families.

In the years leading up to Baker's birth, four thousand Americans were lynched, the vast majority of them Black Southerners who were murdered under what Ida B. Wells denounced as "the same old racket—the new alarm about raping white women."[7] Hundreds of Black Americans died in white-instigated race riots in those years—in Wilmington, North Carolina, in 1898; in New Orleans, Louisiana, in 1900; and in Atlanta, Georgia, and Bronzeville, Texas, both in 1906. In addition to physical violence, Black Americans faced institutionalized separate and unequal facilities in the wake of the 1896 Plessy case.[8]

Baker's account highlights the systemic and brutal nature of the racism that shaped the overall context of her personal reality. On May 28, 1917, word spread that a Black man had shot a white store owner during a robbery. Next, a mob of whites attacked African American homes, businesses, and churches, often burning them to the ground. Baker wrote,

> This was the Apocalypse.... The entire black community appeared to be fleeing like ants from a scattered antheap. "A white woman was raped," someone shouted, and although I didn't understand the meaning of his words, I knew that they described the ultimate catastrophe. The flames drew nearer.... Nearby a white man, his face contorted with hatred, was savagely beating a figure kneeling before him with what looked like a club. Again and again he struck. The only way I could tell that his victim was black was by his raised hands; the rest of him was wet with blood.[9]

The violence had been going on for several days when, on July 1, there was a shooting from a passing car. The following night, residents opened fire on an unmarked police car. The cycle of revenge and attack continued, devastating African Americans' central institutions, including churches, businesses, homes, and schools. An estimated one hundred or more African Americans were killed. The Illinois attorney general indicted eighty-two whites and twenty-three Blacks. Nine of the whites were sentenced, and seven white police officers who were charged with murder were collectively fined $150. Juries convicted ten African Americans of murdering the undercover police officers, sentencing them to fourteen years in prison.[10]

BAKER'S RAGTIME CONSERVATORY

With racial violence as an ever-present backdrop, Baker's recollections of her childhood combine the harshness of her impoverished family's daily life with the delight and reprieve that her musical encounters provided. Both of Baker's parents had been small-time performers, but her mother supported the family as a laundress when Baker's father left. Baker worked as a live-in domestic helper from the age of seven. But she was always creative and actively formulating her own personal aesthetic. She even played at being a director when she created shows at home with her siblings and friends. She wrote in her memoir, "At Saint-Louis, at my mother's, I had organized a small theater in the cellar. I was not yet ten years old. The curtain was made of pieces of cloth tied end to end. I had placed the candles on the tins of 'New Zealand' peaches. The old scraps of candles lit up the steps of the staircase—all three steps—to descend. The audience consisted of a dozen girls and boys, seated at random on boxes and on an old bench."[11]

Baker's aesthetic autonomy included playing makeshift instruments, and she recounted this experience both in her artistic biography offered in *Les mémoires* and in *Josephine*, where she wrote, "Everyone seemed to own an accordion, a banjo or harmonica. Those without enough money for real instruments made banjos from cheese boxes. We played music that to us was beautiful on everything from clothesline strung across barrel halves to paper-covered combs. As soon as the music began, I would move my arms and legs on the treasure we pulled from the trash: tin cans, battered saucepans, abandoned wooden and metal containers. What a wonderful time we had!"[12]

In moments like this, Baker reveals the development of her strong personal aesthetic as a child; by describing it in her book, she asserts her identity as an artist. Baker made herself into an artist by writing these stories and by naming her inspirations and the world around her as collaborators in her developing imaginary. She wrote, "I used to play by stealing my mom's high-heeled shoes and dresses in which I would completely disappear. I seemed to be trapped in a bag, like a diver's suit."[13] She was fond of her grandmother's big hats and long flowery robes, and she often pretended to be her grandmother by wearing her clothes and a red wig. These activities and memories were crucial to Baker's early explorations of her own imagination, and she recounted them particularly in her first memoir to explain where she came from and what inspired her.[14] A youthful Baker brought her flair to whatever objects were available for playing characters and entertaining herself and her friends.

However, her childhood memories were not only of artistic escapades. As an author, she also addressed how much her daily life was affected by her family's poverty. She and her siblings often wandered their neighborhood searching for food or selling coal. These circumstances pushed Baker to support herself and her family at a young age. She recalled, "I had been seven then. . . . Mama had explained to me that we were very poor, that Daddy couldn't find work. As the oldest child, it was up to me to help out. A white woman was coming to take me away. I was to call her Mistress and do as she said. In return, she would give me shoes and a coat." But Baker's work turned out to be dangerous, and this arrangement ended in her being taken to the hospital unconscious, where she was treated for "cuts and bruises" and woke up to find that her "hands were badly burned and [she was] shaking with fear."[15] The little girl's employer was arrested for abusing her, and Baker returned home with her mother, the horrible experience doubtless informing her resolve to build a better life. Feminist scholar Hazel Carby notes that "being a member of a vaudeville show or performing in a nightclub was not attractive primarily because it offered a mythic life of glamor but because it was a rare opportunity to do clean work and to reject the life of a domestic servant."[16] At age thirteen, she worked briefly serving food at the Old Chauffer's Club, a popular meeting place for jazz musicians, as a potential strategy to find a means of supporting herself and her family that was safer.[17] Eight months later, Baker, not yet age fourteen, quit that job when she married her first husband, Willie Wells. However, the union ended shortly after it began, and Baker returned to the restaurant, which put her back in a performers' milieu.

That waitressing job involved service, but it was a formative experience, indirectly exposing her to the musician's life when traveling entertainers would gather for their meals between shows. Fortuitously, this is where Baker met the Jones Family Band, a trio that performed in tent shows and outside the restaurant where she worked. For Baker, the Jones Family Band period served as nothing less than a conservatory of Black vernacular performance, music, and street entertainment. In Paris, Baker's dancing burlesque would be referred to by the catchall term *jazz*, but it came out of older ragtime music.

The Jones band specialized in ragtime—a syncopated, highly modern, distinctly American form of popular music that was current from roughly 1896 to 1918. Known more commonly as a piano style, ragtime also included dance, voice, and other instruments.[18] Associated with the city, ragtime became the soundtrack for a new way of life that was faster paced and on the move; it was about mixing with strangers and engaging new entertainment technologies in the modernity wrought through and alongside Black migrations.

The Jones Family Band introduced Baker to performing, in part because they rehearsed constantly near her workplace. Prior to Baker joining this group of street performers, it was a trio composed of Mr. Jones on a horn, Mrs. Jones on trumpet, and a young girl on the fiddle. From Mrs. Jones, Baker learned to play the trombone, to which she added movement, particularly quickstep dancing and crossing her eyes.[19] This period of study for Baker included grunt work such as carrying the group's trunk.[20] Baker also learned the nuances of catching and holding the audience's attention among all the distractions on the street. Baker studied and incorporated into her routines up-to-date African American dances that she saw at the Booker T. Washington Theater, a successful segregated Black vaudeville venue and single-screen motion picture theater.[21]

The Jones band played music outside the Washington Theater, where Baker would eventually find her big break, her chance to shine on a real stage in front of an audience. It happened that a traveling troupe called the Dixie Steppers needed a new act, and the Jones Family Band was in the right place at the right time to get the gig.[22] Baker's sister Margaret recalled, "With fifteen cents of our delivery money we would regularly buy tickets for the Sunday show at the Booker T. Washington Theater, where the vaudeville troupe called the Dixie Steppers performed before a black audience. . . . Josephine sat glued to the edge of her seat as chorus girls flashed hints of bare skin, comics made faces and a fat singer in a red wig sang the blues. One day [Josephine] announced 'I'm going to talk to the director. Since we're going to have to work someplace, why not in show business? Wouldn't that be fun?'"[23] Although she did not meet the age requirement of fifteen, in pursuit of safer, cleaner, and more fulfilling work, Baker talked her way into an audition.

The Dixie Steppers' show marked a turning point for Baker. In the show, Baker played Cupid in a scene that required her to glide over the stage by means of ropes and pulleys. On the first night, the rigging malfunctioned and left her dangling above the stage. In an early use of the empowering potential of her prismatic comedy style, Baker turned the situation to her advantage, improvising physical comedy that played on the fact that she was stuck. The Dixie Steppers' manager saw Baker's potential as a comedian and decided to keep her with the troupe. Without a regular position in the cast, though, she ended up primarily working as a dresser. Dressers are among the lowest-level employees in the theater hierarchy, responsible for helping performers into and out of their costumes as well as cleaning, mending, and storing the costumes. Requiring close contact and personal knowledge of the performer, the job also provided an education in the opposites of comedy and glamour.[24] With a clear vision of the future she wanted, Baker lamented, "Would Josephine never be born?

While I waited, I almost died."[25] Baker eventually seized an opportunity to get on stage and show off her comedic talent, recalling the event as follows:

> One day a dancer took a nasty fall, causing her knee to swell to the size of her head. Quick as a flash I pleaded, "Mr. Bob let me fill in for her." As it was almost show time, he had little choice. Since I had never danced with the chorus before, the girls were convinced I would have a bad case of stage fright. Strangely enough, just the opposite was true. It was as though I had swallowed a shot of gin. The whistles, the shouts, the bravos, the laughter, the hundreds of staring eyes, were wonderfully exciting. . . . I became the show's "funny girl."[26]

In the band and in the show, Baker learned to perform in and transform the musical idiom of early jazz into her own style with the panache and physical comedy that would make her later performances at the Folies Bergère in Paris so distinctive. The funny-girl character involved dancing like her body was "on fire," as Baker's sister Margaret put it.[27] Bob Russell, the show's director, had initially rejected Baker's dance style, but he later thought she was perfect as a comedy dancer. Baker said, "That same night we left Saint Louis. I was happy to travel and to work. I adored that life. I wished to work more. I was never tired."[28]

BLUES-AND-BROADWAY PRISMATIC

In the wake of the 1917 riots in East St. Louis, Baker became one of the migrating millions. She left her hometown for a series of relocations that included working on the blues women's performance circuit as a dresser for Clara Smith and becoming the breakout comedian of the touring company of the Broadway musical *Shuffle Along*. Baker built her success on a foundation of aesthetic autonomy that she had begun to explore in childhood, and she seized opportunities to work, to express herself, and to perform.

A form of prismatic comedy emerged early in Baker's career as a live performer. In addition to the Cupid number she had performed on the road, as a dresser for Smith, Baker immersed herself in blues music and consciousness, which emerged in song lyrics that brought together opposites. As author Angela Davis explains, "What gives the blues such fascinating possibilities . . . is the way they often construct seemingly antagonist relationships as noncontradictory oppositions."[29] Subservience to desire and autonomous ambition coexist, prismatically. By attending to Smith, Baker was in the company of a solo performer and the archetypal traveling blues woman. Baker was able to observe the way Smith was more than a mere singer; hers was an understated moaning voice framed by a spectacular persona who, like all blues women, worked to suspend the audience between fantasy and reality through sensory overload. Baker wrote that the leading lady was "very black, fat and short. The red wig that was one of her trademarks was gaily decorated with a bow or paper flowers. Her face was layered with purple powder, her teeth were yellow from pipe tobacco. She favored short, gauzy dresses worn over pink tights and was partial to high-heeled shoes."[30] Smith's visual style must have looked to Baker like an outlandish version of her own mother's and grandmother's aesthetics.[31] The key was that Smith made the audience listen, look, and keep looking.

Musicians such as "Mama Smith," as Baker called her, composed, reworked, and performed hundreds of songs in a form of wordplay that was urbane and raunchy yet, due to its emotional fervor, close in sensibility to its rural and spiritual roots. Smith sang plaintive songs that expressed the pain of lost love and in a duet with Bessie Smith sang of "unmitigated disenchantment with the North—even to the point of predicting death from loneliness."[32] The cultural significance of blues singers stems from the way they built Black vernacular oral traditions into the stories, language, and sound—the guttural wail and other nonverbal utterances—of blues songs from a personal perspective. Their work was related to yet distinguished from choral singing or other forms of solo vocalization. The blues women's aesthetic signature came from the individuality of the impression they left in their audiences. In a sense, each woman signed her performances with an expressivity that was exclusive to her yet also part of a broader practice that was shared with other artists.

Baker aspired to the bravado of blues women generally and the sophisticated blues-inspired style of one woman in particular: Ethel Waters, who, in many ways, cultivated a unique style that brought blues to a mainstream audience. In 1922, during Baker's formative years in performing, Waters was at the top of her game. *The Savannah Tribune*, anticipating Waters's arrival, wrote in early May, "Unlike most Blues singers Miss Waters does not seek to impress the audience by the usual method, singing at the top of her voice, she believes that theatregoers prefer melody to noise and largely for this reason her work is most effective. The beautiful gowns worn by Miss Waters are also invariably a subject for much favorable discussion. Good to hear and look at."[33] Waters was a dancer as well, but in an elegant somewhat reserved style different from both the comedy style and exotic style for which Baker would be famous in the 1920s. Baker nonetheless held Waters as a model of performance that elevated the blues style to a more refined presentation that served as reference for her postbananas approach. In homage to (or in competition with) Waters, Baker performed two songs in the blues style on the ship to Paris with much verve—but "not much pitch," apparently. Writes Baker, "I would always remember September 16, 1925. The date of my first real performance—and my first resounding flop."[34] Embarrassed but undaunted, by the 1930s, Baker eventually found her niche singing a light operetta that favored her higher vocal range, and in her later years, her voice resonated in a pleasing, rich alto.

Still, that blues women starred in their own shows provided Baker's own migratory route. She benefitted from their independence, and it doubtless fueled her own ambition. She began to think about the kind of shows she wanted to perform. Baker only achieved something of Waters's 1920s style much later in her career, as seen in her 1940s film role of Zazu in *The French Way*. The aesthetic world in which Baker moved influenced her cinematic prismatic in both direct and indirect ways. Although Baker was not a traditional blues woman, and one could not see the blues explicitly manifest in Baker's Parisian burlesque, a general understanding of this type of performer and her variations clues us in to aspects of her style that might otherwise go unnoticed and that are essential to unpacking her cinematic methods. Particularly crucial was the role of singing and playing sentimental characters in her films.

Travel and mobility were defining markers of Waters's, Smith's, and Baker's lives on the road. In the United States, though "migration for women often meant being left behind," blues women were engaged with the possibilities of mobility.[35] Blues women's effects involved their layered musical aesthetic, their representation as sexual figures, and their traveling. As a popular cultural figure, the blues woman raised controversies around gender and sexuality, which were tied to the fact that she traveled and performed in various cities. She was bound to neither house nor husband. Although Baker was not technically a blues woman, her writing and performance show that the aesthetic of blues women formed part of her atmosphere, and as a traveling performer, Smith provided a model of how traveling by choice, being on a quest, could shape Baker's formation of her own agency. Blues women opened up a performance space for Baker. Her contact with Smith provided Baker with a precedent for her own agentive travel, which she extended to her film characters—travelers all.

The blues designates a type of performing power and personal style that could be adapted as Waters had done. Performing in the music halls of Paris, Baker's instructive proximity to blues women, with Waters as an English-language model, seems to have left a mark on her notions of glamour. Baker fit in with the lavish Folies Bergère style as a dancer, but she became practically the French version of Ethel Waters when, in the 1930s, she included singing and gowns in her repertoire. Waters presented a perhaps more broadly appealing version of the blues woman. Both on- and offstage, blues women used elements of their costume—including jewelry, reflective fabric, beads, and feathers—to present an alluring image of everyday sensuality and power. Baker parlayed this aesthetic into what would become her grande dame persona. Still, the traditional blues women had a lasting impact. They opposed conventional roles for women in that they were migratory, physically imposing, and brash. They opened up new worlds of expression for Black womanhood through the metaphor of their own lives and livelihoods. In addition to Clara Smith and Ethel Waters, Baker's aesthetic models included famous performers Bessie Smith and Ma Rainey. All these women exuded and exploited powerful philosophical, visual, and textural aesthetics, and Baker schooled herself in their performance paradigms of "look-at-me-ness."

Ultimately, blues women's most important contributions to Baker's aesthetic and to the study of Baker's aesthetic are the ways in which they complicate the traditional feminist formulations of the male gaze. Black women, as Andrea Elizabeth Shaw points out, must devise strategies of confrontation and visibility that counter what she calls "racial erasure."[36] Shaw explains that this erasure can take the form of subordinating typically Black characteristics in favor of the appearance of physiological or behavioral assimilation, or it could be the hyperembodiment of Black women through visibility as long as it is limited to sexualized objectification.

Racial erasure is not merely invisibility or unacceptability, however; performance and exaggeration are key components of this process. Focusing on gender differences alone obscures the intersectional operation of race and gender in how Baker was perceived and how she performed. Blues women alert us to the transformative and even radical possibilities of self-objectification and performance—theirs is a counterfemininity to the dominant white and acquiescent Black forms of acceptable womanhood. In using blues women's performances as building blocks for her own burlesque, Baker opposed gender expectations at the intersection with racialized limits of Black women's visibility as women and as Black women citizens. Baker and women like her—Black women of the early twentieth-century stage—actively risked potential repercussions of courting the fetishizing gaze of visual pleasure under Jim Crow with their daring acts of look-at-me-ness, wanting to be the center of attention when it was not safe to do so.

BAKER'S BURLESQUE IN *SHUFFLE ALONG* AND ITS RECEPTION

In the United States, as a Black American entertainer, Baker's immediate contexts, in addition to the blues, were minstrelsy and burlesque in vaudeville—comedy as a Black person and comedy as a woman, respectively. Throughout her career, Baker's burlesque drew from the American vaudeville burlesque variety show and the minstrel show as well as the Parisian music hall and ethnography-related displays in France. Burlesque has, for our purposes, two basic subgenres: the satirical and the erotic, one latent and one overt in Baker's work. Superior comedy or satirical burlesque aims to ridicule, parody, or caricature by physical or grotesque imitation. It involves ridiculing and bringing high or supposedly serious culture down low through the use of comedic parody. Aiming at laughter, satirical burlesque critiques current events or public figures through derisive, exacting imitation. It relies on the audience's sophisticated knowledge of the subject being caricatured and their willingness to venture into murky territory where they can be implicated and exposed, ending up the target. Satirical burlesque ridicules that which it mimics.

Related to but distinct from satire, erotic burlesque features elaborate costuming, rich set design, loose narrative, and plenty of irony. Its performers often have an unconventional appearance, playing against normative expectations in terms of gender, race, or sexuality by mainstream standards. In the United States, Baker's comedic style brought together the burlesque and the physical elements of minstrel comedy, mostly without the use of blackface makeup. The object of her ridicule was the chorus line. It was a friendly roast out of which she built a reputation as a comedic dancer.

In addition to the blues women discussed earlier, Baker's performance milieu was heavily influenced by minstrelsy and blackface comedy, the most popular entertainment of the late nineteenth and early twentieth centuries. The tripartite structure of the minstrel show carried over to the burlesque shows. The first part of these shows typically included songs and dances by women performers and low comedy by male comedians. The second part was in the form of a variety section, where women did not traditionally appear. The final part of the show was usually a spectacular finale. White actors (and later, African American actors for different reasons and in a different register) blackened their faces using burned cork and performed sketches that recycled derogatory clichés about African Americans, often drawn from elsewhere in popular culture. Minstrelsy's social content and its aesthetic thus formed the structure of the minstrel show, which then influenced the formats of both burlesque and vaudeville.

In this second sense, burlesque defines or even celebrates the body as a kinetic, ever-evolving spectacle that satisfies as it re-creates the basic desire to gaze on a pleasing or curious subject. Historically, erotic burlesque aestheticizes and objectifies the skin and plays with how much to show and to see. In the United States, the striptease, in which a (white) performer strategically reveals areas of skin on her body, has dominated knowledge of the burlesque. Yet the burlesque incorporates a much broader theatrical practice, particularly in African American drama and the type of popular entertainment on which Baker's American and French performances were based.

Generally speaking, "burlesque reduced its subject matter, whether drama, myth, or history, to the level of comic and urban domesticity. [It was] a frothy brew of topical songs, legs, limelight, puns good and bad, eccentric dancing and enormous energy. . . . In America burlesque was a nonliterary mixture of skimpily dressed women and eventually strippers and male low comedians, with dancing, songs, comic patter, and an increasing raunchiness frowned upon by civic authorities."[37] Although burlesque waned toward the end of the nineteenth century, it continued to influence vaudeville generally and African American popular entertainment in particular. Baker's career was built on her capacity to remix and reuse such performance strategies, and, as noted in the introduction, performers from Diana Ross (who played Baker and Waters onstage) to Beyoncé appreciate its potential through Baker's adaptation of it.

Burlesque is also illusion that has to do with creating spectacles of inversion and exaggeration for the purposes of entertainment, satire, self-protection, and perhaps revelation. Baker's aesthetic, exemplifying burlesque, features energy, legs, and topical songs. Even celebrity mayhem can serve as a form of burlesque performance. It contains all the stories and images framing the audience's sense of the performer. It involves crafting pop entertainment, disguising person-hood, or fashioning an extraordinary personhood; a star with lights, costumes, music, camera, and dance—production, in other words. Baker's burlesque has to do with absurdity and irony. Burlesque is a performance style that is made and does not hide the fact that it is made up. It allows performers to draw on the ridiculous, the implausible, the spectacular, and the excessive as tactics for navigating the quickly shifting, often disorienting, vicissitudes of popular culture. Baker used that very shaky mixed ground of paradox and ambiguity, especially because it eventually became sexualized, to establish her authorship as a comedic dancer through her deft manipulation of incongruity and the paradoxes in her performance. When Baker joined the traveling troupe of the groundbreaking production *Shuffle Along* in 1922, she gained the opportunity to dance and perform nationally and carried in her muscle memory this rich Black American aesthetic legacy.[38]

Shuffle Along was an extremely important musical with an all-Black cast that introduced the world to luminaries such as Paul Robeson, Fredi Washington, and Baker. As Langston Hughes reflected on the Harlem Renaissance, he wrote, "I remember *Shuffle Along* best of all. It gave just the proper push—a pre-Charleston kick—to that Negro vogue of the 20's that spread to books, African sculpture, music, and dancing.... White people began to come to Harlem in droves."[39] Hughes pointed to the role of the burlesque show in ushering in the Harlem Renaissance and in calling attention to Black writers and the worlds their work seemed to evoke. An astute observer of culture, Hughes recognized the ways in which *Shuffle Along* represented a shift in sensibility among the makers of African American entertainment. *Shuffle Along*'s cocreator, Eubie Blake, put the show in context: "At that time—that is, in the twenties—there was no money to be had for the production of Black shows. Noble Sissle and I had been 'hustling' up and down Broadway for over five years, trying to sell our songs—with no success at all."[40] Moreover, the show epitomized changing tastes among the consumers of Black popular culture. White audiences were now apparently keen to pay money for the pleasure of seeing Black people dancing onstage in ways that gave the impression of being authentic to Black urban culture.

Shuffle Along provided a new crucial site for Baker's performance. In an era when both Black and white actors enacted blackface mimicry through minstrelsy, *Shuffle Along*'s use of actual Black bodies represented a relatively progressive concept of the Black aesthetic and moving forward the issue of Black visibility overall. In a thoughtful article appearing five years after the close of the show attesting to its lasting influence, New York City's *Inter-State Tattler* offered this insight: "Perhaps the next step of the talented comedians will be to reform the content and technique of blackface comedy. Or, in plainer terms, do away with blackface comedy. Dutch, Hebrew, Swede, and Irish comedy actors have practically disappeared from the stage. They still linger on in the backwash of burlesque, but they are fast vanishing from the higher forms of amusement. It is time for the Negro character comedian to go along with them."[41] The writer admired the show for putting dark-skinned girls in the chorus. Important as well is the fact that "the Negro" is one of many ethnic characters and that those ethnic characters involved differentiations among what historian Matthew Jacobson called "probationary white"—that is, white people who were not Anglo-Saxon Protestants and thus underwent a complex probationary period in which their whiteness was manufactured and contested.[42] Caricatures were part of the vaudeville scene, and Baker played her own part in this with a show that was innovative at the time.

In contrast to earlier African American (mis)representations, which drew caricatures from Southern or plantation symbolism, *Shuffle Along*'s music was high energy and combined both rural and urban settings.[43] Although set in a small town, the form and influence of the show suggested modernity and aligned with New York's industrial energy. In particular, this type of burlesque demonstrated a shift in the use of a chorus line. Mainstream or white shows, both in the United States and abroad, tended to use the chorus line as a spectacle akin to a display of dolls either standing still or moving in choreographed straight lines. *Shuffle Along* was especially vernacular, bringing to the stage social dances from the nightclub and juke joint. Baker's comedy end girl caricature fit in with but also departed from the line. Dynamic ragtime and jazz dancing by both men and women came from Black vaudeville via the touring African American performers of the segregated Theater Owners' Booking Association. Dances in the show included soft-shoe, slow-motion acrobatics, prancing, and chorus line kicking.[44] Baker's years with *Shuffle Along* allowed her to experiment artistically and showcase her comedy skills to American audiences.

The production of *Shuffle Along* was Baker's first major experience in crossover entertainment that blended popular music, dialogue, and dancing. The show reworked everyday social spaces such as the dance hall into theatrical and near-ethnographic spaces, revealing African American vernacular culture to new and majority white audiences.[45] With such a variety of dancing inventively presented, it was not long before white chorus lines wanting to imitate the style of Black musical shows learned to dance jazz.[46] The show's slow songs were crucial, too, and exemplified Sissle and Blake's innovations and authorship. Blake continued,

> There hadn't been a Negro show on Broadway since Cole and Johnson's musical comedies. They were the real pioneers—in the very early 1900s.... I think the one single biggest novelty was in a song called "Love Will Find a Way." This was a real romantic number, and at first they didn't want it in the show. See, the thing was that Negroes had never been permitted romance before on the stage. This song was really the first of its kind in a big Negro show. So I think that was a big step for entertainment written by Negroes.[47]

In a Black twist on typical vaudeville comedy, *Shuffle Along* included simple, fast-paced comedic dialogue for scenes set in an all-Black town called Jim Town, and the musical numbers were staged with nightclub backdrops. Blake and Sissle composed the music and wrote lyrics for the songs, while Flournoy Miller and Aubrey Lyles wrote the speaking parts. Finally, *Shuffle Along's* instrumentation consisted of a "thirteen-piece orchestra that included three saxophones, two violins, a clarinet, piano, percussion, etc."[48] The all-Black production ran for fourteen months in New York City before touring to other cities and towns. Baker remained a member of the traveling troupe of *Shuffle Along* for two years, until it closed in 1924.

Newspaper clippings from the era show that *Shuffle Along* brought Baker to a wider audience, and they document that many admired her novel dance-comedy routine that had been gleaned from her formative experiences in St. Louis with the Jones Family Band and refined on the road with the Dixie Steppers and African American blues women performers. Journalists at Black newspapers singled out Baker for her successful performance, debunking the notion that she was nothing before Paris.

As early as 1922, Baker was highlighted—a headliner, no less—in a dance review: "Extraordinary Sensation/Josephine Baker/The Lightning of Jazz."[49] It was no coincidence that Baker was so readily aligned with jazz (rather than blues) in critics' minds. As popular culture came to embrace jazz, it became a framework for describing and critiquing Black performance. Jazz was deemed a highly modern music in many of the quarters that embraced it, and this description draws attention to Baker's kinetic effect of speed and the effects of shock and amazement she inspired in her audiences. This piece points to broad praise Baker received in the United States. When Baker performed for Black audiences, she was understood within a vernacular and comedic and musical context of African American vaudeville culture. Baker's antics earned her the moniker "lightning of jazz," and though she was not the official star, the funny girl was a featured act and a recognized innovator.

Shuffle Along was transformative for the entertainment industry and for Baker. By making herself the center of attention of the show, Baker gained a national profile as a comedy auteur, and she did so in an innovative production that broke away from the use of blackface. The show's coauthors, Noble Sissle and Eubie Blake, put a twist on the chorus line by allowing Baker to create the role of "the comedy end girl." While the chorus line dancers performed their traditional mechanized and uniform motion, Baker broke in the line, mocking the dancers' orderliness and stealing the show by crossing her eyes, dancing with rubbery legs, and generally goofing off. Baker could not have picked a better show in which to do her thing.

By performing in *Shuffle Along*, Baker became part of a show that was critical to the rearticulation of what Black bodies meant onstage in American entertainment, and the experience helped her form her unique funny-glamorous persona. *Shuffle Along* had long-lasting effects on US theater, particularly in the area of dance. The production set expectations of what writers, painters, singers, dancers, and other African American artists would offer consumers: quick-quipping vaudeville comedy and high-energy dance scenes drawn from or purporting to represent working-class urban and rural Black life. As a visual and performative text, *Shuffle Along* was one of the early moments of Black culture as a viable commodity.[50] Baker was lucky to be part of such an

Fig. 1.1. Advertisement for a show featuring Josephine Baker, "the lightning of jazz." *Chicago Defender*, May 20, 1922.

influential show and to share the cultural platform that *Shuffle Along* and other Black-cast American productions provided. Her comic persona would be "the intersection of multiple ideologies and lived experiences . . . constructed by acculturation, individual choice, and industrial imperatives—rather than the person," to borrow from media scholar Bambi Haggins. Baker's later public persona was a glamorous, funny, and provocative amalgamation of Black American women's vernacular performance culture, showcased in her *Shuffle Along* work and Parisian music hall themes.[51]

After *Shuffle Along* closed, Baker joined the casts of *In Bamville* and later *Chocolate Dandies*, both Blake and Sissle productions. A perceptive journalist writing for the African American newspaper the *Cleveland Gazette* singled out Baker's successful performance in *In Bamville*: "And then there's Josephine Baker, one of the funniest young ladies of the moment on the stage. And it is interesting to note that she is a chorus girl. She has been promoted to 'principal' at times in various scenes, but even when she is back in the line the audience is watching her—and applauding her every movement."[52] This quote both paints the picture of Baker's early forays onstage and demonstrates the positive response to her work. She was a hit, to be succinct. And although she might have become frustrated with the labor conditions under which she worked, noting that she sometimes was unpaid and hungry, she did find an audience for her unique brand of dance comedy. The writer did not reference or criticize Baker for minstrelsy, negative stereotypes, or misrepresenting the race—all criticisms journalists made about her later film work.

In the May 13, 1925, edition of the *New York Amsterdam News*, a critic of the show *Chocolate Dandies* wrote, "She is Josephine Baker. Miss Baker is tall, slight of figure and long of limb. She seems as pliable as a rubber band. Her gyrations are comic to the last degree. Some people call her the chocolate edition of Charlotte Greenwood and there are others with long memories who say that she is a bronze counterpart of a celebrated French eccentrique, Pasquerrette, who came to this country years ago."[53] This writer enthusiastically illuminates Baker's stateside popularity as a comedy dancer and exemplifies the type of critical language that was emerging to describe her. Despite these accolades, Baker made a point to note in her written recollections that her name was not listed in the official program for *Chocolate Dandies*.[54]

After *Chocolate Dandies*, Baker appeared in a revue at the Plantation Club starring Florence Mills, with Ethel Waters as an understudy. Baker "stepped out of the line every night to do a specialty dance. One night, producer Caroline Dudley [Reagan] came backstage after the show to recruit for the black revue she wanted to take to Paris," and the tall, pliable comic dancer's performance caught her attention.[55] Dudley offered Baker a role in the show she was organizing in Paris, *La revue nègre*. Dudley offered to raise Baker's $125 weekly salary to $150. At first Baker accepted, but then she decided to negotiate, eventually nearly doubling the initial offer to $250 weekly.[56]

Baker had now come a long way from the starving performer who often went unpaid. And she was no longer performing without a named role. It is tempting to underestimate Baker, giving her little credit as a professional in charge of her career, but her biographies reveal small, crucial moments of self-determination and key instances of creativity that reveal that Baker understood her value as a performer and that she went to Paris as an experienced professional. However, Baker's filmic narrative of the ingenue discovered in Paris was an important part of her overall public persona; it made for a more dramatic and classic story. By her own account in *Les mémoires* and other writings, bolstered with significant traces of what I have recovered of the Black press, Baker's truer story is that of an adventurous young woman artist who had already wanted to go to Europe when Dudley approached her. Baker charted her own course, determined to become Josephine. And her early audiences in the Black American press loved her work.

When Baker set sail for Paris on the SS *Berengaria* in early autumn 1925, her voyage from New York to France was deemed momentous. She was already well known. Appropriately, the *Chicago World* reported the occasion: "On board was Josephine Baker, who has been starring at the Plantation Revue. Miss Baker's place at the Plantation has been filled by May Barnes, formerly of *Runnin Wild* quartet." The reporter praised the "troupe of race entertainers [who were] to star in a special revue in Paris."[57] The American Black press would continue to follow Baker's Parisian career closely, providing a window into what her European migration meant in an African American cultural context. As they wrote about her growing fame in Paris and eventually the release of her first feature film, *La sirène des tropiques*, they came to constitute a critical, if fluid, primary record of Baker's self-invention and circulation as a cultural figure, of a cinematic phenomenon as it took flight.

For Baker and for many others, the Great Migration did not always mean movement toward a US city. The imagination of "somewhere better" included landscapes outside the United States that might have been neither African nor anglophone, and such was the case for Baker. As Baker prepared for Paris, her dance and comedy template for what would become her personal burlesque style had been established. It was all about movement, movement, and more movement. Legs! Crossed eyes! Each move jangled and juxtaposed to the last but was still smooth and topped off with her smile. She would use the dances she had learned as a child in St. Louis and those she had improvised on the road. She would make faces. She would wiggle, shimmy, and shake everything out of order. And she would adapt to her new environment.

PARIS! PARIS!

African Americans had been visiting Paris since the nineteenth century, and travelers such as Frederick Douglass and Booker T. Washington wrote or spoke enthusiastically about their experiences in Paris and contributed to the idea of

France as a safer place for Black people.[58] Baker's own early twentieth-century path had been paved by the two hundred thousand Black American soldiers who saw duty through arduous and unequal labor in the Supply Service in France.[59] "The Great War in France afforded African American men opportunities many had not experienced before."[60] Amid the relief Baker and other African Americans must have felt at being in a place that offered them a refuge from American racism, France's geopolitical role in Africa and the Caribbean retreated to the background. Speaking of his arrival in Paris as a nineteen-year-old stowaway, the boxer Eugene Jacques Bullard exclaimed, "Here I was in the place I had wanted to be in and see all my life. And it was wonderful."[61]

Figures such as W. E. B. Du Bois, who idealized France, were not ignorant of its imperialism and approached the European country with "strategic optimism": "France had conscripted 620,000 soldiers from its colonies to fight the war, often under deeply unpopular and brutal circumstances, and its treatment of colonial labor troops was often as harsh as the treatment Black American labor troops received at the hands of white American officers. Yet for Du Bois—facing a government locked into the patterns of reaction, red-baiting and curtailing civil liberties lauding French democracy as a tactical move seemed necessary to address these problems and thereby maintain the pressure for reform in the United States."[62] The cultural residue of French colonialism complicated Baker's mythic Paris. The trafficking of cultural objects from the continent to Paris made it "a charged site" of Black internationalism.[63] For this discussion of Baker, Paris is best understood as a "dialectical wish-image of Paris as a site of idealism and unrest," a sweet conundrum.[64] In African Americans' writing about France, we see the "use of France as a rhetorical figure for a truly egalitarian and democratic poetics . . . the acquisition of French as a gateway to new and progressive subjectivities."[65] When Baker relocated to Paris, her comedy-dance performances took on new meanings for new audiences and for her.

"That Paris rather than New York, London or Berlin should be the city where these notions, such as negrophilia, black liberation, et cetera, were played out is understandable, if not predictable," writes art historian Petrine Archer-Straw in *Negrophilia: Avant-Garde Paris and Black Culture in the 1920s*.[66] The performances of African American entertainers in Paris serve as a bridge between the African shows of the late nineteenth century and Baker's Africanist and so-called tropical shows of the early twentieth century. The negrophilia, or commercializing love of Black culture, that Baker exemplified was a collective obsession that preceded Baker, and the film *Zouzou* (1934) shows just how profoundly long-standing exoticism influenced the characters written for her and their French reception. Archer-Straw continues, "Paris' modernity was characterized by its openness to Black culture and jazz in particular, the improvised and anarchic musical form that seemed to sum up the unpredictability and anxieties of a new age."[67]

Such a double-edged dynamic provided that sense of freedom and cultural validation so many African American expatriates like Baker sought and reveled in, in contrast to the restrictions and violence in the United States. Archer-Straw writes, however, that while Black Americans were "reflected" and rarely "depicted," they are evoked as an "invisible presence in a multitude of negrophiliac images and texts from the era."[68] Paris was not perfect. Baker was highly visible and in the specificity of her persona as Josephine, appears to be both an exception to and confirmation of Archer-Straw's observation. Yet again, she represented the exception to her race because she often performed solo onstage as a singular phenomenon, but for many she also epitomized a racial type. Baker's performances onstage and on film were among those texts that isolated the Black figure and fetishized Black culture. This unsettling modality underpins Baker's success abroad, though it is overlooked, whether by her own accounts or by critics past and present. She operated between two limiting kinds of perspectives, and I find that, ironically, it was the cinematic aspect of her career, with the fewest examples, that allowed for a measure of play within those boundaries.

The new Paris of the interwar years involved both France and Black America, and the idea of Blackness. In retrospect, the immense popularity of Black American music and dances such as the Charleston was conflated with diasporic Blackness overall. This trend clashed and then melded with the traffic of objects, such as sculpture, from Africa and elsewhere in the French empire. Still, the Parisian story provided an alluring image of the sweet life of cultural recognition and freedom from violence that was incredibly and rightly important to the overall formation of African American modernity and modernism.

To be sure, Baker loved Paris—"its noise, its mystery, its mysteries"—and it loved her back.[69] For Baker, Paris was a party. In her memoirs, she wrote, "At night, champagne, joy, fever, more dance, flowers, women, dancing. Never brutal, never stupid, never vulgar, long live Paris! However, I know there are poor people, and I do think about it."[70] Her newfound wealth and celebrity defined her world. Designers, producers, and other prominent figures showered Baker with luxurious gifts, and she changed apartments several times, experiencing a voluntary mobility few African Americans of her era could scarcely imagine. Such experiences were reflected in the narratives of her films. The world she had left behind in the United States was still on her mind, perhaps reflected in the way that the characters she played were young women of modest means who were somewhat on the margins of glittering Parisian society and looking to make a change.

Mademoiselle Baker's world now involved international writers and artists, expatriates, royalty, and European tourists passing through Paris. She was surrounded by artists who sought her as a muse and found her to be someone crafting her own mastery, her own story. Acclaimed American mobile artist Alexander Calder paid tribute to Baker in one of his earliest wire sculptures in 1927. She was both a muse and an artist. Baker's Paris was a city of movement—not only in the dancing onstage but also in the flows of people from various places. The architect Adolf Loos designed a four-story house for Baker, which, though never built, remains an inspiration for generations of designers and students.[71] These relationships opened up new possibilities for Baker's own creativity.

In some ways Baker's story is the story of Black American migration. She left St. Louis in search of a better life. The journey opened opportunities of self-fashioning through performance jobs. She ran *to* something as much as she ran *away*, and so her migration within the United States and certainly her migration to Paris was an act of creativity, daring, and imagination—just as it was for millions of Black Americans leaving untenable situations.

The Parisian venues Théâtre des Champs-Élysées and Folies Bergère attracted a foreign clientele from around Europe, so Baker's audience consisted of an international cross-section of music hall attendees. When Baker and *La revue nègre* arrived in Paris, negrophilia, a fantasy-driven appreciation of African diaspora art and performance in the context of colonialism, was already underway. Yet Paris was a site of "black ideas" as well as Black fandom.[72] Historian of Black internationalism and literature Brent Edwards writes, "The significance of Paris in this period is not a question of sheer population size. Instead, as Raymond Williams has argued, the European metropole after the war provided a special sort of vibrant, cosmopolitan space for interaction that was available neither in the United States nor in the colonies. . . . Paris is crucial because it allowed boundary crossing, conversations, and collaborations that were available nowhere else to the same degree."[73] Due in no small part to the writings of the Black American press, Paris came to represent "certain extensions of the horizon."[74] Negrophilia did not foreclose Black creativity and initiative in this moment.

Even the ways in which information about Baker circulated was a product of this effervescence, this outpouring of Black performance in Paris. Foreign correspondents were in fact part and parcel of the phenomenon of Black

Fig. 1.2. Josephine Baker standing next to
her automobile. © Bettmann/CORBIS.

success in Paris that they reported on. During the 1920s and 1930s, Jamaican-
born Black American author and journalist Joel Augustus Rogers was for a
time the European correspondent for the *New York Amsterdam News,* while
the *Baltimore Afro-American* and the *Chicago Defender* relied on a number of
reporters and contributors, many of whom did not have bylines. Smaller, more
regional papers sometimes used correspondents but more often maintained
their ability to report entertainment news from Europe and the daily goings-
on of Paris by printing articles from the Associated Press newswire or other
services, sometimes with added commentary. Covering Baker (among other
European-based Black performers) helped make American newspapers international in scope, increasing their profile and prestige as they cultivated and
fed readers' curiosity. Baker became a recurring news story, and her location
in Paris aroused interest in the possibilities of life abroad. The Black press was

a psychosocial space for Black formation and helped promote the idea of Paris as a racial refuge.

African American newspapers and their correspondents were agents of Baker's publicity and, by extension, promoters of Paris and cowriters of the Parisian mythology. Through their writings about Baker and other successful entertainers, they portrayed Paris as a haven where African Americans could pursue the sweet life; a cosmopolitan life cut off from dominant, white-American perceptions of Black American identity; a life relatively unencumbered by the racist restrictions and social insult that were commonplace in the United States. The sweet life was merely an expectation of common decency and safety from harm in public life. The *New York Amsterdam News*, along with the *Chicago Defender* and the *Baltimore Afro-American*, enthusiastically covered Baker's Parisian career. The performer gained publicity in these papers, and, for an American newspaper otherwise oriented toward informative activism, such as the *Defender*, Baker was a rich source of not only entertainment but also cultural discussion and hope. Black journalists stationed in Europe helped create an occasion for Black newspapers' wide international and interdisciplinary scope.

CONUNDRUMS OF BLACK SUCCESS IN PARIS

The phenomenon of African American success in Paris, fueled by African American internationalism and French negrophilia, would vindicate African American talent and inspire the French. Writes historian Tyler Stovall, "When one searches for the roots of the Jazz Age in 1920s Paris, one must consider the impact of energetic rhythms and haunting melodies overheard on the dusty plains of war-torn France."[75] The Black American expat community lived mostly in Montmartre, a working-class neighborhood toward the north of Paris, and it was made up of a variety of performers, especially jazz musicians. The African American soldiers set Baker's stage in two related but different kinds of performances. Baker and the music she danced to were not entirely novel to her Parisian audiences. In 1918, James Reese Europe's 369th Infantry Regiment band had played concerts in Nantes, Angers, Tours, and Aix-les-Bains and had helped create a jazz audience in France. As Stovall documents, later that same year, Europe's group debuted at the Théâtre des Champs-Élysées, where no less than the president of the republic was in attendance. Other regiments also had touring jazz bands, and Black American performers came to give concerts during the war.[76] Black American soldiers had brought their cultural wares to France and shared them with the population;

thus, when Baker debuted in 1925, word of the beautiful music, crazy jazz rhythms, and sheer physical energy of Black Americans had preceded both her and *La revue nègre*.

Apart from Black Americans, the presence of Africans and the resonance of events in the Caribbean influenced Baker's career in Paris. Senegalese and West African soldiers had served as a colonial augment in the French army during World War I. Tunisia had been a French protectorate since 1881. Martinique was still a colony in the 1930s, becoming a department in 1946. The long wake of the 1804 Haitian revolution and the US occupation of Haiti between 1915 and 1934 were in the background, and the specter of the Algerian independence movements beginning in the 1940s was on the horizon. Baker's aesthetics and the understanding of her cultural position was not so much as an American but as a figure on to which could be projected interpretations, ideas, and stories drawn from colonialist thinking. As a Black American, Paris was for Baker a site of success. As a Black diasporic figure, her situation was more complex. Paris was in this sense a refuge both real and imagined, and it was through her film characters that Baker best embodies the contradictions that emerge from this setting. Baker walked into a narrative that was, in many ways, paved by Black men in the diaspora, and she changed it as she performed onstage and on film.

Baker served as a metaphor and medium in French attempts to resolve the long-standing tension between the country's liberating principles and its colonizing activities. Through Baker, France could see itself through the eyes of the Black American refugees it harbored. Black Americans could perform their identities, their chosen notions of Blackness, with pleasure, even if that included the negrophilia of others; they were finally free to embrace the very romance with Blackness that many American and French whites have always enjoyed. Paris was the site of a Black romantic, where expressions of Blackness became synonymous with expressions of freedom. The Black American community in Paris was formed out of this shared expression. Thus, Black Americans' expatriation to Paris is significant not only because they achieved success that they might not have found in the United States but also because their work and lives constituted new creative networks for Black artists. The phenomenon of Black American success in Paris is the result of a mutually beneficial relationship between the French and Black Americans rather than simply one group's escape from racism.

France was always at odds with its status as a colonial empire both within the metropole and out in the territories. Blackness played a constitutive role in the invention of modernist Parisian cultural identity by acting as a mediator.

At issue is whether Black American entertainers and self-declared refugees of American racism performed Blackness in a way that was particularly convenient for the French. Each major wave of Black American expatriation—prewar, postwar, and contemporary—differs from the others and thus reflects social and economic shifts both in France and the United States. These shifts indicate France's changing needs, which were met in part by Black Americans as icons, as political refugees, and as pleasant relief.

As Baker's work in France was reported in the Black American press, her success served as a trope of freedom and assimilation within a larger conversation about a better elsewhere for African Americans. The travels of African Americans—especially performers, writers, scholars, and artists—between New York and Paris during the 1920s and 1930s charted the international dimensions of the Harlem Renaissance. Neither exclusively contained in Harlem nor a literal rebirth (because it was the continuation of cultural trends that had begun in the nineteenth century), this early twentieth-century cultural movement was national in scope, encompassing cities in the South (such as Memphis), the Midwest (Chicago), and the far West. While the Great Migration is characterized as an American movement from south to north, many people also crossed the Atlantic—some for military service in France and other foreign locations, others (those African Americans with the resources to do so) to Europe as tourists, and still others to Africa to establish themselves as missionaries.[77] Through military bands, such as the one led by James Reese Europe, and through the spectacle that everyday Black soldiers must have created for French villagers who had never seen a Black person, African American troops followed in the footsteps of the Fisk Jubilee Singers and paved the way for the phenomenal success of Black jazz musicians, Broadway-style productions such as *La revue nègre*, and Jo Baker, the girl from St. Louis.[78]

Michel Fabre, the late historian of Black American writers in Paris, has described the desire of African Americans at home to share in the international achievement of the expatriates as a desire for a form of "recognition" through embracing "symbols of black American enjoyment of the warm welcome extended by the average French citizen."[79] Through images of Black success and freedom in Paris, in some ways folks at home recognized themselves as contributors of culture, makers of valuable culture, which refuted accusations of inferiority and offered grounds for denaturalizing American racism. The myth of a liberating Paris is manifest in the figure of the jazzman, as it is in Baker's *sauvage* persona. Baker contradictorily inhabited, as a diasporic figure, a Black American performer playing a French colonial figure, first onstage and eventually on film.

This modern African American appeals to these constituencies because he or she is in a sense politically, morally, artistically, and sexually distanced from colonial guilt, Old World musical traditions, and conservative social mores. Indeed, French colonial guilt, French racial envy and fascination toward Black (American) people, and Black American expatriates' desire for modernity were managed by the consumption among white Parisians of a particular brand of the free Black in Paris that both Black American performer-products and white audience-consumers invented. Black Americans and white Parisians conspired to support a myth of the free Black in Paris.

France's relationship to Africa and the conflict between its rhetoric and actions drove the phenomenon of Black American success in Paris. For it was the combination of (fantastical) references to ideas of ancient Africa through artifacts and to modern Black America through music—bypassing actual, contemporary Africans—that African Americans like Baker uniquely permitted and that made Baker and Black American jazz so compelling to Parisians throughout the twentieth century, but particularly in the 1920s and 1930s, the height of the second era of colonial wealth and expansion.

At the same time Baker's performance became Africanized in Paris, what was seen as Blackness (of Africa and the Caribbean) was being run the other way through Baker; it was being commercialized, modernized, and, to some extent, Americanized via Baker's exotic and glamorous persona. Americanness and Africanness presented two different kinds of exoticism, but together they fulfilled audiences' dual fascination with the United States and with Africa—and the critique of American racism provided a form of superiority.

As they were constitutive of colonial cinema, Baker's characters were drawn from preexisting types, recycled from her shows certainly, but from those which proliferated throughout imperial Paris, bubbling up from what Elizabeth Ezra called its "colonialist unconscious."[80] Examples include associating Black bodies with menial labor and entertainment as well as idealizing the particular body parts or even the Black body in general.

As an American performer in a colonial context, Baker entered into an ongoing and capacious narrative for Black and brown bodies. She brought to this narrative references to minstrelsy, ragtime, jazz, cakewalking, one-shot films, popularized anthropology, eroticized pseudo-scientific curiosity, and appropriations of many kinds and motivations. In her films, Baker did not take on the roles of great characters of African American history and myth. She made musical comedies, and she played ordinary women thrust into the spotlight. Yet there is something glamorous and mythic about how she amalgamated her stereotypes by her sheer energy and desire to be seen.

In March 1928, *Amsterdam News* correspondent Andrew Rosemond wrote, "Although Josephine Baker has left Paris, the book and notion stores are still featuring her pictures. The beauty shops are advertising 'Bakerfix,' a preparation (for the hair) which she sponsors. Excepting Lindbergh, Josephine Baker is probably the best known American in Europe."[81] A few months later, he reported to American readers on the proliferation of Baker likeness: "One wonders at the powerful attraction of Josephine Baker on the French public. The windows all over town are still full of her pictures and many people still buy them. Many patrons of the theatre think that she has the most beautiful body in the world."[82] Observers measured her success by such unprecedented visibility by a Black woman and in the multiplicity of her image to be consumed by white Europeans. Baker's image in shop windows is part of the prismatic Black presence in Paris. The narratives and characterizations across Baker's cycle of films, discussed across the next three chapters, constitute the reflexive patterns of the cinematic prism, with internal repetitions and the recycling of preexisting colonialist material that would yet also recall her humble origins in St. Louis.

NOTES

1. Hotchner, *Papa Hemingway*, 52–53.

2. Lydia Nichols and Tracy Laguerre, *Josephine Baker's 111th Birthday*, Google Doodle, June 3, 2017, https://www.google.com/doodles/josephine-bakers-111th-birthday.

3. Guterl, *Josephine Baker and the Rainbow Tribe*, 7.

4. Josephine Baker, *Les mémoires*, 43–44. "Il est pleine de chemins de fer, pleins d'usines qui fume pas dessus toute les maisons et il fait froid."

5. Wilkerson, *The Warmth of Other Suns*, 9.

6. Rudwick, *Race Riot at East St. Louis*, 3.

7. Wells, "Chapter I: The Offense," 4. Wells used sharp sarcasm combined with careful journalistic documentation in her writing against lynching.

8. See Lofgren, *The Plessy Case. Plessy v. Ferguson*, 163 U.S. 537 (1896) resulted in concrete circumstances associated with Jim Crow, such as separate public facilities for white Americans and African Americans. However, both performance and perception played integral roles in the enforcement of these policies. The plaintiff, Homer Plessy, was one-eighth African descent and was classified as Black under Louisiana law. His physical appearance required visual analysis and relied on the interpretation of the looker.

9. Baker and Bouillon, *Josephine*, 2–3.

10. Robinson, "East St. Louis Riot of 1917."

11. Josephine Baker, *Les mémoires*, 52. "A Saint-Louis, chez ma mère, j'avais organisé un petit théâtre dans la cave. Je n'avais pas encore dix ans. Le rideau était fait de pièces d'étoffes ajustées bout à bout. J'avais disposé les bougies sur les boîtes de conserves 'pêches de la Nouvelle-Zélande'. Les vieux bouts de bougies éclairaient les marches de l'escalier—toutes les trois marches—pour descendre. Le public était composé d'une douzaine de filles et de garçons, assis au hasard sur des caisses et sur un vieux banc."

12. Baker and Bouillon, *Josephine*, 6.

13. Josephine Baker, *Les mémoires*, 52. "C'est moi qui jouai; j'avais volé des chaussures à talons hauts à mère et une robe dans laquelle je disparaissais, tellement elle était large. J'avais l'air d'être prisonnière dans un sac, dans un habit à air pour scaphandrier."

14. Josephine Baker, *Les mémoires*, 58. "Ma grand'mere était une grosse dame avec de grosses fleurs. Elle portait des robes à traîne, des manches à gigot en soie et un grand chapeau avec un tout petit trou au milieu où était logé son chignon. Ce chapeau est la plus belle chose que j'ai vue. Il était tellement gai à voir. Naturellement, un jour, je me suis déguisée en 'ma grand-mére' mais avec des cheveux rouges faux. Je mis la robe à traîne, enfilai de grosses manches, mais le chapeau, Ah! quel chapeau! Laissez-moi rire."

15. Baker and Bouillon, *Josephine*, 3–4.

16. Carby, "Women, Migration," 34.

17. Rose, *Jazz Cleopatra*, 47.

18. Berlin, "Ragtime." For history and criticism, see Waldo, *This Is Ragtime.* For a broad philosophical examination of the piano music ragtime and its significance in African American culture, see Johnson, *Autobiography of an Ex-Colored Man.* Initially published anonymously in 1912, Johnson's novel explores themes of migration, passing, identity, and violence through the emotional turmoil and experiences of a protagonist who is of African descent but passing for white.

19. Rose, *Jazz Cleopatra*, 48.

20. Baker and Bouillon, *Josephine*, 15.

21. "Cabanne in Arms over the Proposed Club for Negroes: Will Ask for an Injunction Restraining the Erection of the Buildings on Delmar Boulevard by the Egyptian Club for the Entertainment of Colored Visitors to Fair," *St. Louis Post-Dispatch*, March 20, 1904. Public space and culture were major sites of racial formations and contention. The Washington was a segregated African American theater that seated 506 spectators and operated from 1913 to 1930. On March 20, 1904, the *St. Louis Post-Dispatch* announced that a group of businesses had acquired permits "for a theater, music pavilion and restaurant, the three buildings to extend from 5847 to 5891 Delmar Boulevard." White property owners expressed

concern that "a negro club there will certainly cause great depreciation in Cabanne property generally."

22. Rose, *Jazz Cleopatra*, 48.

23. Baker and Bouillon, *Josephine*, 14.

24. Rose, *Jazz Cleopatra*, 49.

25. Baker and Bouillon, *Josephine*, 24.

26. Ibid., 25–26.

27. Ibid., 15.

28. Jean-Claude Baker, *Josephine: The Hungry Heart*, 34.

29. Davis, *Blues Legacies and Black Feminism*, xv.

30. Baker and Bouillon, *Josephine*, 21.

31. Rye, *Grove Music Online*, n.p.: "Born in Spartanburg, South Carolina, 1894, Clara Smith began working in vaudeville around 1910, and by 1918 was a principal performer on the Theater Owners' Booking Association circuit. For the next five years she toured, mainly in the South, before traveling in 1923 to New York, where she sang at clubs in Harlem and made her first recordings exclusively for Columbia." She died in Detroit in 1935.

32. Davis, *Blues Legacies and Black Feminism*, 84.

33. "Ethel Waters, Famous Blues Singer, Coming," *Savannah Tribune*, May 4, 1922.

34. Baker and Bouillon, *Josephine*, 45–46.

35. Carby, "Women, Migration," 11–13.

36. Shaw, *The Embodiment of Disobedience*, 3.

37. Booth, "Burlesque." Burlesque is a critically studied American theatrical form of comedy and body performance. Key texts include Allen, *Horrible Prettiness*; Schteir, *Striptease*; Liepe-Levinson, *Strip Show*; Baldwin, *Burlesque and the New Bump-n-Grind*; and Davis, *Baggy Pants*.

38. White theater owner John Cort, who eventually produced the show, was broke, but he had an available music hall on Sixty-Third Street in Manhattan. This is where the show opened on May 23, 1921.

39. Hughes, "When the Negro Was in Vogue," 224.

40. Bobbi King, Southern, and Blake, "A Legend in His Own Lifetime," 151–56.

41. Lewis, "Theatres."

42. Jacobson, *Whiteness of a Different Color*, 57.

43. Rose, *Jazz Cleopatra*, 55.

44. Perron, "Dance in the Harlem Renaissance," 23.

45. This is a quality that Baker incorporated in her Paris shows, except that she alone represented Blackness.

46. See Malone, *Steppin' on the Blues*.

47. King, Southern, and Blake, "A Legend in His Own Lifetime," 152.

48. Ibid, 151.

49. Display ad 33 in the *Chicago Defender* (national ed.), May 20, 1922, 8.

50. Stearns and Stearns, *Jazz Dance*, 224–25. After *Shuffle Along*, African American social dances such as the Charleston, the Black bottom, and the buck and wing would be elevated to the stage, where they were choreographed and received as Black vernacular art.

51. Haggins, *Laughing Mad*, 5.

52. "Sissle and Blake 'In Bamville,'" *Cleveland Gazette*, May 10, 1924.

53. "A Chorus Girl Who Really Stood Out and Won Acclaim," *New York Amsterdam News*, May 13, 1925, 6. Charlotte Greenwood was an American vaudeville and early film actor.

54. Josephine Baker, *Les mémoires*, 68.

55. Rose, *Jazz Cleopatra*, 63. Dudley was a socialite who had the financial means to become a producer.

56. Josephine Baker, *Les mémoires*, 72.

57. "European Trip Dodged by Will Marion Cooke," *Chicago World*, October 29, 1925.

58. Quoted in Stovall, *Paris Noir*, 46.

59. Figures from Stovall, *Paris Noir*, 5.

60. Whalan, "Only Real White Democracy," 53.

61. Stovall, *Paris Noir*, 4.

62. Whalan, "Only Real White Democracy," 56.

63. Braddock and Eburne, *Paris, Capital of the Black Atlantic*, 3.

64. Ibid., 11.

65. Whalan, "Only Real White Democracy," 55.

66. Archer-Straw, *Negrophilia*, 18.

67. Ibid.

68. Ibid., 19.

69. Josephine Baker, *Les mémoires*, 92.

70. Ibid., 95.

71. As recently as 2018, an essay on the Baker house appeared in *Architectural Review*; see Slessor, "Loos and Baker." See also Farès and Atkinson, "The Josephine Baker House"; and Shapira, "Dressing a Celebrity."

72. Edwards, *Practice of Diaspora*, 79. The lyrics are from a song that museum curator and occasional pianist George Rivière wrote for Josephine Baker. It reads, "And morning and night, my head / is full of black ideas / All the women want to assume the airs / of Josephine Baker."

73. Edwards, *Practice of Diaspora*, 4.

74. Ibid., 4.

75. Stovall, *Paris Noir*, 22.

76. Ibid., 20–21. See also Fabre, *From Harlem to Paris*. For a recent take on cultural exchanges between Black American and French jazz musicians, see Jackson, *Making Jazz French*.

77. See Griffin and Fish, *Stranger in the Village*.
78. See Jackson, *Making Jazz French*.
79. Fabre, "International Beacons," 122.
80. Ezra, *Colonial Unconscious*, 99.
81. Rosemond, "News of Paris," March 21.
82. Rosemond, "News of Paris," May 23.

TWO

SHOUTING AT SHADOWS

The Black American Press, French Colonial
Culture, and *La sirène des tropiques*

BLACK FILM IN THE UNITED States was formed both in relation to the representational failures of mainstream white cinema and as a creative response to the vicissitudes of American life. Filmmakers shared a clear sense of purpose, while personal artistic dreams found expression and flourished. The early Black American press and early Black American filmmakers often worked together in advancing race films, formulating the intellectual project of Black independent film, and improving Black representation in mainstream films. Black film was a dynamic part of larger Black cultural movements and was itself a long-term, sustained manifestation of experimentation in early American cinema.

African Americans redefined American cinema as they redefined American cities, a process film historian Jacqueline Stewart called "migrating to the movies."[1] During the Great Migration period from 1900 to the 1930s (and continuing in waves through the 1970s), race movies addressed the Black community's needs for dignified representation and secular forms of collectivity and leisure in their new environments. Bill Foster had founded the Foster Photoplay Company in 1910. The Lincoln Motion Picture Company had been established in 1916. And Oscar Micheaux had organized the Oscar Micheaux Book and Film Company in 1918 with the profits from sales of his memoirs and novels. Theirs were the films that would largely define race films and help create a specific brand of Black filmmaking. As historian Cara Caddoo writes, "The popularity of cinema in black life continued to generate new industries and cultural practices."[2] In other words, the cinema ushered in sources of entertainment, employment, and ways of being for audiences as well as critics and filmmakers—and their common objective was to influence the independent cinema to address issues that impacted daily life. Allyson Field's work on nonextant films traces the audiovisual productions of the 1910s, particularly those of Hampton and Tuskegee Institutes.[3] In *Returning the Gaze: A Genealogy of Black Film Criticism, 1909–1945*, media scholar Anna Everett opens a window on critics' and filmmakers' shared goals of encouraging the independent cinema of the era, pointing out that "buoyed by the relative successes of the black press's oppositional campaign against *The Birth of a Nation*, African American elites and masses set out to redefine their relationship to the cinema beyond the bounds of protest literature and a disaffected spectatorship."[4] Made by African American actors, writers, and directors, race films addressed segregated African American audiences and engaged issues of concern to African Americans—such as youth education, temperance, the unfair economics of tenant farming, mob violence and the crime of lynching, and the dangers of city life in the north—all issues that were generally disregarded in Hollywood films. These films and their promotion reflected the new cultural formations and ambitions brought about by the transformations and upheavals of the Great Migration. As millions of Blacks came into perceived competition with whites for limited resources, cities that were once seen as avenues for better education and economic advancement became spaces of both opportunity and oppression, and this dynamic played out in popular culture.

The Black press sought to align themselves with "fledgling" race films and filmmakers: "As early as 1913, the black press initiated a high-profile campaign to promote and celebrate the exploits of upstart black filmmakers dedicated to re-inscribing cinematic images of blackness that authenticated African American progress and development."[5] Film examples from the period include Foster Photoplay's *The Railroad Porter* (1913) and the Lincoln Motion Picture Company's now-lost *The Realization of a Negro's Ambition* (1916). Black audiences wanted to enjoy the movies, too.

Baker's films are paradoxically both peripheral to and central to multiple cinema cultures. Independently produced Black films where African American characters and worldviews were centered, French cinema of the 1930s that sought to balance "hegemonic ideologies about the exotic Other and an escapism that frequently refutes these ideologies,"[6] and Hollywood films in which Black actors were merely the "shadows": these cinema cultures mark out a peculiar and shifting parabolic curve, making it difficult to situate Baker's work in a straightforward way.[7] Her films encompass musical, comedic, and romantic genres within a colonialist framework, containing both the promise and the frustrations of these cinematic ventures, and as we study the "Black Pearl" as an artist,[8] they incite necessary but difficult discussions on the limits of individual representation without structural change.

Fig. 2.1. Advertisement for *The Siren of the Tropics* targeting African American audiences. *Baltimore Afro-American*, October 19, 1929. Reprinted by permission of the AFRO-American Newspapers Archives and Research Center.

The significance of Baker's films arises precisely from their outsider position—from *her* outsider position. Baker reflects prismatically on—and shows various aspects of—the hopes, roles, blind spots, and queries of the idea of the modern new Negro of the 1920s, not (only) as a representative Black figure in an all-white context but as a fragmented one, often playfully putting on and putting off the exhilarations and alienations of a world in the city, on the move, and beyond Jim Crow's segregated insularity. Baker's positions outside Hollywood, outside race films, and outside 1930s French cinema define what might have been and show the expat film star's contributions more clearly.

Baker's films would circulate in the United States, but they were shaped by Paris's famous music halls where Josephine Baker performed; those halls were often settings for "race" shows, ethnographic exhibitions, or human zoos referred to as the *village nègre* ("negro village")—a public display of Africans, indigenous people, or nonwhite people as a stand-alone event or as part of an international trade show such as a world fair or colonial fair. Human zoos were ordinary, easily accessible, and popular displays that provided entertainment for the public as well as human subjects of study for race scientists. The exhibits were usually held outdoors in zoo-like settings.[9] In 1878, *Les Zoulous* played at the Folies Bergère, and in 1892, a musical revue called *Au Dahomey* (starring not Africans but American vaudevillians Bert Williams and George Walker) played at the Casino de Paris as well as at American venues. Displays such as *villages noirs* ("Black villages") or *villages sénégalais* ("Senegalese villages") multiplied at the turn of the century and continued to be successful until the mid-1920s. French historians Pascal Blanchard and Nicolas Bancel have documented the popularity of "human zoos" during the early years of mass entertainment. They write that during the 1870s, "'savage' populations were presented in enclosures with exotic animals (ostriches, camels, monkeys, et cetera)."[10] The exhibits were at the height of their popularity in the period from 1877 to 1890 and were visited by millions of people. The best known among them were "les Indiens Kalina" in 1882, "the Somalis" in 1892, and "Dahomeans" in 1893.[11]

"Un village nègre au Champs de Mars" was a late nineteenth-century living diorama produced in a Parisian public park in which a Black culture's supposed daily life was exhibited for the entertainment of visitors, who played the role of lay anthropologists. Not a one-time occurrence, such displays took place over a number of years and featured African groups such as the Ashantis and the Dahomeans. One particular *village nègre* featured people and cultural practices of Sudan. It might be surprising that the French display was not specific to a French colony, but colonial culture encompassed a range of nonwhite groups and nations. In this particular exhibit, there was a French brasserie at one corner of the scene where visitors invited villagers to sit with them and talk, interactivity being a key aspect of the display.[12] This simulation of a Sudanese village required 350 uprooted men, women, and children who had been transported to Paris from Africa. The compensation, if any, that the people might have been offered or provided is not reported. For religious and architectural "precision," organizers built a mud mosque in the center of the village and maintained fidelity to the village's planning by building mud-clay houses and arranging them around the mosque. They even went to the trouble of constructing an artificial lake to replicate what was meant to represent the Sudanese landscape. However, the lake also served as a curious kind of wishing well into which visitors would toss coins; village-diorama children would dive after them while other "natives" glided by in dugout canoes.

In its fabricated re-creation of village life, the diorama juxtaposed the Sudanese village and the French capital, making striking contrasts and enhancing the frisson of the participation-spectacle. Ultimately, the *village nègre* plays with the idea of Africans coming to Paris as immigrants and colonial subjects in a fashion similar to the exoticism of Baker's films. By spectacularizing everyday aspects of their culture, the exhibit distanced the participants (and those they represented) from French daily life. Unnaturalized in this way, the participants' role was to perform themselves. Fundamentally, it is a scene of containment through exposure, Othering those on display.

The term *village nègre* suggests that the reproduction was a composite of any and all African villages. What does it mean for colonialist exhibition in general and for Baker's roles that specificity is erased in the name of greater "precision" and "authenticity"?[13] The *village nègre* is a key example of the ethnological entertainment backdrop from which Baker emerged, particularly in regard to its strategy of display. The *village nègre* calls for collapsing a wide variety of African ethnicities into one composite Black representative—despite *L'illustration*'s reported claims of specificity. This idea of *black* as a general term, rather than signifying particular ethnicities, became a code that developed through other *villages nègres* and manifested itself in Baker's performances.

"From music-hall to the screen is only one step," opined the December 31, 1927, *Paris-Soir* review of *La sirène des tropiques*. The film relies on Baker's dancing and music hall–infused celebrity and features physical comedy in her scenes with other actors. Baker plays Papitou, who lives "down there in the tropics." She becomes infatuated with André Berval (Pierre Batcheff), a French engineer who has been sent to the island, ostensibly for a surveying project, by a scheming Parisian marquis who has designs on André's beloved, Denise. André proves himself heroic in Papitou's eyes when he rescues her from the unwanted advances of Alvarez (Kiranine), a drunken, disreputable landlord in league with the marquis. In return, Papitou saves André's life when she discovers the marquis's plot to prevent André from ever returning to Paris. Thanks to Papitou, André is able to leave the islands, but she secretly follows him by stowing away on the ship. Such is the synopsis of Baker's feature film debut.[14]

La sirène des tropiques takes on an ethnographic visual rhetoric, especially during the opening sequences that establish location. The first shot is a slightly angled wide exterior shot that shows goats and people milling about on a sandy road that passes several grass-covered circular structures decorated with what appear to be Afro-Caribbean sculptures. Next, a medium wide shot shows groups of adults and children seated in circles, one of whom is weaving a basket. A third shot is wider than the first and shows people, goats, and two men on

Fig. 2.2. Josephine Baker as Papitou and Pierre Batcheff as André Berval in *La Sirène des Tropiques*, 1927. AKG-Images.

horseback moving in various directions. Foliage frames the background and foreground. The plants are indistinct and do not appear to be typically "tropical." The roofs of the dwellings all have the same type of African-like mask on top, and one of the buildings occupies the foreground of the shot. The shots do not feature any one individual but offer "slice of life" views of a group. This brief sequence establishes the location and supposed cultural context where most of the action will take place. The set appears to be created in the manner of a music hall backdrop with vague references to a roughly conceived tropicality. Baker confirmed in her recollections that "a 'native village' hastily constructed in the studio served as our set. Its freshly built straw huts absolutely glistened."[15]

Baker's first dance sequence comes twenty-six minutes into the film. Titled "Night," it is a version of her stage burlesque that begins with a montage of a dozen shots of a dancing Black man surrounded by a crowd of people, including musicians. The featured dancer is Joe Alex, who had been Baker's dance partner in *La revue nègre*. Eventually, Baker joins the scene, and she dances alongside him. He seems to be coded "traditional," first by the trope of the African mask that is seen in the first shot in this sequence. It is on the right side of the frame, close to the foreground. The dancer is dressed similarly to the surrounding crowd, and the camera focuses as much on him as it does on the crowd. What is on display here is not only the dancer but also his context, those who watch him, similar to *la danse des bananes* footage.

With the circles of performance and spectatorship blended, Baker does not make a formal entrance. She appears suddenly in a brief shot (missing footage may account for its abruptness) that is followed by a longer one in which André, her soon-to-be love interest, is seen observing her. Baker is dressed in her typical, if more modest, exotic costume: sarong, blouse, *les créoles* (large hoop earrings), and scarf. She dances her signature choreography. Although the dance sequence is brief and visually straightforward, it marks a turning point in the narrative. Papitou will overhear details of a plot to kill André. Rhetorically, the re-creation of nighttime dances, a native gathering, and a tropical setting references the constructed nature of the *village nègre*.

BETWEEN GLAMOUR, COMEDY, AND RACE

A fascinating unintended attraction of *La sirène* is Baker's contrasting performance styles in her attempts to act like a silent film star while maintaining her own comedic style and choreography from her earlier live performances. When Papitou is still on the island, she is seen in a blue-tinted dream sequence that follows a red-tinted dance sequence. Focused on Papitou's face and seminude body, the camera lingers over Baker's body. Baker's comedic and dramatic sides are both on display, but the camera is always focused on her body. André and Alvarez appear in superimposition as figments of the dream, while the camera fixes on Baker's sleeping face and her twisting and turning in her hammock. She wakes and looks around with some exaggerated expressions as if looking at her own thoughts. Next, she stands and walks toward the camera to part a beaded curtain, leaving her hands outstretched and thus striking one of her alluring poses. The stillness and sensuality of the image contrast with earlier shots of her physical comedy in which she is constantly moving and overacting with goofy facial expressions.

A few scenes later, Baker returns to her roots in physical comedy. At the ticket agency, Papitou leaps onto the railing to get to the front of the line. She is next seen in the ticket line, bumping and pushing other customers with her rear end. At the ticket window, she does not have enough money. Cut to Papitou swimming toward the ship. A crew member hears her shouting and pulls her up to a porthole. They struggle at the window, but eventually she is pulled in,

Fig. 2.3. Baker's character Papitou alternates
between alluring glamour and goofy comedy.

spitting out a big mouthful of water. She tumbles into the room, disheveled,
wet, and confused.

The title card that represents her speech—"Harakko! Krikri! La-oo-ya!!!
(War cry of the island natives.)"—functions as an example of the film's burlesque of ethnographic representation. Previously, Papitou's speech had been
represented as a poor imitation of a type of Creole. In American film, the representation of the dialogue of African American characters was a major point
of contention for critics at that time. Here, the "war cry" is unfortunately meant
to be taken as part of the comedy of the scene.

Papitou's plan is to stow away on the ship. Her rescuer quickly becomes a
would-be captor when Papitou escapes. A chase ensues, and Papitou tumbles
into the coal room of the ship. Disoriented, she waits a moment before deciding

Fig. 2.4. Josephine Baker as Papitou negotiates passage to Paris.
AKG-Images.

Fig. 2.5. Baker's silent film debut showcased her physical comedy gifts.
AKG-Images.

Fig. 2.6. Baker as Papitou, a stowaway disguised with coal on a Paris-bound ship. AKG-Images.

Fig. 2.7. Baker performs ablutions in a bathtub scene. AKG-Images.

to climb the stairs to find a better hiding place. Covered in black coal, Papitou cautiously walks on the deck. She is surprised to bump into a paying guest, who is also surprised. This passenger reports what she has seen to the captain. Meanwhile, Papitou overhears the search party and runs to find a new hiding place. This leads her to the kitchen, where she climbs inside a large container of flour. Now that the captain and passengers are searching for someone "all black," Papitou is all white, covered with flour. A frightful sight, she meets a passenger, who runs to inform the captain: "She is now all white. A ghost!" Finally, Papitou sneaks into a cabin, where she discovers a bathtub. While passengers follow the trail of flour she has left, Papitou is seen in the bathtub, and it is there that she is eventually discovered in a spectacle of nudity and naturalness in another sultry, glamorous framing.

Once she arrives in Paris, Papitou takes a job looking after children. While she is entertaining the children, she is discovered by two producers who attempt to recruit her for their music hall show. She refuses to perform unless they find André, her love, the engineer who had saved her life and with whom she hopes to reconnect in Paris. The producers succeed in locating André and bring him to the theater. However, instead of bearing a declaration of love, André brings news of his engagement to another woman. Baker's solo dance performance occurs after Papitou has found out that her cherished Frenchman does not love her. Although the film has the makings of a romance, Papitou's feelings are unreturned. The plot's progression is not toward romantic bliss—at least not for the ostensible star of the film, who is more famous than everyone else in it—but rather toward occasions for her dancing. Following the engineer was merely a device for getting her to Paris, where she would be discovered and placed in a show. *La sirène des tropiques* restaged Baker's live performances rather than creating a narrative and characters where she could grow and be central to the story. Importantly, Papitou does not express any ambition to be in a music hall show. She purely desires love and attention, which she audaciously demands as a condition of her performance. On another level, Baker's grief takes the form of resignation to the fact that Baker is in the B plot of the movie despite starring in it.

The film continues its trajectory toward the big payoff—Baker dancing onstage in one of her music hall costumes. Papitou, isolated and rejected by André, takes to the stage. The intertitles introducing the performance read, "And that night, as she dances for the last time in Paris, as she pretends to be gay, she mourns her lost love, her illusions, all the sweetness of her youth." Papitou's sadness is contrasted with her supposedly happy dancing, in an example of the incongruity that literary critic Glenda Carpio defined, discussed in chapter 3. A shot of the audience shows the accolades Papitou receives. Instead of the intimacy and romantic love she demanded, Papitou gets public applause as cold comfort. Rather than becoming part of French society through a partnership with the engineer, she has been assigned a role onstage as the entertainment. The dance is a prime example of Baker's grief, as the performance is driven by both her character's longing for and rejection by André.

This dance sequence contains qualities that are consistent with Baker's dance films that were recorded at the Folies Bergère: speed, Africanist bent knees, and the way her costume creates multiple spheres of motion with parts that move independently of her body while reflecting light. The dance sequence is an example of the way that the story provides context and creates meaning around Baker through her film character by reference to her stage performance. The theatrical context in *La sirène* is a reference to Baker's real performance career, and, indeed, she dances not only as Papitou but as herself, performing her signature movements. Baker's dancing in *La sirène* tends to be filmed theatrically, with tableau shots that show her from head to toe on a stage in a theater or on a makeshift stage.

Cinematic dancing today generally includes perspectives—such as close-ups on the feet or face, slow-motion, or freeze-frame—that are not accessible to the live audience. In Baker's era, theatrical framing more or less replicates the setting, which is often a music hall, and also the wide perspective that frames the stage for viewing audiences. The camera's look imitates the view that a live audience member might have. Significantly, however, Baker's dancing is full of figurative cuts and edits—quick changes and an illusory continuity. The world in the film and the world beyond it are layered over each other when Baker dances. We can see the performance—what she actually does—while the story provides a constructed layer of meaning for Baker's performativity.

The story of *La sirène des tropiques* is about much more than the film's plot and content. The reception of the film in the United States among the Black press, and their anticipation even before they saw it, reveals much about the dreams that were attached to the film. And the film is about Baker as an actor as much as it is about the character she played. Baker is always in triplicate as the character, the actor, and her offstage persona. Each shot of the film encompasses the intersecting worlds of Baker's stardom. And by playing types and repeating her characters, Baker synthesizes various stories of exotic women who serve, as explained in the previous chapter, as three types of stars: glamorous movie star, songstress, and quirky comedic auteur.

BLACK AMERICAN RECEPTION OF *LA SIRÈNE*

Six years before Baker returned to the United States, *La sirène des tropiques* had its American premiere at the Lafayette Theater in New York on September 22, 1929. Discussion of the film had begun in early September and centered on Baker's celebrity, using the trope of her life's story and the film's production notes. The film was two years old by the time it came to New York. Viewers experienced the film as though it were from another era of cinema. *The Jazz Singer*, released in October 1927, was the first feature film that was shown as a talkie. A major hit, it was made with Vitaphone, the leading sound-on-disc technology of the day. So-called silent films were almost always accompanied by sound, whether it was a lecturer, phonograph, or live musical accompaniment. Early sound processes involved converting sound to light waves reproduced on a photographic stripe. Vitaphone was an analog system that used sound-on-disc technology where the phonograph records were played on a turntable set within the film projector. Synchronous sound for film would soon become the standard for the movies. In 1929, Baker brought an outdated silent film to American screens at the dawn of talkies.[16]

La sirène's favorable reception thus depended on Baker's fame and the degree to which the film satisfied the critical frameworks of the Black press and fulfilled the ideal of dignified cinematic African American representation. *La sirène des tropiques*, though, was both a French film and a Black film. The dialogue was entirely in French, the filming took place in France, and it was set in the French "tropics." Yet its lead role was played by an African American star. *La sirène des tropiques* thus offered the potential for redefining what constituted a Black film in the United States. But the potential went largely unappreciated at the time.

Hype for Baker's first feature began in the summer, with an article in the *New York Amsterdam News* titled "Josephine Baker Here Soon in Film." The article, likely copied from a press release, exclaimed that *La sirène des tropiques* was "the most elaborate production made during the past year by any European film company, . . . said to have broken all box-office records" in Paris. The piece further highlighted that the production was shot on location in Martinique for three weeks. Finally, the article mentioned the cost of insurance.[17] All these details were meant to create high expectations for the film's production value and to place it on par with Hollywood productions. Like the music hall aesthetic that it referenced, the film would be an elaborate, expensive visual spectacle. The press also discussed the film's place in the new environment of sound. The *New York Amsterdam News* reported that the film would "be synchronized to an original score written by Negro musicians." Joe Jordan is listed as the composer, with Gold Pictures Corporation sponsoring a "plan to road show the seven-reel feature picture."[18] Gold Pictures engaged a singing ensemble of twenty voices to furnish the vocal accompaniment.[19]

Baker's films were viewed in light of her preexisting celebrity in the French music hall as well as in the context of African Americans in Hollywood, such as Bill Robinson, Louise Beavers, and Nina Mae McKinney. When it was brought to the United States, *La sirène des tropiques* was presented in the African American press in relation to Black-cast American films such as *Hearts of Dixie* (1929) and King Vidor's *Hallelujah* (1929), in which McKinney costarred. Baker and McKinney were explicitly linked and compared, as in this excerpt from the *Inter-State Tattler* in 1929: "With the advent of the talkies and the remarkable success of Nina Mae McKinney, the Negro is making a firm bid for recognition on the spoken screen. Tus [*sic*], we find Josephine Baker, the sepia girl from Harlem, who set Paris agog with her sensational dancing, making her initial bow in the film titled 'The Siren of the Tropics.'"[20] The film was not discussed as a French film or a colonial film. Producers certainly hoped to capitalize on what they recognized as the beginnings of a trend in Black film with broad appeal. The Black American press had been proud to report that the British film journal *Close-Up* devoted an entire issue to *Hallelujah* and the whole "vogue of the Negro film." This news entered documented Black film history via the *Indianapolis Recorder* under the headline, "*Close-Up*: English Cinema Monthly Devotes August Number to Negro." The article says of the *Close-Up* issue, "A number of writers state that the Negro is only at the beginning of the contributions he may eventually be enabled to make through the motion picture."[21] This article speaks to the desire for an opportunity to join the great American myth-making machine from a position of independence and pleasure—of oppositionality. At the same time, a picture was emerging of what the ideal Black woman star looked like. "Lovely Nina Mae McKinney" appeared in a Pittsburgh fashion show wearing the gorgeous clothing "with grace and distinction."[22] With this type of reporting, the Black press created and enhanced the available critical vocabulary for talking about Black film. The papers encouraged belief among their readers in the hope that African Americans would be able to participate in the American film industry on equal footing. The cinema was a potent symbol of and vehicle to experiences of modernity and prospects for African Americans. Making a film was metaphorically remaking the world.

La sirène des tropiques departed from race movies in that it was viewed in terms of its potential to improve the standing of Black professionals in Hollywood.

Indeed, "talkiedom" had apparently been looking with intense interest to the Harlem performers in hopes of finding someone with star power to portray the rapidly mounting scripts. An article describing the Parisian debut of *La sirène des tropiques* stated that "the opening night [brought] an audience composed of royalty, resplendent with jewels and title"; after the screening, they "literally swamped her with congratulations and assured her that she had firmly carved a niche for herself in the Hall of Filmdom."[23] Baker offered a vision of a Black cinema that was commercial and Hollywood-adjacent.

Eventually, in mid-September, the *New York Amsterdam News* reported the film's upcoming screening at the Lafayette Theater: "The picture will be thrown upon the screen promptly at twelve o'clock, to be followed by the many stars of the stage and champions of the boxing world. The picture was made in Paris with many scenes being taken in the French islands of Martinique and Guadalupe, and . . . since the showing of the picture at the French capital a great deal of curiosity has been aroused here, especially since the publicity given the arrival of the film in this country."[24] The claims about filming in Martinique and Guadalupe were overstated; the African-style huts for the film had been built on the less exotic lots of the Épernay studios, two hours outside Paris. This was not the only tidbit of inaccurate information in the press surrounding the movie.

As the film traveled to select locations during the fall of 1929, the *Chicago Defender*, the *New York Amsterdam News*, and the *Baltimore Afro-American* each published reviews. In addition, the *Afro-American* ran a three-part series on Baker's life story. Thus, although the star did not appear in person at the American screenings of *La sirène*, she promoted the film indirectly by feeding the press stories about her life. In one of these stories, Baker described her early days of traveling with the cast of the 1921 musical *Shuffle Along*: "After leaving *Shuffle Along* . . . then *Chocolate Dandies*, I was no longer a chorus girl given a featured number. I was a feature player in my own right! I had grown used to seeing my name in lights . . . but there always remained some of the thrill which I experienced the first time."[25] Baker's repeated accounts of her life emphasize aspirational values of adventure, liberty, wealth, and personal transformation. These values, along with the glow of Paris and her achievements there, were at the heart of her appeal in the United States. She personified the hopes of newly urban African Americans and fulfilled moviegoers' desire for a bona fide movie star about whom they could say, "Don't fail to read next week's account of how Josephine Baker became the worshipped and beloved Siren of Paris!"[26] Promoters spared no superlative in selling *La sirène des tropiques*. It was "The Greatest Attraction in Our History—the Sensation of Paris, featuring Josephine Baker," in the usual exaggerated language of advertising.[27] It was "the most amazing spectacle ever filmed."[28] Nevertheless, the actual reception of *La sirène des tropiques* in the African American press departed from the royal welcome it reportedly received in Paris and from the rhetoric of boosterism.

The *Afro-American* screen-review column provided a frank appraisal of *La sirène des tropiques* that reads, in part, "Omit the dancing of Josephine Baker from her photoplay, 'La Sirène des Tropiques,' now playing at the theatre, and you have just another picture. Leave it in (and that's why the picture was made, we guess) and you will find after witnessing some rather amateurish acting of white principles in a plot hoary with age, that you've not spent such a bad evening."[29] The reviewer's critical rubric included the values of African American cinema, with particular attention to handling of race relations. The review took issue with the romantic plot in the following terms:

> Though the theme of the picture was advertised to show racial equality, the picture falls short of that. While it is true that Miss Baker is seen in the arms of the Nordic, it is only because she has flung herself there, and not because he has made any effort to draw her to his French bosom. Not once in the entire picture does one see the white actor kiss Miss Baker, nor does one see him make any declaration of his love for her. The love making that is done, is done by Miss Baker, and that, to us, was very weak and almost servile.
>
> ... As a picture showing "Jo" doing the Charleston, and undressed in a costume of feathers or bananas, the photoplay has its merits. It is something new, but its temperature is quite a number of degrees below perfection.[30]

Overall, the review seeks to balance the reasons to see *La sirène* and reasons why it might be disappointing. But its failures as race film point to the particular responsibility that many cultural journalists placed on the cinema. In *La sirène*, Baker's performance provided a satisfying spectacle: "It is something new." However, the deeper investment, the article suggests, is in how the film demonstrates racial equality. It was hoped that the plot would model racial equality in the area of romance, where Baker's character would be the celebrated object of desire in the film. The revolution in romance here would have been for "the Nordic" to pursue Miss Baker passionately.[31]

In September, Jamaica's *Gleaner* ran a brief notice: "Josephine Baker, the coloured singer who has been a sensation in Europe for the past season, will be seen in La Sirène des Tropiques, a film which was made in Europe and which will be synchronized by an orchestra aided by a singing ensemble of twenty voices. One-third of the film will be in colour."[32] The text, which emphasizes the high production values of spectacle—Baker herself among them—repeats other advertising language verbatim. In January, another notice in the *Gleaner*

Fig. 2.8. Papitou in her tropical dwelling prior
to her departure for Paris. AKG-Images.

described the film: "Now that *Hallelujah* is set in both Broadway and Harlem
districts, another Negro film is being made. Josephine Baker, the Harlem girl whose
dancing made a tremendous hit in Paris, is appearing in *La Sirène des Tropiques*. This
picture is now being synchronized."[33] Notably, the *Gleaner* contextualizes Baker's feature with *Hallelujah* under the category of "Negro film," defined by Baker's presence.

Baker gave the film further cultural significance by expressing how important it was to her: "'La Sirène des Tropiques' is dedicated to my friends in America. I have thrown all of myself into the making of it, and those who may wish
to see me, will find me to my best advantage in this picture. Whatever I may do
in the future, this will always be the most gratifying experience of my life!"[34]

In March 1930, roughly six months after the Harlem opening, the film was
still playing on the East Coast. "Josephine Baker, bronzed race star, who has

taken Europe by storm, is the star of 'La Sirène des Tropiques,' the photo-play that will be shown at the Lafayette Theater Tuesday and Wednesday." The weeklong bill included a western and "a heart touching story of a little [Russian] peasant girl."[35] This quote provides evidence of both the film's screen-ing and its programming context. Its inclusion among mainstream genre films suggests the ways in which Baker's international stardom functioned to create a specific niche for her in American mainstream movie fare.

Baker's movie roles associated her with intellectual activities—one of the core values of Black films. The centerpiece of Baker's performance remained her dancing body. But the combination of dance and acting widened the audi-ence's views to include Baker's capacities for thought, language, and emotional expression. (In the later films *Zouzou* and *Princesse Tam-Tam*, her mastery of spoken French would be on display.)

For Parisian audiences, this film updates the familiar *village nègre*. *La sirène des tropiques* is a Caribbean film as much as it is a French film or a "Negro" film in the sense that, at least in the early sequences in which Baker is still on the island, there is a strong sense of the setting. This setting referenced Baker's identity as Creole, which was established by her stage performances and the perceptions of journalists and audiences, thus providing her a lasting associa-tion with the Caribbean.

AMERICAN ACTORS AND BAKER'S VISIBILITY

The film careers of Baker's African American contemporaries Nina Mae McKinney, Ethel Waters, Fredi Washington, Elisabeth Welch, Hattie McDaniel, Evelyn Preer, and Lena Horne reflected, as they also shaped, the field of possi-bilities available to their Parisian colleague in the 1920s and 1930s. As Charlene Regester writes, "As black women during the first half of the twentieth century struggled to transgress the borders of Otherness and emerge as Hollywood actresses in their own right, the mainstream cinema industry erased, margin-alized, and devalued them, denied them cinematic voice, and reduced them to the body."[36] A comparison to the other African American leading ladies, however circumscribed their careers might have been, can help us pinpoint Baker's strategies, objectives, and achievements as well as her limitations as an actor. These women did not all perform in films in the same way. Like Baker, many were primarily (or at least initially) singers or dancers. But the careers of these other Black women actors were less sustained than Baker's. They typ-ically appeared in only one or two starring roles, as McKinney did (even though they acted in many films); they tended to play the same characters repeatedly, as Hattie McDaniel did; or they made a clear break from one type to another, as Ethel Waters did when she went from glamorous songstress to somewhat homely roles, portraying ordinary matrons.

During the 1920s, Waters was a wildly famous blues singer of tremendous influence. The *Savannah Tribune*'s music critic joked that one of her performances unfortunately drew a small crowd—of three hundred people. He continued, "Her renditions went big and her interpretation of blues singing was indeed refreshing. Her stage demeanor was most pleasing and her departure from the shouting, hollowing [hollering?] sort of blues singers we have been accustomed to hearing was a source of much pleasure to the local music lovers."[37]

Because she was based in Paris, Baker was left out of most of the coverage of the American "galaxy of well-known stars."[38] However, from our perspective today, we can see connections that were not evident at the time. The group included Preer, Baker, Waters, Washington, and McKinney, as well as Adelaide Hall and Florence Mills for a time. Their performances featured a unique expressivity, whether it was a voice, dance style, or acting mode, and they appeared in the cinema, theater, and concert hall with dynamism and sophistication. Their use of feathers, fur, jewel-toned dresses, and other attention-getting textiles drew on burlesque and on classic Hollywood glamour for women. They selected costumes that highlight the body's form and insist on being looked at. Such performers, like the blues women discussed in chapter 1, enacted their visions of themselves and the world through personal gesture, voice, and movement. Baker was unique in that she performed in multiple genres while being diasporic as an African American woman entertainer based in Paris. These women all appeared in films but maintained careers as singers. In Baker's case, she moved from dance star to film star to recording artist.

Baker's dichotomies and paradoxes occurred over ten years, and her acting roles constantly referenced the complexity of her persona, arising from her locations in films, in music halls, and in European colonialist settings. It is precisely through embodying the Black Venus caricature in its many forms that Baker reflects on and makes visible the underlying conundrums of her own creativity and that of her peers. Baker is exemplary of a modest constellation of Black women actors, yet she also stands above and apart as the lead in her French productions and a crossover star in a variety of media and for a diverse transnational audience.

Waters, Horne, and Washington all appeared in mainstream American films. Baker's films were French, foreign-language productions. Welch's half dozen films from the 1930s were British, and she was known as the "sepia songbird of Europe."[39] In 1925, Baker and Welch performed together in *Chocolate*

Dandies in New York.[40] They later both left the United States for Europe but took divergent paths there. Welch did more singing, and Baker did more dancing, and their films relied on these performances, at least initially in Baker's case.

Preer appeared in race films, which were independent American films exhibited for primarily African American audiences before 1950. Though they were part of a small and marginal film market in the United States, race films circulated internationally. Domestically, they were directed toward a segregated audience of Black people, yet these films are complex in terms of ideology and taste. Race films for African American audiences valued Preer differently than did mainstream films. In *The Brute* (1920), *Within Our Gates* (1920), and *Homesteader* (1919), for example, Preer was film pioneer Oscar Micheaux's leading lady. She is a parallel star to Baker, but Preer was the more admired actor. Preer, a principal member of the Lafayette Players, was described as "a beautiful, professional Negro actress."[41] By contrast, in *Blonde Venus* (1932), starring Marlene Dietrich, Preer acted in a role that, like Hattie McDaniel's similar role of a maid in the same film, was not credited. Such roles represent the kind that Baker feared. Both actors appear as servants, called only by their first names, who cross paths with Dietrich's character and mark her descent into an indecent life and the distance she has traveled from the life she had been living when the film began. Although it would be true of many actors taking bit parts and working their way up, Black women actors tended to always play the same bit part—maid or singer (not that they couldn't steal the show)—and they are often uncredited. Given this context, it is significant that when Baker appeared on film, she got top billing.

BAKER'S CINEPHILIA

Baker was herself both a consumer and a maker of movies, and her reflections on the cinema express her curiosity and optimism as well as trepidation about the medium; the high stakes of Black representation were clear to her. Yet Baker was an unlikely muse for race films or for any other type of African American film endeavor. Her early efforts were awkward for her, and she and her collaborators used film simply to record one of her Folies Bergère performances to promote the theater. For instance, in 1926 and 1927, Baker recorded *la danse des bananes* and other brief excerpts from her appearances at the Folies Bergère that would be compiled in both the 16 mm *Josephine Baker, Star of the Folies Bergère* and in *La revue des revues*, eventually released as a DVD. Baker was aware of how African Americans were depicted in the cinema, and she was motivated in part by the same set of representational circumstances and desires that stirred Black moviegoers, critics, and filmmakers in the United States. Even at the height of her fame in 1926, Baker feared Hollywood would reduce her to what she called "mammy roles."[42] Instead her "greatest wish" was to create representations that were "beautiful and true," and she wanted to shine as a glamorous star of the cinema.[43] Baker was a critical participant, discerning what was beautiful to her from what was not.

In Baker's words, the experience "turned out to be less fun than I'd anticipated. It involved doing exactly what I'd done for the past two years: getting into an egg decorated with marabou feathers, stepping out again, dancing with my bananas."[44] She missed the warmth of the audience's presence. Jean-Claude Baker, one of her adopted sons and biographers, elaborated: "She had not enjoyed those brief flings, the lights had burned her eyes, she had looked at the cameraman when she should have looked elsewhere, but she wanted to learn the new medium, 'because my greatest wish is to act in a great film, beautiful and true.'"[45]

Despite her initial unease with motion pictures, Baker accepted the opportunity to perform in a feature-length silent film. Henri Étiévant, a stage actor who trained at the National Conservatory of Dramatic Art of Paris, would direct it. Giuseppe "Pepito" Abatino, Baker's manager, approached her in her dressing room at the Folies Bergère and presented *La sirène des tropiques* enthusiastically.[46] Because prominent novelist Maurice Dekobra had based the script for *La sirène* on Baker's persona, Baker perhaps viewed the project as a risk of redundancy. But it played to her strengths and was bolstered by the prestige of her collaborators.

As noted above, *La sirène des tropiques* was released in France in 1927, and the American premiere followed in 1929. In the United States, Baker's feature debut circulated with race movies in Micheaux's milieu, and it was advertised in the Black press. Advance advertising and subsequent reviews of *La sirène* reveal how deeply the film critics of the Black press were invested in boosting Black film stardom. The *New York Amsterdam News* declared, "From across the sea comes an ominous rumble of thunder. The dark cloud of hope on the horizon is Josephine Baker."[47] Baker's Parisian celebrity invited cinephiles to imagine a new Black cinema in the space between Hollywood and race movies. And the anticipation of *La sirène des tropiques* and the film production itself would be a great cinematic drama of its own.

La sirène des tropiques would be a frustrating experience with many highs and lows both for Baker and for critics in the Black American press. Baker described her role with some disdain: "I played the part of a West Indian girl named Papitou, who longed to come to Paris and was astonished when she couldn't pay her boat fare with beads. A real featherbrain." Baker found the work tedious, with "hours of waiting," and too close to the work she did at the Folies, writing ruefully in the director's voice, "'It's time for your belly dance.' Because naturally Papitou danced exactly like Mademoiselle Baker of the Folies." She referred to the sequence in *La sirène des tropiques* where, as a stowaway, she first jumps into a bin of coal and then is pushed into a second bin of flour as "riotously funny."[48] Overall, however, she hated *La sirène des tropiques*, writing, "The finished film brought tears to my eyes. Was that ugly, silly person me? What a total waste of time!"[49] Baker cited two fundamental challenges she faced at the time: her lack of fluency in French and her uncertainty about how—and even whether—to translate her music hall performance for the camera. Her frustration being unable to read the French script she was supposed to follow is understandable: "Nobody bothered to have it translated into English."[50]

Like many early movie viewers, Baker was fascinated by the cinema, but she was also skeptical of the new medium. She was, after all, a live performer: "For a long time I did not believe in talking pictures. . . . It seemed to me impossible that one could speak sensibly, sing, shout at shadows . . . that this would be anything but gruel for cats around a screen. But in 1929, I witnessed in Vienna the filming of a boxing match. The public screamed. The people were barking. Everyone insulted everyone. It was funny. When the film was projected, there were the screams I had heard. I was dumbfounded, won over."[51] In the poetry of the phrase "speak sensibly, sing, shout at shadows," Baker clearly describes the way she felt when she tried to act in a film. It must have felt unnatural to try to project her live stage performance to a camera rather than to an audience. In her later years, she discussed her filmmaking experiences in an interview with the Canadian Broadcasting Corporation, saying, "I found it cold and I need warmth; I need people."[52] With so few moments where Baker speaks about her own experiences, such comments constitute revelations of her aesthetic sensibility and needs as a performer. Baker has, above all else (even above her considerable talent and commitment to hard work), an eye for what is good and what is not, and knows what she enjoys and what she does not.

La sirène des tropiques was Baker's first feature film. She took on the project during a time when performing in front of the camera was challenging for her, but at the same time, the very idea of cinema inspired her. She wrote, "Cinema is black art: image, dance, sun, night. In the future, I will go to the movies every day. I'll have a cinema at home."[53] Folies Bergère manager Paul Derval arranged for a series of Baker's performances of the Charleston to be filmed under the title *Excursion to Paris*.[54] Baker writes, "I've always loved the cinema, so I was thrilled when a compatriot, Rex Ingram, decided to film our Folies show."[55]

Baker's performances were filmed and perhaps released under various edits and titles.

The feature *La sirène* was a film created with her in mind.[56] The success of Dekobra's interwar novels—including *The Madonna of the Sleeping Cars*, which was made into a movie in 1928—attests to his stature and, by extension, to Baker's standing in French entertainment. In a review of the film, *Paris-Soir* noted that Dekobra was not one to look down at the screen like other literary types. The entertainment magazine noted that the screenplay did not lack technical skill and that Dekobra had long recognized the power of motion pictures.[57] *La sirène* was directed by Nalpas and prominent stage actor Henri Étiévant, who went on to direct two more films: *La symphonie pathétique* with Nalpas in 1928 and *Fécondité* with Nicolas Evreinoff in 1929.

TRACING BAKER'S CELEBRITY IN THE PRESS

Baker's films reframe and recast her live performances. Filmed in black and white, they record Baker's choreography, graying out her use of color, thus leaving a major aspect of her performance to the viewer's imagination. On film, Baker often appears to have worn white or silver and used feathers and rhinestones to add drama to her appearance. As minimalist as Baker's signature hairdo was, it exemplified the kind of eye-catching burlesque hairstyle confected from wigs, hair dye, pomades, and other styling products. In Baker's cinematic prismatic image, she is revealed little by little and then hidden, and this process repeats throughout the film. Baker's or her character's racial, ethnic, national identity is the device by which she was separated from society—the audience—and thrust into the spotlight onstage, finally fully revealed as Josephine Baker of the Folies.

Baker's capacity to be recognized and reproduced arises from her performativity. Baker from St. Louis is the performer. Baker from Martinique and America and everywhere is Baker's burlesque, layered, reflecting personae, while there is something essential and always recognizable about her. As an entertainer on film, Baker's movements become semiotic gestures. Baker is herself, and she is a commentary about herself. As her film characters referenced her stage performances and because of the repetition of certain movements, Baker is put into a larger context and projected on the screens of all our imaginations.

Baker's public life continued to be discussed through a series of articles documenting various scandals. The year 1928 began with an "astonishing mess" and a new opportunity for Baker's publicity prismatic. In *Les mémoires de Joséphine Baker*, her first coauthored autobiography, published when she was twenty-two years old, Baker is quoted as saying in reference to war veterans that she was afraid of "crippled" people. When she was confronted about it, she disowned the book: "Scared out of her wits by the newspaper men who invaded her dressing room in the Folies Bergère and barked questions at her concerning her 'insult' to the veterans, she cried: 'The book? I don't know anything about my book. I never wrote nor read a line of it.'" Her collaborator, Marcel Sauvage, spoke up right away in his own defense: "There is no way for a lady who can neither read nor write to pen a book other than by the method of hiring a collaborator. I submitted the manuscript, page by page, not to Josephine, who couldn't make any sense of it, but to her admirer and man-of-all-jobs, the elegant pseudo count [Pepito Abatino]."[58] Sauvage provides insight into his relationship with Baker and what he is willing to say about his collaborator. He describes the process of the partnership, in which he claims that while Baker is the subject, Sauvage and Abatino translated and arranged her words. She perhaps did not read French well enough to critique Sauvage's manuscript, so she turned over that duty to her manager, Abatino.

The incident as a whole reflects Baker's awkwardness in the press, but, more importantly, it demonstrates how ethnic framing served as a defining, if at times fanciful, rubric. The article goes on:

> Americans cannot easily conceive the fame which has surrounded Josephine since her humble arrival and first experience in a Montmartre boarding house for chorus girls several years ago. People do not usually write their memoirs until their declining years. Mistinguett and Yvette Guilbert are writing theirs in their sixties. But Josephine's were out before she had turned twenty, and all because this India rubber dancing girl timed her arrival in Paris to coincide with the first insane fad for the Charleston. Her book has sold like hot cakes. The other part of the story is that the heir apparent of Rouzbedi-Klahm, one of the few remaining independent Zambesian principalities, sought a genealogical connection. The Prince, with the help of a member of the French College of Charts and Heraldry, has assembled a long file of papers tending to prove that Josephine Baker, St. Louis dancing girl, is, in fact, the great granddaughter of a former King of Kouzbedi-Klahm, banished by the English and an enforced emigrant to America, where his patronymic was changed to that of Baker.[59]

Baker's many narratives of her life did not reference Africa: "It is for this reason, explain her friends, that Josephine has so anxiously seized the occasion, provided by the 'Gueules Cassees,' to repudiate her memoirs."[60] Baker's first film was released within a moment of mixed publicity while she was on an international tour. Although Baker repudiated the memoirs, they were nonetheless mediated primary sources of her creation and construction. My framing of the books is not that they provide pure views of Baker but that they open a portal into her process of making up her performative self.

Celebrity news about Baker mixed gossip and news about her personal life with stories related to her career. When Baker's film *La sirène des tropiques* was released in France in December 1927, press coverage in January consisted of reviews along with the odd report of something scandalous Baker had said or done. The film was covered in major news outlets the *Chicago Defender*, the *New York Amsterdam News*, and the *Baltimore Afro-American*. The *Defender* reported, "Josephine Baker, the entertaining idol of the French people, has launched into films and the French people have styled her 'the Colored world's sweetheart' or 'Harlem's new princess.'" The reporter points out, "This movie is unique in at least one respect. It was filmed entirely between the hours of 4 and 7am." Baker was often accused of being late to the set, but her schedule was clearly unusual: "As soon as Josephine finished twisting in "[Shuffle] Along' at the Folies Bergère, she pounded into her limousine [illegible] to her own night cabaret to dance and ogle at drowsy champagne drinking Americans, Argentines, Berliners and whoever else paid. That task done, she went to the studio where a sleepy cast always awaited her."[61]

Baker's celebrity often clashed with but sometimes fueled the emergence of Black film. Baker personified its promise: "Josephine hopes that the film will travel around the world to encourage the black race to make its own films, and incidentally, to elect her queen of the Colored favorites."[62] Reception of *La sirène* in Paris was reportedly quite positive, but the reporter made a point of mentioning the film's inadequate treatment of race relations. The *New York Amsterdam News*'s article read, "Josephine Baker, 'The Celebrated Black Venus,' has entered the movies and is meeting with splendid success. A film in which she is starred has been showing at the Aubert Palace on the Grand Boulevard for the last month and still the place is crowded day and night. . . . So far as the 'color' part of the play is concerned, it is rather conventional, being the old story of the native girl who falls into hopeless love with a white. But apart from this it has touches of splendid originality." The rest of the review focuses on Baker's acting: "Miss Baker is splendid throughout with her frolicsome and original ways. Her dancing is much better than at the Follies, and she is by far the most natural person in the entire cast. Many other Negroes appear in the cast and they too are very good, particularly in the native dances. Most of the white persons in the cast, except Alvarez, are stiff and self-conscious in comparison."[63]

Fig. 2.9. Now in Paris, an ardent Papitou declares her affection for André.
AKG-Images.

This was a rare acknowledgment that Baker was not the only Black actor in the film, although she operates in its narrative world as the Other.

La sirène des tropiques was released just before Baker set off on an international tour of Europe and South America. Although the United States was not on her schedule, as her home, it remained part of her identity.[64] Baker's popularity in France and throughout Europe brought positive attention to Harlem and the nightclubs of her early career. "Writers infused a new and romantic glamour to the Black Belt. It was reported 'hot.' Josephine Baker's Parisian popularity was something else to wag tongues about the district, for she was a product of the black and tan cafes."[65] Although her celebrity in the United States was a product of her residence abroad and her international travel, the potential of her return figured into her stardom as well. Indeed, "the lithe, brown former Harlem chorus girl, Josephine Baker, continuing her conquest of the European music halls, is scheduled to open [in Sweden] Friday at the Oscars-theater. While the rumor goes the rounds of Broadway that she will soon return to the States."[66] Another article notes, "Negotiations have already been begun with the management of the Lafayette Theatre to bring Miss Baker [to Amsterdam] and then star her on Broadway."[67] Baker's celebrity in France bolstered her coverage in the United States, and her movements around the world were followed closely.

BAKER ON TOUR

Baker's tour began with an unexplained visa denial in Poland.[68] In Austria, the Vienna Roman Catholic Church held three services for three days "in atonement for outrages on morality allegedly committed by Baker at St. Paul's Church, which adjoins the Johann Strauss theatre where the Negro dancer has been appearing. The sensational dances of Miss Baker, American Negro, have brought many protests against her scanty costumes."[69] Her "exotic nude dances" were the target of a boycott. The Jamaica *Gleaner* reported that Dr. Jerzabeck, a leader of the clerical party and a practicing physician for twenty-five years, said he was opposed to Baker's appearance, not because of her color or nationality but because she appeared before the public "dressed only in a postage stamp." The question of whether Baker was a worthy artist came up, too. Jerzabeck said, "Her dances are devoid of any real art, consisting only of grotesque distortions and writhing grimaces. . . . We are asked to pay 100,000 shillings to see nudity when 100,000 workmen are walking the streets of Vienna searching for employment and food." The social democrats replied sarcastically that the cleric should see to it that none of his "bourgeoisie friends" sees Baker perform.[70] In the end, protests against Baker were successful mostly in generating publicity.

In Vienna, Baker created news both by what her critics feared she would do and by the tomfoolery she did manage. For instance, the *New York Amsterdam News* reported that Baker "has created great interest here by driving in a dogcart drawn by an ostrich through the city streets."[71] Baker created a fuss everywhere she went. Her "brown lithe body . . . won her fame and fortune throughout Europe, [and she] was given such a boisterous welcome here Wednesday that several women were injured and a number of windows smashed."[72] She danced in "a few feathers [and] the *London Daily Mail* carried the information that Miss Josephine Baker, the colored dancer, whose alleged immodest attire shocked the people of Budapest, made her appearance that night in a costume revealing only her face and arms."[73]

At one point during this tour, Baker inspired a poem, "Black Sun of City of Light," which led to a duel between her manager and one Andrew Czlovoydi.

Fig. 2.10. Josephine Baker created a scandal driving a cart drawn by an ostrich through city streets. General Photographic Agency/Hulton Archive/Getty Images.

The two men apparently fought with swords, and "Miss Baker put in an appearance and accompanied the scene with screaming."[74] Celebrity news on Baker continued with a lawsuit over dog ownership. Apparently, she was walking in Paris with a wolfhound when a certain Madame Grasset, seeing them, claimed the dog had been stolen from her. The matter went to court. The judge proposed that the dog be brought to court to see which person it preferred. Baker was out of the country at the time of the hearing, so the test could not be performed. The dog was awarded to Baker provided she would promise to take the animal out of France.[75] The trivialities continued with an incident in Berlin, where Baker's temperament was on display: "Baker failed to appear on stage. . . . While the crowd was surging in the lobby and crying for their money, the dancer was heard in an argument with her husband, Count Pepito Abatino, behind the scenes. She was seen to throw her costumes into an automobile and speed away from the amusement house."[76]

That Baker was a Black American among other Americans abroad—and, by some accounts, more famous than they were—was a newsworthy angle. Baker's fame in Paris made her a crossover success back in the United States.

In his nationally syndicated column, O. O. McIntyre wrote, "News drifts back from Paris that the most successful entertainers there so far this season have been Americans. Among those mentioned: The Dolly Sisters, Josephine Baker, Helen Morgan, Harry Pilcer and Earl Leslie. But the trouble is they don't pay them much over there."[77] This last line perhaps asserts American economic superiority, but overall the article gives an idea of Baker's professional context in the late 1920s.

J. A. Rogers of the *New York Amsterdam News*, reporting from Paris, helped keep Baker and other expatriate entertainers in the news. He published a sensationalist article in which topless dancing was referred to as nude dancing: "The Paris ladies, who by the way, are mostly English girls, do wear a garment of about 1/50th of an inch larger and thicker than the piece of ham one gets in a railroad sandwich." Rogers's more serious aims were revealed as the article put Baker in the context of nude dancing: "In 1925 at the Folies-Bergère it was Benglia, the magnificent Negro, dancing with one of the white ladies clad in the above mentioned unmentionables. This year it is Josephine Baker, dressed in two tiny tufts of red and yellow feathers, back and front. This, I have been told, took the place of three or four bananas which looked as if they would fall off any minute. There is also a moving picture at the Folies with nudes, and then ever so many more nudes." But Rogers gets to the heart of the matter when he describes interracial "nude" dancing. He offers several examples before remarking, "It is easy to understand now why the Kluxers got ready to give a hempen reception to the boys when they got back from 'over there.'" Rogers uses nudity as a hook for the reader and a trope for scandal and social reversals in Paris. This article is about the sight of interracial couples, especially Black men with white women onstage and in dance halls. Rogers claims to be a tour guide of sorts, writing, "I have been taking some of the Negro tourists to these dance halls so that they may see for themselves."[78] Interracial socializing was a newsworthy spectacle for Americans in Paris, and at the same time, with Baker's marriage—hoax or not—Paris was a scene of crossing taboos. Baker's persona was an affront to social taboos and mores.

Baker's coverage in the American press included articles that were metacritical—that is, they analyzed her coverage in other papers. In an article in the *Broad Axe*, a journalist quoted and critiqued an article about Baker.[79] The article is critical of the way Baker's racial identity was reported by other elements of the press: "And now they would have us believe that Josephine Baker is a Filipino lady. Word is going the rounds in Europe among the Americans that everything is alright now with 'Mme. Baker,' for she is a foreigner 'and, you know, my dear, it just couldn't be that any European count would marry one of our Negro girls. Impossible.'"[80] Note that, although the story of her marriage to Abatino has been disproved, it still plays a significant role in Baker coverage.

A certain Mrs. Stuart who ran a cabaret that Baker had helped to establish had said, "Josephine is Filipino by birth, but of course an American citizen. She is not exactly beautiful but is intensely fascinating to know."[81] The question of Baker's origins is at the heart of this article, and maintaining Baker as a key figure in the case for vindicating Black culture internationally—ambivalent and problematic an enterprise though it was—was crucial. Baker's ethnic authenticity must be maintained in order for the community to continue claiming her and her status. Baker might well have endorsed this story if she had not initiated such a fabrication, but the paper defended her actual racial/ethnic identity as a way to share in the credit for her success.

The Baker phenomenon inspired increased interest in Black film production. Maurice Gaugin, a French producer, came to the United States to recruit performers for a new revue. The *New York Amsterdam News* reported, "The admiration for the Negro's art,' said Gaugin in a recent interview, 'is more apparent in Europe than in America, despite the fact that Americans continually shout that their country is a great democracy. The individual Negro in Europe is looked upon by the most aristocratic and autocratic individuals as a human being, and only in rare instances are expressions of prejudice heard—and in these instances the fanatical statements come from people of little consequence.'" Gaugin continues, "I have seen Josephine Baker many times, and I agree with French critics that she possesses personality and gifts that must certainly lie in other performers of her race. I hope to find and develop other artists of her caliber while I am in the States." Baker's signification operates through her uniqueness and singularity on the Parisian stage, and her identity is burlesqued through news reporting. Gaugin has specific aesthetic goals. He wants to combine Black art and elaborate staging: "The French impresario claims that there is no reason why the Negro should be expected to demonstrate his art in tumbledown and dilapidated theatres where the acoustics, lighting, comfort of the players and audiences are lacking."[82] Furthermore, he wants to bring these shows to white audiences instead of limiting them to African American audiences.

Baker, the most famous Black American expatriate, wanted to establish new roots in Paris—feelings that she parodied in her films. The year 1927, Baker's second year in Paris, was dominated by the news of her marriage followed by the news of her nonmarriage, and finally with the French release of *La sirène des tropiques*, her first feature film. Throughout early 1928, there were reports of the film's production and reviews by the Parisian correspondents of African

American newspapers. These reports intermingled with news of Baker's first coauthored autobiography and accounts of her reception when she performed outside Paris. However, most of the news in 1928 concerned Baker's world tour. *La sirène* was not shown in the United States until 1929, when it became a part of Baker's stateside film historical narrative. In 1929, Baker's silent film, viewed along with modern sound films, had King Vidor's *Hallelujah* (1929) as a contextual anchor.

Baker's career was lauded as a historic phenomenon in and of itself. To many journalists and other onlookers, the reality of an African American woman who established herself as a success in doing something other than service showed that "the black woman [was] holding her own as a star of the first rank beside the white woman."[83] Yet almost a century later, Baker's luminous and influential films now specifically and ironically reveal her reflexive aesthetic and multisensory visual style, despite how they were received at the time. They opened a critical gateway toward (re)defining cinemas of the African diaspora.

The significance of Baker's films is rooted, primarily, for general audiences in the fact that Baker was an international celebrity. *Zouzou* and *Princesse Tam-Tam* are remembered precisely and only because Baker was in them. She shines above her costars Jean Gabin and Albert Prejean. But an expanded understanding of Baker today centers on her cinematic prismatic image, which necessarily extends off-screen to include, for example, the rapturous stories and fevered speculation printed about Baker in newspapers and the blurring of her person and persona that such coverage made inevitable. These ideas are woven throughout this book and become the focus of a deeper discussion in the next chapter.

As cinema made Baker a global phenomenon, her stardom held particularly positive meaning for African American observers at home. As an entertainer who had garnered European adulation, she became someone who could represent African American humanity and vindicate African American talent. The African American press enthusiastically followed Baker's travels and reported on her performances as well as offstage constructions. The *Baltimore Afro-American* and the *New York Amsterdam News* announced Baker's film screenings amid ongoing conversations around the projects of independent African American cinema, Black-cast Hollywood films, and rare lead or supporting roles with African American actors. Cultural critics in the Black press advertised and discussed Baker's films as they did race films. Baker was a fresh and unique hope for Black representation in an emerging American cinema culture. African American spectators wanted to see their lives portrayed on the silver screen with dignity, but they faced a media environment toxic with racism.

That Baker found the heights of her career abroad in France enhanced her significance to African Americans in the United States. Her transnational and cross-genre film historical context, marked by her own travels and those of her film characters in fictional plots based loosely on her persona, expanded the physical, cultural, and thematic parameters of African American cinema. Where the independent films of Oscar Micheaux, the Colored Players, and Spencer Williams pictured a somewhat insular Black world addressing community concerns outside the Hollywood system, Baker's films opened a lens on the lone Black figure negotiating white worlds, reflexively recycling material from her own life.

Not just any one image, Baker is a cinematic prism consisting of many representations joined at acute angles to one another. Her image is refracted, and as we turn it in the light, we see an oscillating structure of gestures, gazes, and characters on-screen and off-screen reflecting on and reflective of Baker's iterations in film, newspaper, and dance. Neither a single image nor a static representation, Baker is, rather, a dazzling manyness, a structure of spectacles formed from multiple media.

Baker's own recycling and reimagining of stereotypes she inherited and regenerated, in light of her ingenuity, created conundrums within her cinematic prism. On one hand, Baker exemplified the colonialist-patriarchal idea of the Black woman—crazy, hypersexual, and primitive. Yet on the other hand, Baker's dancing conveys power, creativity, and liberation. Was Baker's entertainment career a critique on colonialism, a product of it, or both? Was Baker a fetish, exploited by her own performance in a European patriarchal and colonialist milieu, or was she a glamorous innovator deserving of legendary status?

NOTES

1. Stewart, *Migrating to the Movies*, 3.
2. Caddoo, *Envisioning Freedom*, 5.
3. See Field, *Uplift Cinema*.
4. Everett, *Returning the Gaze*, 107–8.
5. Ibid., 111.
6. Kennedy-Karpat, *Rogues, Romance, and Exoticism*, 179.
7. Regester, *African American Actresses*, 1.
8. Baker was known variously as La Bakaire, a play on the French pronunciation of her last name, as well as the Black Pearl, Bronze Venus, Black Venus, and Creole Goddess.

9. See Blanchard et al., *Colonial Culture in France.*

10. Blanchard and Bancel, *"Le Zoo Humain,"* 35–37.

11. Blanchard et al., "Creation of a Colonial Culture," 4.

12. "Un village nègre au Champ de Mars," *L'illustration,* June 15, 1895, 508.

13. See Karp and Lavine, *Exhibiting Cultures.* Essays in this collection discuss the construction of ethnic identity through the objects of museum displays. The authors explain how iconic materials representing the Other serve as a prosthetic link to that culture's past. For a detailed discussion of the role of American photography, see Shawn Michelle Smith, "Photographing the 'American Negro.'"

14. For a thorough comparison of Baker's and Pierre Batcheff's exoticisms, see Powrie and Rebillard, "Josephine Baker and Pierre Batcheff." Powrie points to roles in which Batcheff notably plays a Slav character and discusses the actor's origins in the press.

15. Baker and Bouillon, *Josephine,* 72.

16. Thompson and Bordwell, *Film History,* 214.

17. "Josephine Baker Here Soon in Film," *New York Amsterdam News,* July 31, 1929.

18. "To Synchronize Picture in Which Baker Woman Stars," *New York Amsterdam News,* August 14, 1929, 9.

19. "Baker Picture Now Looms," *New York Amsterdam News,* September 4, 1929, 8.

20. Butler, "The Theatre."

21. "Close-Up English Cinema Monthly Devotes August Number to Negro," *Indianapolis Recorder,* September 21, 1929, 3. The Black-cast musical *Hallelujah* was Vidor's first sound project and among the earliest major Black-cast Hollywood features. For foreign audiences, *Hallelujah* appeared to be a living tableau of Black American culture because of several factors: The filming took place on location in Memphis, Tennessee; it enlisted the expertise of local preachers and choir members; it appointed an African American assistant director in charge of cultural accuracy, infusing the melodramatic tale with African American Southern cultural practices; and a realist aesthetic was used to tell the story. In Paris, the prospect of viewing *Hallelujah* was received as a gateway to the origins of jazz and the essential qualities of "real" Black American culture.

22. "Nina Mae McKinney Will Be in Pittsburgh Apr. 18," *Negro World,* April 19, 1930.

23. "Baker Picture Now Looms," 8.

24. "First American Showing of Josephine Baker European Picture at Midnight Show," *New York Amsterdam News,* September 11, 1929, 9.

25. Rochambeau, "Josephine Baker Captured Paris," 8.

26. Ibid., 9.

27. Royal Theater advertisement in the *Baltimore Afro-American*, October 12, 1929, 8.

28. "The Greatest Attraction in Our History—The Sensation of Paris, featuring Josephine Baker," *Baltimore Afro-American*, October 19, 1929, 8.

29. Review of *Sirène des tropiques, Baltimore Afro-American*, October 26, 1929, 9.

30. Ibid.

31. Ibid.

32. Movie Man, "Around the Movies," *Gleaner* (Jamaica), September 28, 1929, 36.

33. Movie Man, "Around the Movies," *Gleaner* (Jamaica), January 4, 1930.

34. Rochambeau, "Seeking New Thrill," *Baltimore Afro-American*, 8.

35. Lafayette Theater, *Baltimore Afro-American*, March 1, 1930, A8.

36. Regester, *African American Actresses*, 1.

37. "Ethel Waters, Famous Blues Singer, Coming," *Savannah Tribune*, May 4, 1922.

38. "Duke Ellington Heads Howard's Attractions," *Washington Tribune*, April 29, 1932.

39. Snelson, "Harlem."

40. Advertisement for Werba's Brooklyn Theatre, *New York Age*, May 16, 1925.

41. Lewis, "Theatres."

42. Haney, *Naked at the Feast*, 138.

43. Jean-Claude Baker, *Josephine*, 151.

44. Baker and Bouillon, *Josephine*, 72.

45. Jean-Claude Baker, *Josephine*, 151.

46. Baker and Bouillon, *Josephine*, 72.

47. "Baker Picture Now Looms," 8.

48. Baker and Bouillon, *Josephine*, 72.

49. Ibid., 73.

50. Jean-Claude Baker, *Josephine*, 151.

51. Ibid., 166–67.

52. Les Archives de Radio-Canada, "En 1968, rencontre avec Joséphine Baker, artiste légendaire et femme engagée," uploaded June 18, 2020, YouTube video, 57:01, https://youtu.be/mwbejBfmwgA. Baker is speaking with Fernand Seguin, host of *Le sel de la semaine*, first aired March 18, 1968.

53. Josephine Baker, *Les mémoires*, 141. "Le cinema c'est l'art nègre: images, danses, soleil, nuit noire. Plus tard j'irai tous les jours au cinema. J'aura le cinema chez moi."

54. Haney, *Naked at the Feast*, 138.

55. Baker and Bouillon, *Josephine*, 72.

56. Ibid., 141–42.

57. "Les films de la semaine: La sirène des tropiques," *Paris-Soir*, December 31, 1927, 5.

58. "Astonishing Mess Josephine Baker Gets Herself Into," *San Antonio Light*, January 8, 1928, 79.

59. Ibid.

60. Ibid. "Gueules Cassees" refers to wounded servicemen.

61. "Josephine Baker in Films," *Chicago Defender*, January 21, 1928, 7.

62. "Paris Theatre Crowded a Month for 'Jo' Baker Film," *Baltimore Afro-American*, February 18, 1928, 8.

63. Rogers, "News European Writer," 8.

64. "'Jo' Baker May Return to U.S.," *Baltimore Afro-American*, March 31, 1928, 6B.

65. McIntyre, "New York Day by Day," 2.

66. "Josephine Baker Goes to Sweeden [*sic*]," *Baltimore Afro-American*, July 21, 1928, 9.

67. "Josephine Baker May Return," *New York Amsterdam News*, August 1, 1928, 6.

68. "Poland Denies Passport to Josephine Baker," *Chicago Defender*, January 12, 1929, 1.

69. "Services to Atone for Dancer's Acts," *Charleston Gazette*, March 12, 1928, 7.

70. "Indignation in Vienna over Nude Dancer," *Gleaner* (Jamaica), March 14, 1928.

71. "Josephine Creates Furore by Driving an Ostrich," *New York Amsterdam News*, April 11, 1928.

72. "Slav Women Hurt in Rush to Greet Josephine Baker," *Baltimore Afro-American*, April 28, 1928, 8.

73. "Acid Thrown in European Theatre: Hungarians Protest against Appearance of Josephine Baker," *New York Amsterdam News*, May 23, 1928, 7.

74. "Poem to 'Jo' Baker Forces Lovers' Duel," *Baltimore Afro-American*, May 26, 1928, 9.

75. "Josephine Baker Wins Court Fight over Her Dog," *New York Amsterdam News*, October 31, 1928, 6.

76. "Josephine Baker Again Causes Crowd to Riot," *Chicago Defender*, December 8, 1928, 1.

77. "Short, But Not Especially Pithy," *Davenport Democrat*, July 17, 1927.

78. Rogers, "Sexiest Spot in Paris," 15.

79. Cameraman, "Colorful News Movies," *Broad Axe*, April 9, 1927.

80. "Is Josephine a Filipino?," *New York Amsterdam News*, August 10, 1927, 11.

81. Ibid.

82. "Noted French Theatrical Impresario Coming Here to Present Negro Shows," *New York Amsterdam News*, December 7, 1927, 13.

83. "Paris Finds Women Can Do Something Else Besides Act as Servants," *Baltimore Afro-American*, February 7, 1931.

THREE

—◊—

UNINTENDED EXPOSURES

Baker's Prismatic Ethnological Performance in *Zouzou*

WITHOUT SAARTJIE BAARTMAN, THERE COULD have been no Josephine Baker. Baartman's performance and history offer a theoretical framework for examining Baker. If Baker's Zouzou, the eponymous protagonist of her second feature-length film, embodied the scientific and social stereotypes of the early twentieth century, Saartjie Baartman, the "Hottentot Venus" of the early nineteenth century, presented an example of racial burlesque that combined science with entertainment, anthropology with freak show. Baker's portrayals of both Zouzou and Fatou burlesque a preexisting character. Baartman's involvement in the 1810 "Hottentot Venus" exhibition in London was itself part of an ongoing discourse about so-called Hottentots, southern Africa specifically, and Black women generally, and it had a quasieducational purpose as an alibi within an entertainment context that involved a variety of spectacles.[1] In this discourse, Baartman's identity was changeable, and what she meant to her audiences shifted as her locations changed from London to Paris. Like Baker, Baartman was surrounded in myth and half-truths.

UNPACKING BAARTMAN'S PRISMATIC

Born in 1789, Baartman, a member of the indigenous Khoikhoi people of South Africa, was about twenty years old when she arrived in London under dubious circumstances, the details of which can be found partially through court documents and their summaries in the press. Baartman was presented not as an African, a Negro, or a Black woman, but as a specimen of a "tribe" from a location near the Gamtoos River. Such precision separates her from Baker, though the two have been readily associated in scholarship of the last decade as two iconic Black women who embody the problems of Black female performance. Each woman's case illuminates the other's, but their social situations differed in several important ways.[2]

Bells Weekly Messenger of London ran this detailed announcement of the "Hottentot Venus" exhibition:

> Just arrived and may be seen between the hours of twelve and four in the afternoon, at No. 225 Piccadilly, from the Banks of the River Gamtoos, on the Borders of Kaffaria, in the interior of South Africa, a most correct and perfect specimen of that race of people. From the extraordinary phenomenon of nature, the Public will have an opportunity of judging how far she exceeds any description given by historians of that tribe of the human species. She is habited in the dress of her country, with all the rude ornaments usually worn by those people. She has been seen by the principal literati of this metropolis, who were all greatly astonished and highly gratified with the sight of so wonderful of a specimen of the human race. She had been brought to this country by Hendrick Cezar, a Native of the Cape, and their stay will be but short. To commence on Monday the 24th. Admittance Two Shillings each.[3]

The article highlights the show's main attraction, which was to provide an opportunity to observe a live specimen of a group previously known only through written descriptions and illustrative sketches. Indigenous populations had been a fascination for European explorers since the sixteenth century: "From the sixteenth to the eighteenth centuries the manners of representing Hottentots varied widely. . . . By the mid eighteenth century, a stable configuration had emerged that Sara Baartman would be obliged to act out in dress and in performance on her arrival to Europe in 1810."[4] Travel writers and illustrators of both the sentimental and the scientific modes struggled to depict the Khoikhoi, or Hottentots, "accurately" while negotiating the "unsettling tension between the Hottentot's savage culture and the beauty of his body" in their own perception.[5] Art historian Z. S. Strother's account, "Display of the Body Hottentot," in *Africans on Stage: Ethnological Show Business*, leaves little doubt that when Baartman debuted in London, "she came into an ongoing problem of representing Hottentots. To make matters more complicated, her display intersected with a venerable system of representation established for the public exhibition of people in the 'freak show.'"[6] This intersection made Baartman available for readings as both a type (all Hottentots are this way) and a freak (no human could be a Hottentot).

Sociologist Zine Magubane clarifies the significance and instrumental role of London in Baartman's case, pointing out that, in this city, "the line between science and show business was easily and often traversed."[7] Quoting historian

J. N. Hays, Magubane continues, "Lectures on biological subjects could draw on another London resource in addition to the talent of the medical community. They could exploit London's position as the center of entertainment, spectacle, and display."[8] As the *Bells* article indicates, the "Hottentot Venus" exhibition was located in Piccadilly, an area that had been a fashionable residential district at one time, but by Baartman's day, it had become a commercial thoroughfare.[9] In the intervening centuries, the district had become associated with nightlife, entertainment, and prostitution. Haymarket intersected with Piccadilly, and the following description makes clear the neighborhood's late eighteenth-century character:

> In the 1780's the street [Haymarket] was noted for curious exhibitions. George Baily advertised a monster "brought from Mount Tibet," which was considered "to approach the human species nearer than any other hitherto exhibited, and is supposed to be the long lost link between the human and brute creation." In an adjoining house there was also a cow with three horns from Berkeley in Gloucestershire, and a calf with two heads and two necks; they had been exhibited to the University of Oxford and to the King at Windsor, "who allowed them to be the greatest curiosity in the Kingdom."[10]

The Hottentot Venus's appearance in this location, even forty years after the calf with two heads in 1810, suggests that the area was still a destination for burlesques of many kinds, including racial burlesque. That the Hottentot Venus was showcased in this type of popular entertainment setting leaves little doubt as to the nature of her exhibition—and from this perspective, the article's use of the term *literati* to describe her audience seems ironic.

The freak show or human oddity spectacle typically consisted of a person with a perceived deviation from a supposedly normal body or cultural type who stood on a raised platform (sometimes in a cage), while the ringmaster or exhibiter stood to the side. The barker provided background and justification for the show. To draw attention, he "barked," or shouted, a story about the person on display. Occasionally, a freak show featured a single figure, as in Baartman's case, but at times it was one spectacle among many attractions, as in a circus or other multidisplay outdoor exhibition. The format of these venues, especially the darkness that hid the spectator of the circus (or cinema), provided the safety necessary to inspect the bodies onstage. This is the exact staging we see at the opening of the film *Zouzou* as the scene recalls this entertainment history.

In the narrative of these ethnographic spectacles, the circus barker often figured himself as a colonial explorer who had gone deep into the wilderness and brought back treasures—evidence of his bravery, patriotism, and eye for scientific and aesthetic wonders. He permitted the viewers to align themselves with him. Throughout their international history, ethnological spectacles constituted commercial exhibitions with pretenses toward educating audiences in venues that included theaters, fairs, amusement parks, and circuses. As opposed to the colonial exhibition or the museum, the viewer of singular human oddity is not guided through architectural space and, as in the case of racialized and gendered Others like Baartman, attends this kind of spectacle to see and confirm what he or she has already heard. The freak show offers its audience physical proof of rumor and proximity. The curious viewer could even touch the evidence, the body. The sort of show that featured Baartman further objectified a person by isolating him or her from normal frames of reference.

Racial exhibitions tended to expand cultural distance as well as the sense of difference between viewer and freak, and it is this principle that ties Baker to Baartman most closely. The distance between the presumed racial freak and the viewer, however, was complicated by the question of evidence; seeing was not enough for believing. In Baartman's case, spectators could touch her. Rubbing the skin, pulling the hair, poking the body, and other tactile tests were meant to verify reports—or better, to test hallucinations about racial Others.[11]

Although direct references to Baartman do not arise in Baker's historical archive, the two are linked in contemporary analyses of both women. Both are viewed as touchstones or metaphors for thinking about the Black female body, discourses of beauty, and formations of power and desire. At Venus 2010, a milestone conference on Baartman, scholars and artists linked the Hottentot Venus to the question of dignity and liberty in Baker's star image. Such a comparison allows us to see both similarities and crucial differences between Baartman and Baker. An audacious Baker thrust herself into the spotlight, whereas Baartman's publicity is regarded as akin to slavery, and indeed British abolitionists sued for her release (which she refused).[12]

In this comparative analysis of Baker and Baartman, the twentieth-century performer walked into a space populated by both American minstrelsy and colonialist negrophilia and transformed it. It was a risky space in which she was able to maintain control. The mechanism of that transformation is cinema. Where the movies should have ossified Baker's performance in common stereotypes, Baker instead performed a prismatic cinema reflection so resonant and empowering that it ultimately became an icon for later performers and artists, including Diana Ross, Beyoncé, and Julia Bullock.

More than one hundred years separated Baartman and Baker, but their European audiences responded to them in not dissimilar ways. Baker's body might have been fetishized, but she was not specifically exhibited among human and animal oddities. Yet she is continually associated with pets in both *Zouzou* and *Princesse Tam-Tam* as well as with her personal off-screen menagerie (for example, she has been photographed with a cheetah), perhaps referencing human zoos and race studies. On the other hand, both Baartman and Baker found themselves the embodiments of a preexisting imperialist fantasy. Both Baartman and her "imaginary daughter"[13] performed in the context of "all that people thought they knew about Hottentots" and about *les nègres*, respectively.[14] Baartman sang and danced only rarely, and her mode of stillness allowed audiences to stare at her, exploring the tension in early ethnological exhibits between science and entertainment, between the goals of education and those of astonishment. The combination of close looking and touching provided evidence for the attendees and consumers of porno-scientific entertainment. Baartman performed almost like a living wax figure.

Many concrete details of the Hottentot Venus exhibition were revealed when a published account of her trial appeared in *The London Times* in the fall of 1810. Baartman herself was not on trial; she became the plaintiff in a case brought to court on her behalf. On November 26 and 29, 1810, the newspaper ran two articles reporting on a civil action taken on behalf of Baartman, who was "exhibited to the public under circumstances of peculiar disgrace to a civilized country." Disgrace to Baartman as a person was not mentioned directly, however. The African Association, which brought the case, felt that its members "had every reason to believe, that the unfortunate female in question was brought away from her own country without her consent, was kept here for exhibition without her consent, and that the appearance of compliance which she evinced was the result of menaces and ill-treatment."[15] Each article claims to represent Baartman's deposition and the affidavits that were gathered by the attorney general pending trial, but as summaries, the articles contain slightly different, though not entirely contradictory, details. They paint as full a picture as we have about the conditions under which Baartman was displayed, and they offer representation, through the interpretation of an attorney and a courtroom journalist, of what she thought about her situation.

Baartman's case was brought before the court not by abolitionists but by the African Association for Promoting the Discovery of the Interior of Africa, which sought to play "a leading role in opening a new phase in the exploitation of the Continent."[16] Referred to in the *Times* as a "society of benevolent and highly respectable Gentlemen," the African Association sought to "put [Baartman] under proper protection while she remained here, and restore her to her country by the first conveyance that offered." The article does not address how initiating Baartman's case would advance the association's objectives in Africa. The organization's stated goal was to "deliver her out of the restraint in which she was supposed to be; and to allow certain persons speaking her own language to examine her."[17]

According to the *Times* article, among the affidavits filed was one by a Mr. McCartney, the secretary of the African Association, which provided a description of the exhibition. It said that the show consisted of "a stage raised about three feet from the floor, with a cage, or enclosed place at the end of it; that the Hottentot was within the cage; that on being ordered by her keeper, she came out, and that her appearance was highly offensive to delicacy." Few details are given after that point. The article continues with McCartney's deposition, stating that, in his presence, "The Hottentot was produced like a wild beast, and ordered to move backwards and forwards, and come out and go into her cage, more like a bear in a chain than a human being." McCartney acknowledges that since he could not speak to her in her language, he "could only judge from appearances. Those appearances, however, were convincing." He described Baartman's affect as marked by "deep sighs; [she] seemed anxious and uneasy; grew sullen, when she was ordered to play on some rude instrument of music."[18]

The case was an application for habeas corpus, which orders that a detained person be brought before a court or judge, at a specified time and place, to determine whether such detention is lawful. During this visit to the Hottentot Venus, it was ascertained that Baartman spoke Dutch and that, in the interest of giving "her the means of expressing her own feeling of the state in which she was," Dutch speakers would interview her, "unrestrained by the presence of Cezar," Baartman's captor. Later in the article, Baartman's costume was described in order to ascertain the "indecency" of her exposure. The attorney general then addressed the court: "My Lord, she is dressed in a colour as nearly resembling her skin as possible. The dress is contrived to exhibit the entire frame of her body and the spectators are even invited to examine the peculiarities of her form." The court replied that its duty was to "ascertain how far the exhibition gives her pain as a sentient being." The rule was granted, and an interview with Baartman by a Dutch speaker was arranged.[19]

The *Times* article printed on November 29 reports that the interview with Baartman lasted three hours and that "the questions were put by persons who spoke Dutch, and no person immediately connected with the exhibition was present." Though her words are rendered in the third person, the article offers a valuable impression of Baartman. For instance, the deposition found that she was supposed to receive a share of the exhibition money. While Cezar said that he had permission to exhibit her for two years, she said that the term was to last six years. The rest of the article reads as follows:

> She had left her own country when extremely young. She was brought down to the Cape by the Dutch farmers, and served Peter Cezar. She then agreed with Hendrick Cezar to come over to England for six years. She appeared before the Governor at the Cape, and got his permission. Mr. [Alexander] Dunlop promised to send her back rich. She was under no restraint. She was happy in England. She did not want to go back; nor to see her two brothers and three sisters, for she admired this country. She went out in a coach on Sunday for two or three hours together. Her father was a drover of cattle, and in going up the country was killed by the Bushmen. She had a child by a drummer at the Cape, where she lived two years. The child was dead. She had two black boys attend her and would like warmer clothes. The man who shows her never comes till she is just dressed, and then only ties a ribbon round her waist.

Baartman's statements as rendered in the summaries, especially that "she was under no restraint," led to the dismissal of the case. The court found that Baartman was not being held unlawfully. She would remain with Cezar.[20]

Baartman's mediated voice was translated from Dutch to English, then rendered in legalese, and finally transmitted through a summary printed in the newspaper; her self-expression, if that is what it could be called, has many references. Baartman's performance continued in the legal context, and the fact that the affidavit avoided describing details of the show, in the interest of "delicacy," is suggestive. In a precedent to Baker's writings, Baartman's voice, even mediated, comes through urgently and marks out a necessary critical inquiry into Baker's life and its refractions.[21]

In "Exhibit A: Private Life without a Narrative," architect J. Yolande Daniels reflects on Baartman's relationship to physical spaces and what it suggests about her social situation. Imagining Baartman's archive as a concrete space, Daniels contemplates temporal spaces as knowledge gaps in Baartman's archive, focusing especially on the "gap in time between the close of the London exhibition in 1810 and the opening of the Paris exhibition in 1815. During this time when the exhibition toured, Baartman was baptized in Manchester in December 1811. Given this fact, it seems possible that within the schedule of the human exhibition, time was made for domestic constructions. Baartman was believed to have married and to have conceived one or two children."[22] Such implied spaces, particularly those domestic ones of Baartman's personal life, offer what Daniels calls "alternative spaces" that may "bridge from this site of alienated spectatorial urbanization to private dwelling space. This gesture is not to posit an idyllic point prior to a somewhat diasporic urbanization, but to entertain the likelihood and ramifications of private space."[23] Daniels argues, "In resisting the construction of a narrative for Baartman, the structure of the characteristic exteriority in which she was framed—a condition particular to objects—is highlighted. Once scale shifts to include an interior—a private space—the possibility for the construction of subject positions has arisen."[24] Baartman's biographer, Rachel Holmes, presents significant details of Baartman's public life, yet the years following Baartman's baptism remain mysterious to her, too: "[Baartman] remained visible in the press, politics, and popular culture, but the real Baartman disappeared almost entirely from public view, suggesting that her baptism was precipitated by an important development in her personal life, of which there is no record."[25]

On the other side of this theoretical and mysterious bridge of private space, Baartman found herself once again on display—this time in Paris. It is unclear whether she was exhibited and slept in a decent space that offered adequate protection from the weather, if not privacy. The *Bells Weekly Messenger* index documents her arrival around January 1, 1814.[26] In late 1813, an animal exhibitor named Réaux arrived in Paris with Baartman in his sponsorship. He set up both lodgings and an exhibition space for La Vénus Hottentot at 15 rue des Petits-Champs, where spectators could see her for three francs between 11:00 a.m. and 9:00 p.m.—twice the number of hours that were required of her in London. Baartman found herself living in a street that ran "parallel to the north end of the Palais Royal gardens, amid the terraced streets, glittering arcades, and white colonnades of the Palais Royal, Paris's theater district and mecca for amusements. The building at 15 rue Neuve-des-Petits-Champs had a well-known exhibition hall on the ground floor and accommodation above."[27]

In London Baartman had been displayed among human anatomical oddities, but in Paris she became part of a spectacle that presented itself as scientific discourse. Baartman's body was occasionally fetishized and sexualized in London. She sometimes wore a tight dress, but at other times—and always in posters—she appeared in a revealing costume that "was a pastiche of exotica designed by exhibitors, fancifully mixing Xhosa or other beadwork with fringed garters, skull cap, and bowed shoes."[28] Baartman also appeared in private homes in both London and Paris. In London, the Hottentot Venus led to discussions of liberty, decency, and property marked by the actions of those who sought to end the show.

In Paris, in contrast, Baartman was exhibited unto death, and in death, as a sexualized anatomical oddity and natural science curiosity. The Palais-Royal exhibition continued for eighteen months, ending only when Baartman became ill and eventually died:[29] "The winter of 1815 was bitterly cold and harsh. Saartjie died at 7 Cour des Fontaines during the night of Friday, December 29. Réaux did not call a priest."[30] The London *Champion* newspaper ran this notice: "That important personage, the Hottentot Venus, died at Paris on the 1st December, after an illness of three days. Her body has been sent to the Museum of Natural History at Paris for dissection. Her disorder was the small-pox. Her physicians prescribed to her for a catarrh, a pleurisy, and a dropsy. She was ill eight days."[31] Despite the different dates recorded for Baartman's death in this article (December 31) and by Baartman's biographer (December 29), the short piece of journalism productively sheds light on the real conditions experienced by Baartman's overdetermined and abused body.

Baartman's corpse continued to inform the French public's understanding of racialized bodies. After her death, Baartman's body was transported to what was then the Musée de l'histoire naturelle, where, as Holmes and others have written, Georges Cuvier, the preeminent scientist specializing in comparative anatomy, conducted her dissection. In 1817, Cuvier delivered a paper to his colleagues in which he showcased Baartman's genitals and explained what he had learned about the Hottentot woman from studying her body.[32] The Musée de l'Homme, the successor to the natural history museum, showed Baartman's dissected body parts in jars so that viewers could see her remains up close. Her brain and genitals were the centerpiece of the display.[33]

The so-called educational dioramas contained spectacular elements and exploited the physical differences between the "natives" and the spectators by placing them in close proximity. The displays encouraged ordinary spectator-citizens, who might also visit a world's fair or colonial exposition, to practice a layperson's anthropology for their edification as well as their entertainment. Baker's performance in *Zouzou* drew on both types of ethnological spectacle, exemplifying the tenacity of racial entertainment and the way that cinema draws on and competes with other forms. *Zouzou* is cinematic ethnography repackaged and mainstreamed in a musical comedy. Baartman provides the shadow to Baker, framing and underlying her Folies Bergère performances, shaping what they projected to her audiences, perhaps unbeknownst to her.

In the early nineteenth century in London, Baartman's exhibition was tied to theatrical presentations of human (and sometimes animal) anatomical oddities, while the African Association found in her the personification of questions of liberty. Baker's assemblages were different from the single-emphasis and illustrative function of ethnic representations that characterized early racial burlesque. The differences between Baartman and Baker are as important as the overarching themes that connect them. While Baker embodied colonialist entertainment in the 1920s, she certainly neither invented nor patented this cultural form. In France, racial burlesque took the shape of its particular social context as the French near equivalent of American minstrelsy.

Baker, like Baartman before her, did not initiate exoticist performances of her supposed fictional ethnicities and sexual proclivities; these women stepped into preexisting colonialist narratives and were obliged to play the parts assigned to them. Whether the program was intended to be quasiscientific display, entertainment, or both to audiences, these performers permitted the fantasy of contact between distant lands and audience members—or more precisely, between the peoples of colonial empire, the nonwhite world beyond, and the ruling nation's spectator-citizenry. But there is an important distinction to be made between ethnographic dioramas and the freak shows in which Baartman performed: the dioramas sought to display a context, a type of community and various elements of its daily life, whereas Baartman was taken out of context and given fictionalized settings open enough to receive the projections of the viewers.

BAKER'S EXOTICIST PRISMATIC

The surviving film material of Baker's banana dance at Folies Bergère, the performance for which she is best known and which I examined in the introduction, provides a rare if mediated opportunity to examine Baker's eclectic and anthological dance style outside of a feature film narrative. Yet the banana dance, the focal point of Baker's fantasy sequence in *La folie du jour*, set on a Caribbean banana plantation, is itself part of a story drawn from Baartman as well as characters from colonialist literature. Baker's performance in *Zouzou* is nested in prisms with preexisting colonialist types. Baker's characters Fatou, Papitou, and Zouzou are repetitious, drawn from a shared core of types, informed by Baartman and taking form in a variety of expressions of colonialist culture.

Baker's Zouzou evokes her music hall character of Fatou, who in turn evokes Fatou-gaye, an African woman character at the center of the romance plot in the French novel *Roman d'un Spahi* (1881), known in English under multiple titles including *A Spahi's Love-Story* (1907) and *The Sahara* (1921). Written by French novelist Julien Viaud under the pseudonym Pierre Loti, *Roman d'un Spahi* went through dozens and dozens of editions, helping to cement the author's reputation for living an adventurous life as well as penning romantic travel writing and exoticist fiction. In the novel, a European everyman, Jean Peyral, is engaged to a girl from his village, but before the wedding takes place, he is sent to Africa. There he meets Fatou-gaye, "a negro girl, half goddess, half monkey," as she is described in the introduction to the 1907 English edition.[34] Unsurprisingly, Fatou is sexualized; for the genre, her appeal is a sign of Peyral's denigration under the African sun. However, Loti's prose conveys Jean Peyral's perhaps genuine attraction to Fatou-gaye and to the desert landscape. At the same time, he is also repelled and wants to return home to his fiancée. Such back-and-forth communicates Peyral's sexual confusion and the larger cultural ambivalence reflected in it. *A Spahi's Love-Story* crackles with descriptions such as, "Fatou-gaye knew what catlike caresses to lavish on her angry lover,—how to throw round his neck her black arms with their silver circlets, finely moulded as a statue's, how to press her naked bosom against the red cloth of his jacket, to rouse presently the hot fevers of desire, that would make him forget and forgive her transgression."[35] Fatou-gaye here functions as a test for the preservation of Peyral's European character. Loti writes of Peyral, "It is one of those strange passing moments, when memory is dead within him, when this land of Africa seems to wear a smile and the Spahi surrenders himself."[36] Landscape and character meld. A similar formulation becomes essential to the templates of exotic Othering in the films that Baker becomes a part of. In playing Fatou, Baker portrayed a new version of Fatou-gaye, a citation of the already-made or the stereotype of nonwhite women as available, enticing, and the stuff of an ambivalent goddess-monkey sexual fantasy.

Historian Richard M. Berrong writes that of the dozens of works Loti published, *Roman d'un Spahi* "is perhaps the most difficult of his works to read. The Senegalese men are often portrayed as handsome and noble, but the women, who again have no real voice of their own, come off too often as savages. . . . Jean Peyral's affair with one of them, Fatou-gaye, is presented as degrading."[37] Such characterizations exemplify what cinema scholar Elizabeth Ezra calls the "colonialist unconscious," the largely unspoken images, feelings, and representations through which white Europeans negotiate their ambivalence about the presence of the Other, a vacillation marked primarily by a "will to dominate."[38] Like Fatou-gaye, Baker's Fatou was a figure of fascination and implied desire. She was both intimate and distant, illustrating the duality of the colonialist unconscious; in *Josephine Baker, Star of the Folies-Bergère and the Casino de Paris*, Fatou was a figment of the plantation boss's own mind, representing his desires, yet dancing in front of him, she remained at a remove, unable and uninvited to cross the boundary into his world.

Filming mediates Baker's body in *Josephine Baker, Star of the Folies-Bergère*, turning her into the prismatic Fatou, and given these interrelated references to dance and literature, the Creole Goddess's image can no longer be seen as merely a straightforward reflection of the performer's personhood or even as simply a person playing a character, although those functions still operate in Baker's image. Rather, all those images are prismatically combined in a multisided image. Baker plays many characters at once, and they constitute the prismatic animating figure of an emerging cultural imagination of Africa, or negrophilia, in France, fueled by fantasy, here centered on the filmic Fatou, Fatou onstage, and Fatou in literature.

Baker dances within a prism of looks that frame and multiply her banana dance through multiple perspectives. At first, the rectangular gaze of the camera goes unnoticed, but when we see Baker, as Fatou, from multiple points of view, the frame of each spectator builds one gaze linked to another at angles. These include the camera's gaze plus the points of view of the watching audience and the characters in the scene who fixate on Baker's percussive movements. The film spectator watches Baker dance for the onstage characters who watch her. Because there is no visible theatrical audience in the film, these onstage viewing characters function as the film viewer's surrogate audience, facing the theatrical audience, the camera, and viewers of the footage. But at times Fatou turns away from the camera and its aligned perspectives, performing her dance for the plantation boss and the drummers and workers.

In some film shots, Fatou is shown only in profile. These shots are balanced by medium shots of her facing the camera. The viewer and camera are interconnected in a reflexive use of point of view. Baker (as Fatou) is the dominant, manifest spectacle, but the latent spectacle and the one that defines her cinematic prism consists of the architecture of gazes and how those looks become meaningful referents to Baker's changing cultural position.

In the prism, the bananas around Baker's waist operate symbolically on multiple levels. They represent consumable agricultural commodities; Baker herself, as an entertainer, is also a consumable commodity. The film of the banana dance is meant to be seen as entertainment, too, and thus is consumable in a third way. The bananas, imitation kitsch bananas, nevertheless cannot be eaten; as symbols they evoke particular places and specific agricultural processes, adding meaning and humor to Baker's performance, as discussed earlier. *Zouzou,* built on Baker's colonialist persona, reflects on and refracts Papitou from *La sirène des tropiques* and Fatou (with her literary precedent) from *la danse des bananes* in *Josephine Baker, Star of the Folies Bergère.*

REFRACTED COLONIALIST PRISMATICS

Released seven years after *La sirène des tropiques,* Baker's second feature-length film and first sound film, *Zouzou,* also sought to bank on Baker's international fame as a live performer and to retell the story of her rise to stardom in Paris from her humble beginnings in St. Louis. *Zouzou* was promoted in "the English-speaking world" by a well-coordinated advertising campaign. Baker's publicity team created a multipage "newspaper" to ballyhoo the film, describing *Zouzou* as "chock full of Laughs, Tears, Drama, Music and Songs." Baker was the "golden bronze Sarah Bernhardt of today." Several pieces in the booklet were purported to have been written by Baker, including a poem and a short first-person essay on her superstitions. A piece titled "Josephine Baker as Seen by Josephine Baker" is a list, or a kind of poem, that outlines the story of her life and life principles, such as "I do not drink. I do not smoke. I have a religion." Lines such as "I earn much" and "I love sadness—my soul is sad" suggest a degree of introspection and self-awareness. But what is remarkable about the promotion is the lack of reference to race. Other than the comparison to Bernhardt, the text speaks in such general terms that it is difficult to discern a specifically racialized narrative.[39] Perhaps that was the goal. As Baker sought to expand her stage career to include song and high fashion, she embraced a brand of global glamour that would translate in multiple contexts, although she would continue to play colonial women in films and include references to Africa and the Caribbean in her stage shows. Still, it is race that provides the logic for *Zouzou*. Understanding one of Baker's most critical precedents illuminates the narratives that framed Baker's reception and her pursuit of a more modern and global brand.

Zouzou cites and reflexively explores Baker's Parisian alter ego and Baker's career within a specifically colonialist context that is seen throughout her films. But viewers would be mistaken to view the character of Zouzou as merely a version of *La sirène des tropiques*'s Papitou, whom we last saw pleading her love case to the already-engaged André. Zouzou can be seen as Papitou's double in the sense that both *Zouzou* and *La sirène des tropiques* (and the later *Princesse Tam-Tam*, for that matter) recycle Baker's makeover story: An ordinary but talented girl with moxie is transformed into a Parisian lady and music hall star. In fact, *Zouzou* can be seen as something of a sequel to *La sirène*; the character Zouzou could be Papitou, now settled into a young migrant's life in Paris, working at a laundry but still yearning for love and the thrill of performing onstage.

Zouzou, however, has her own particular and peculiar backstory, as each iteration of La Bakaire is set in a new location amid new characters. The foundational makeover plot is there, but this film engages with the whiteness of romance in Baker's cinematic world, which, though still indirect, was as apparent to the keen observer as it was to the Black reviewers of *La sirène*. What sets *Zouzou* apart is the juxtaposition of Baker and her costar Yvette Labon, who was blonde, fair-skinned, and luminous under the flattering cinematic lighting structure designed to make her shine. My reading here looks at the Zouzou image as a surface, an illusion constructed of light and shadows, with Baker as a visual and aesthetic system refracted within it. Baker, as the ostensible star of this film, becomes lost in some ways amid the white romance, the light that favors blonde hair, and a narrative that ultimately cannot imagine her as its desirable, desiring subject.

In Zouzou's backstory, she was once a child performer in the Cirque Romarin, acting alongside a little boy, Jean (Serge Grave), who is passed off as her twin brother. Having left the circus, the adult present-day Zouzou works as a laundress, mixing with music hall entertainers when she delivers their cleaned costumes and linens, reminiscent surely of Baker's days as a dresser with the Dixie Steppers and Clara Smith. Zouzou's routine is disrupted when her long-lost "brother" Jean returns after his military service, and, perhaps in admiration of his seeming worldliness and bravery, she falls in love with him. However, Jean sees Zouzou as his sister and instead develops romantic feelings for Zouzou's best friend, Claire. Jean and Zouzou see their relationship differently, and their incompatible interpretations of who they are for each another ultimately lead to Zouzou's crisis of exposure.

Zouzou opens energetically with a high-angle mobile camera that pans across a nighttime scene at the fairgrounds. The viewer first sees a carousel in motion, then a crowd milling about, and finally a stage where a quirky chorus line is performing. Two minutes into the film, there is a cut to a couple of boys sneaking around the performers' trailers. One boy climbs up to a window to peer inside and then calls his friend. Cut to a close-up of a young Zouzou making funny faces at herself in the mirror. Cut to one of the boys making a joke about Zouzou. The English subtitles on the US Kino version translate the boys' dialogue as "See how strange she looks!" But what they mean by "strange" is unclear. Do they mean that Zouzou does not look like a typical girl? Does she not look French? Does she look like a foreigner? Is it strange that she is looking at herself, not noticing them? Is it the way she is dressed? Is it strange that she is in the dressing room rather than onstage? What is certain is that the specific nature of this moment of self-regard takes on different meanings for Zouzou, the film audience, and the young Peeping Toms. As a reflexive moment of look-at-me-ness, it doubles as a site of visual pleasure for the film spectator and for the boys.

After a break, the mirror sequence continues, offering multiple views of Zouzou—from behind, in front, and in miniature at the upper left corner of the frame. This three-part prismatic imagery references the anthropological method of photographing subjects in a direct frontal view, a direct rear view, and a direct profile. The scene frames Zouzou as one caught up in her own image but also as somewhat of an oddity. When the boys sneak a look at her, they make Zouzou at once desired, taboo, and vulnerable, since she is unaware that she is being watched. Zouzou is twice taboo as a desired object that must be viewed in secret and, as we learn later, as evidence of interracial sex. Are the boys looking at Zouzou because she is of mixed race, wondering "what" she is? The illicitness of their voyeurism casts her as an object of fascination and fear. The sequence places Zouzou in a cinematic prism.

The mirror sequence is intercut with Zouzou's introduction onstage by Papa Mêlé (his name is an adjective meaning "mixed," which comes from *mêler*, meaning "to mingle" or, when referring to races, "to mix"). Zouzou performs with her supposed twin, Jean, in the Cirque Romarin, and Papa is the ringmaster. The children's "act" consists of standing still and allowing themselves to be on display as living illustrations of Papa's circus fiction. Papa tells the audience that Zouzou and Jean are twins born of a Chinese mother and an Indian father in a union that took place on a Polynesian island far, far away—this despite the fact that Jean is played by a young actor who looks white, not mixed race, and Zouzou is played by an actor who appears to be mixed race of African descent. Though not impossible, Papa's claims point to the fictions at play in the spectacle of the children's racial origins, their bodies, for the circus.

Papa Mêlé's race story serves as the voice-over and dominant narrative for interpreting Zouzou. The children were unwanted because of their colors, Papa Mêlé says, so he has rescued them and raised them as his own, in the circus. Cut to the young Zouzou looking at herself in the mirror. Because Zouzou is still in her dressing room gazing at her reflection and applying her makeup, the twins miss their cue, and Papa Mêlé is compelled to improvise. Papa Mêlé explains to the circus audience, "Freaks are allowed to be late once in a while. They aren't made like us." Thus Zouzou is dehumanized and placed outside the norms of society. "We," meaning the audience, should not try too hard to understand them because they are "mysteries." "Where would we be without them?" asks Papa Mêlé. Clearly, we would be without a contrast to an imagined normalcy. The "mutant" in exhibition serves to define the line between "normal" spectators and the dark, empty depths of freakery. So, too, the role of those particularly marked by ethnicity is, in this scenario, to limn the borders of difference—in this case, between spectators and spectacle, normalcy and oddity. This opening sequence establishes the key themes that the film will develop over the course of the narrative as contrasts between Claire and Zouzou sharpen.

The film viewer and the circus audience are finally presented with the twins. Like the Folies stage, the elevated stage in the film becomes a wide field of fantasy in which the children appear to be exotic creatures under the shining lights. They look ill at ease and out of place. Jean is still smarting from his fight with the bullies who were spying on his sister. The audience looks on in astonishment, delight, and superiority at what to them is simply entertainment. When the children take the stage, it is apparent that there is nothing unusual about them; a young white actor and a young multiracial actress play characters whose visual contrasts are heightened by showing them next to each other. The scene is given meaning through Papa's story of their origins, in which he frames the children as freaks of both nature and culture.

This opening sequence is a paradigm that sets the terms of the film. The twins enter in costume and take their places on either side, and slightly downstage, of Papa Mêlé. Rather than framing the children theatrically, at a distance, and thereby taking cues from both anthropological photography and theatrical presentation, director Marc Allégret positions the camera at an angle that shows both the audience and the stage, although he cuts between the two as well. Papa Mêlé stands with his hands firmly on the children's shoulders in a gesture of ownership, familiarity, and exhibition. His very hands appear to generate the children/performers/objects as the spectators look on and listen to the ultrapatriarch who is father/director/owner. Papa Mêlé narrates the children's existence. According to Papa, the indefinite tones of their complexions cursed the twins, but the circus gave them value and a home. The twins' performance involves simply being objects of the audience's curiosity and inviting projection. The performance is to be looked at. Standing next to each other, moving minimally, and allowing the audience to look at them, the twins' bodies are defined and dynamized through the exhibition's juxtapositions of girl/boy and Black/white. The children are distinguished, moreover, by their ethnicities and genders. Jean wears a sailor suit and a hat, Zouzou a grass skirt, sleeveless blouse, and crown of flowers.

What does Jean's sailor suit signify if not assimilation to the West and colonialist sea exploration? Fictionalized in Papa's narrative as one captured and rescued from across the sea, the little boy wears the uniform of his captors. His costume references life on the seas, which represents the fulfillment of childhood ambitions. Later, a sequence that contains a medium shot of Jean working on his model ship paired with an extreme close-up of the model confirms that Jean is in control of his path despite his current position as passive circus object.

By contrast, Zouzou's blouse is perhaps her costume's only Western reference, worn possibly for the sake of the movie audience's sensibilities. (The anthropological audience would have been accustomed to seeing "ethnic" females of all ages displayed seminude.) Unlike Jean, Zouzou wears a costume that refers back to the unspecified Polynesian island from which the twins are said to have come. Though Jean and Zouzou are both on display, Zouzou is the sole bearer of their make-believe ethnicity. Furthermore, only the girl, Zouzou, is shown looking at herself in the mirror. Jean reacts to bullies in the audience, makes model ships, and dreams of his future; Zouzou remains caught up in her own image.

Zouzou's opening sequence resembles colonial narratives in which the display of captives was routine. Colonial dioramas were typically held in the open air and showcased in natural daylight, yet enclosed in spaces separate from everyday life. In the freak-show setting, they were usually contained within a bordered village (which the people in the display were not allowed to leave) or perhaps on an elevated stage. The audience had the benefit of a comfortable physical proximity from which they could see the person or persons on display in a low-tech, realistic setting but with the protection of a visible or invisible barrier.

Zouzou's circus sequence takes place at night. Lights on the stage illuminate the performers, and the audience stands to watch in the open night air. The film later features Baker in an elaborate shadow-dance sequence, and the bridge between it and the Cirque Romarin in the early portion of the film is the music hall. The circus and the music hall are both low-cost, high-spectacle forms of entertainment for the working masses. Typical shows in both venues featured a series of unrelated acts that might include jugglers, dwarfs, dancers, contortionists, comedians, musicians, and, as we see in *Zouzou*, a singing and kicking chorus line composed of several women of similar height and weight. Most of the performers in the Cirque Romarin wear shiny costumes, and one female dancer wears an elaborate headdress of feathers. They represent old-fashioned and silly precursors to Baker, calling forth a certain nostalgia for the direct intimacy and contact associated with live performance in contrast to cinema's selective framing and spectatorial distancing. Baker's colonialist stage persona, despite its innovative features, recalls an earlier Black woman exoticist sensation: Saartjie Baartman, stage name.[40]

Early in the movie, Zouzou is presented as an object even in her own eyes—enamored, and perhaps trapped, by her own reflection—whereas Jean is the subject of his self-made narrative of future manhood. In the remainder of the film, the adult Zouzou, though she works in a laundry, is depicted as never really having left the stage. She appears in two song-and-dance sequences for nontheatrical audiences (in an apartment for a child and in the laundry for her coworkers). Jean leaves the stage and serves in the military. On his return to Paris, he takes a backstage position at a music hall where Zouzou delivers linens.

In the rising action to her shadow dance, a major production number in the film, Zouzou plays dress-up with some of the chorus girls, and they put her in a shimmering, one-piece leotard. Perhaps noting a glow (from the costume? from Zouzou's emotions?), the girls tease her about being in love. Zouzou confesses her affection for Jean, who happens to be a lighting technician at the music hall. When she is dressed and powdered, Zouzou seeks out Jean to show herself off. When Zouzou enters Jean's work area, the camera is positioned over his shoulder, so we cannot read his facial expression. The scene lacks the pretense of privacy; instead, their interaction is clearly public.

In a device of deflection, Jean's coworker, whose delight is obvious, stands facing the camera at a three-quarter angle between Jean and Zouzou. We can read Jean's pleasure reflected in Zouzou's and the coworker's faces. Marked as a strange and possibly illicit object at the beginning of the movie, Zouzou is portrayed now as an exotic, delightful creature under an adoring gaze. A soft-focus close-up on her face confirms the new regard that we viewers should have for her. But Baartman haunts this encounter.

Jean tells Zouzou to stand on the stage, explaining that he has to test his spotlight. He gives her directions. She turns in profile and turns around in the light in a manner analogous to an ethnographic subject under observation. The difference is that Zouzou appears to enjoy the spectacle that she and Jean are collaboratively making of her.

The two friends are playing a game, but the terms of the game are quite different for each player. Zouzou displays her body—a dark-skinned girl in a bodice of diamonds—glamorized and newly exciting even to her. Zouzou loves Jean, and from her point of view, the heat and light of the spotlight substitute for the gaze she desires from him. Jean sees a curious, sexy creature of entertainment emerging from where his humble "sister" had been. However, Zouzou is always beyond the category of romantic interest for Jean, and she remains an object at the fair. He continues to direct her, and, childlike in her delight, she becomes absorbed in the game and seems intrigued by the enormous projection of her shadow on the stage's back wall.

Zouzou improvises a dance sequence of full-body movements that cover large sections of the stage as well as smaller, detailed gestures. At first, she shakes her head and wiggles her fingers. As she becomes bolder, her dance becomes more physical and more imaginative with each movement, and she interacts with increasingly broad proportions of space. She walks on her hands and feet with rump in the air. She drops to the floor with one leg bent in front and the other dragging behind in imitation of soldiers crawling through trenches with their rifles drawn; she flails her arms and legs in profile and then full front; she twirls and crosses her hands over her knees—all signature Baker moves. Throughout the sequence, Zouzou's body is framed with a few close-ups of her face or other parts of her body. The dance's drama derives not only from Baker's movements but also from the contrast between the woman and her shadow. The shadow dance visually flattens out the character's body and history within the narrative, emptying her out for new fictions, representing Baker's status as what Elizabeth Ezra has called "a floating signifier of cultural difference."[41] Adding visual and narrative tension, the shadow cast behind Zouzou is a flat, black graphic that is reminiscent of some drawings of Baker and allegorically represents the idea of projected fantasy.

Now expected to move and display the capacities of her unique body, Zouzou clowns around onstage. Now a director, not a coethnographic object, Jean tells Zouzou how to move and creates a shadow puppet show using Zouzou's body. The narrative of exotic origins is updated to match the modern times, and Zouzou is an ordinary assimilated Creole laundress revealed as a natural dancer. Absent the mirror, Zouzou turns from the spotlight and looks up at her ephemeral, weightless, hollow presence, so much larger than herself.

In *Zouzou*, the basic elements of the ethnographic circus act and the principle of the *village nègre* are recast as a music hall number. We see a version of the narrative in which the colonialist brings a human curiosity from afar. Jean's exhibit implies an exoticizing ethnological gaze that exploits Zouzou's physical appearance. Possibly lost in the sounds of rising orchestral music, which seems to come from a rehearsal off-screen, and in the prospect of Jean's pleasure in watching her, Zouzou does not notice when Jean raises the curtains on her. She continues to dance for several beats and then freezes in midturn with her arms out and knees bent toward each other in a pose of embarrassment. What she had believed to be a private or at a least personal exchange (Zouzou barely acknowledged Jean's coworker) between herself and her love interest is revealed as a public exhibition, and she is the unaware star. Zouzou gets turned into Baartman. Frightened at the suddenly public nature of her dancing, Zouzou escapes, climbing a ladder up and out of the frame, with Jean shouting after her to return. We have witnessed Zouzou's glamorization in a reversal of the melodrama's logic where the public is made private. This transformation serves the interests of her amused male transformer/director, Jean, who now has the point of view.

Jean is not the only one to witness the spectacular shadow dance. The director of the music hall has been watching the scene unfold, and he wants Zouzou to replace his temperamental star, who has run off to Argentina in search of her lover. Again, physical curiosity and ethnic difference are combined into an event of astonishment, but it now has a glamorous cast thanks to the glittering bodice and the spotlight's transformative powers. Zouzou is seen through the lens of burlesque as a beautiful, larger-than-life spectacle. In a sense, the shadow-dance sequence is a visual statement of what happens when a human figure is burlesqued cinematically in that it is enlarged through the projection of light and inscribed by the myths and fantasies of the viewer.

Zouzou departs from Hollywood's method of filming musical numbers. The production number featuring Baker in a birdcage shows female dancers' aesthetic value as decoration through high crane shots and framing that abstracts their bodies, though to a lesser extent than we might see in the visually striking synchronized dancing and high-energy camera work and editing that characterize the Hollywood aesthetic. Overall, the production number in Baker's musicals tends to be less mechanical and less linear in its aesthetic compared to Hollywood musicals of this period. There is no tap dancing, and when Baker makes her entrance in the birdcage, all other dancing ceases. After a plaintive song, she dives out of the cage into the waiting arms of a line of male dancers. The star is not integrated to the number, as she is in her earlier films. Isolation and singularity—double-edged uniqueness—are key components of Baker's persona in *Zouzou*. She strikes a triumphant pose, with arms in the air as if she has just freed herself by singing. As another dance number begins, Zouzou is already back in her dressing room worrying about Jean. *Zouzou* then departs from another convention in that Baker and the dancers do not appear together again.

The particular formulation of Baker's stardom is similar to that of the characters she played in that they relied on her celebrity persona and gave her top billing but then undermined her as a protagonist. Jean's storyline relies on Zouzou and uses Zouzou rather than elevating her. Zouzou is more of a tool in the storyline, with her performance enabling the funds to release Jean from jail. Baker as an actor was thrust into the spotlight with none of the support she would require to truly shine in the roles. Baker's performance rather burlesqued the Black Venus narrative but also succumbed to it. As an African American performer, Baker brought with her the history of Black performance she had gained as a dancer in *Shuffle Along*. This legacy was one of her strengths, since it is where she developed her auteurism around comedy dance and improvisation. In the film, Baker's Zouzou allowed her burlesque to blend comedy, parody, and glamour, but ultimately she moved in the narrow, if prismatic, confines of the ethnographic roles outlined by her predecessors. Baker came to public attention as a dancer, and the ways she used comedy (primarily in the form of facial expressions) to play down her sexuality—or just as likely, to play it up—carried over into her screen roles. Moreover, Baker was known for having performed the Charleston, which is characterized by whirling arms and legs. This combination made Baker a visual prism where her film character, her offscreen persona, the preexisting narratives of Black women, and her other film characters all refract one another.

In *Zouzou*, the pairing of the twins' race and gender permits a fiction unique to each of them. Which parent does each twin take after? What is Indian or Chinese about them? The answers are neither and nothing. Jean and Zouzou look basically white and (light-skinned) Black, respectively. The film highlights Zouzou's skepticism toward Papa's story in the following dialogue:

Jean (to Papa): Zouzou doesn't think we're twins.
Zouzou: It wasn't the same stork that brought us, was it?
Papa: Of course it was the same stork. But that clumsy bird dropped you in
    the chimney.

Papa's absurd explanation underscores the ignorance around race and ethnicity that this film is based on. From the beginning of her career in Paris, Baker played ethnic female roles. The colonial women she represented were only vaguely outlined, although in tribute, I have chosen to take them seriously in this book. As an American expatriate of African descent who performed in French, eventually gaining French citizenship, Baker seems to have believed in and acted out notions of assimilation and transcendence across racial lines in her career as in her life. Papa Mêlé's story about the twins makes no sense whatsoever, even within the realm of his private logic, unless we see Zouzou and Jean as equal parts in the whole of the old man's utopian tale of a paradoxically raceless yet thoroughly racialized society, illustrated with live models. In many ways, Baker served to manage opposites and soothe cultural anxiety about their possible integration. Zouzou wanted to be a star, and she is certainly ambitious. In fact, Zouzou wants assimilation and integration through being in a couple with Jean, but she finds that society has only one role for her: entertainer, an Other that is compulsory spectacle as illustrated in the shadow-dance sequence.

If *Zouzou* followed the conventions of backstage musicals, Zouzou and Jean would have fallen in love and taken the stage together in a romantic, show-stopping number in the happy ending. Instead, Zouzou performs alone. Jean and Claire, Zouzou's best friend and visual counterpoint, are united because Zouzou provides information that gets Jean out of jail. It is amazing that the star of the film is marginalized by its racial and gender politics and her key plot point is service to others.

At the film's climactic moment, Zouzou sees her friends embrace in a long shot, immediately followed by a close-up of her face showing her reaction of shock and disappointment. Zouzou turns away from Jean and Claire, and the camera tracks her as she runs past posters (material actually used for Baker's performances) that announce her performance. Rather than enjoying her notoriety, her fame is superficial and meaningless to her. Zouzou's rise to stardom increases rather than diminishes her status as an outsider by granting her a place on the stage and labeling her as merely an entertainer. Baker played characters who were Caribbean, and her skin color permitted multiple interpretations of her ethnicity. Her characterization as an Other, an ethnographic curiosity, highlights the musical romance conventions of cultural assimilation, except that rather than finding unity of differences or overcoming obstacles, Baker's characters remain maligned, disqualified from coupling, and alone, unchosen. On-screen Baker plays a character who seeks the interior of that experience.

Baker received top billing in *Zouzou*, but liberal attitudes toward race did not preclude limits on the producers' expectations about Baker's acceptance among an international audience (including Americans). On film, Baker could not get the guy, despite her well-documented legions of fans and the fact that she was a French sex symbol. Instead, Baker is Parisianized and elevated to the gilded cage of an entertainer's stardom, to the chagrin of today's audiences. The extras on the DVD of *Zouzou* include interviews in which commentators such as author Margo Jefferson and Lynne Whitfield, who played Baker in *The Josephine Baker Story*, lightheartedly lament the fact that Baker does not get her man. Although the closing scenes of *Princesse Tam-Tam* (discussed in the next chapter) suggest that Alwina/Baker formed a family with Dar, it is difficult to ascertain what is dream, what is reality, and who the narrator is in that film.

In *Zouzou*, Jean is forever looking at other women while Zouzou is out of view, pictured on her own and even blending in with the background. Jean holds both the literal spotlight in the shadow dance sequence and the power to establish Zouzou's importance in the film. In that dance sequence, Baker is shadow to herself; in other sequences, she is Claire's shadow. Thus, she follows the pattern of Black women's filmic visibility even when she is meant to be the star and despite this being a moment when her talents are showcased. None of it matters in terms of who is truly desirable in the film. The film's sun continues to shine in the direction of the white woman character. Desire follows Jean's gaze, and his gaze is never on Zouzou until he turns her into a spectacle.

In her cinematic prism, Baker's images perform a double signification between the character on-screen and the star persona behind it. This duality creates a compelling tension that superimposes Zouzou onto Baker. Like Zouzou, Baker was an outsider in a largely homogeneous French community. Her presence threatens its white French nationalistic identity while providing the force that strengthens the bond between community members. Zouzou's unrequited love is tied to the ways in which she is refused integration. Driven by spurious racial theories, the film introduces interracial families in the context of the circus and its notions of freakishness, adoption, and biracial status. The staging in a circus context creates a representation of Papa Mélé's family as not just unusual but as abnormal, following the racist logic of race science. Visually, Zouzou stands out the most and appears to be the adopted child who does not belong. This status is borne out as the film's plot depends on Jean's capacity to pass for a normative white man, leaving his circus beginnings behind. He romances Claire, who looks like him, excluding Zouzou, who does not and cannot.

Zouzou is the outsider of Jean's romantic intentions with Claire. Jean's origins disappear into the diegetic past while Zouzou's are inscribed on her skin, and she cannot rewrite them. In the end, Zouzou and the threats of racial mixing she represents are resolved and put in their proper place as Jean ignores Zouzou as a romantic possibility and partners with Claire "to form a natural (i.e., white) proletarian family" rather unlike the circus community in which he was raised.[42] Thus, "having constructed racial difference as Otherness, 'intermixing' becomes an unthinkable act, any desire for which has to be repressed" or, indeed, sublimated into the desire to look at the Other as entertainment.[43] Zouzou's place in the community is onstage as a spectacle, making possible other characters' pleasure and helping forge bonds between them. It is reasonable to conclude that Baker is trapped or flattened into this situation, but her deployment of burlesque creates a negotiation, a discourse in which Baker's ambitions as an artist and her desires for community and connection as an Other somehow coexist in dynamic, rather than immobilizing, contradiction.

What is most compelling and striking about the film's racial politics is its adaptation of anthropological or ethnographic aesthetics into what is essentially a backstage musical. The melodramatic focus on the personal lives of a few individuals and the trajectory from the laundry to the music hall takes on the resonance of an allegory because of the way the film treats Zouzou. References to the cabaret, circus, and music hall are suggestive of the era's passion for popular entertainments, including colonial-inspired ones. *Zouzou* links nineteenth-century displays and investigations of foreign people in both scientific and entertainment venues with twentieth-century updates of these displays via Baker's primitivist/colonialist twist on the performance aesthetics of the music hall and the stylistics of the musical film: "They're born dancers," says one character while looking at an anonymous dancing "native" while Jean writes a postcard to Zouzou.[44]

Although the shadow dance is modernist in many ways, the shadow itself, hovering in the background and tracking Baker, offers a way to think about Baker's early performance history, particularly her relationship to Baartman and to minstrelsy. The shadow operates almost like a minstrel mask, a flat stereotype devoid of subtle facial expression that is both apart from her and stuck with her. Consider that minstrelsy highlights the superficiality of the identity it perpetuates since it is a made-up representation based on black makeup and imitations of preexisting stereotypes. The reality is, as Eric Lott has pointed out, "Black performance itself, first of all, was precisely 'performative,' a cultural invention, not some precious essence installed in black bodies."[45] It is superficiality itself. From *Shuffle Along* to *Zouzou*, Baker worked on international stages and in film against her origins in the United States. Minstrelsy, as James Weldon Johnson wrote, "fixed a stage tradition which has not yet been entirely broken. It fixed the tradition of the Negro as only an irresponsible, happy-go-lucky, wide-grinning, loud-laughing, shuffling, banjo-playing, singing, dancing sort of being."[46] When African Americans later began to participate in minstrelsy, the caricature became even more deeply engulfed in the bizarre. But Baker's films work to offer, as *Zouzou*'s press book promised, laughs, drama, and songs that depart from this tradition. She finds strategies of being entertaining without the shadow of race and minstrelsy.

Even as Baker incorporated French flair and burlesque glitz into her vaudevillian routines, and even as she became a Paris institution in her own right, the burdens of Black (mis)representation would haunt her reception in the United States and in France. They made of Baker a tangle of ambivalences that speak to the complexities of belonging, belonging to, and recognition in diverse societies. The figure of Baker enables us to envision the ruptures and anxieties that underlie Black identity and, by extension, the reality of Black cinema as a deeply conflictual institution and as a cultural practice—and as illusion. Baker makes possible a revised understanding of Black cinema such that it is transnational and full of rupture, driven by anxieties of misrepresentation and desires to belong.

Ultimately, Baker and Black cinema reveal much about each other, as a relation between enigmas. Baker is a paradox of power and powerlessness, authorship and stereotypical script. But her biographer Jean-Claude Baker reminds us not to underestimate her: "Some have suggested that she was being exploited, that white men had put onstage their fantasy of a noble African girl, but it was not so easy to exploit Josephine; you couldn't make her do anything unless she was convinced the public wanted it."[47] Baker certainly took a number of gambles in walking the line between being laughed at and sharing the laugh. Despite her marginalization in her own films, Baker was not a joke. She was funny, the purveyor of jokes, and the conductor of humor. She was the reason the films were made and the reason we remember them. Baker's comedic approach, combined with her mastery of burlesque's acting precepts, offered her a measure of control over her own intentionality. She is luminous and funny despite the context. Burlesque in the larger sense was, for Baker and for some of today's entertainers, a necessary and shrewd strategy of power in an absurd hall-of-mirrors media culture. Burlesque theorizes the spectacular revelation and transformation of self and recognizes Baker's daring insistence on her own deft and knowing visibility in a hostile environment of racial and gender inequality.

Baker's performance depended on ideological relics, aesthetic artifacts, and frozen notions of the primitive and the exotic Other. And yet Baker was also a subject, dynamic and acting on those old stereotypes. In Baker's burlesque, she was prismatic and in pieces. She brought together her public persona of La Bakaire and her film characters Papitou, Zouzou, Alwina, and Zazu into multiple and simultaneous incarnations that reflect her shifting response to different and incoherent onslaughts and critiques. Although it is compelling to defend Baker's agency, to define her wholeness, the reality is that Baker's fragmented authorship offered a potent and brave strategy of facing and navigating oppression in ways that protect the creative soul and establish shelter within which to flourish.

If we see Baker as the true author, the authority, of these films, then her appearances onstage can be appreciated not as scenes of banishment but as generative havens of solitude, imagination, and artistry. Baker's characters may not win the affections of the mediocre white men who reject them, but when the film progresses to the climactic number, and Papitou, Zouzou, and Alwina take their respective stages, each woman gets to be the artist; she gets to be Josephine Baker.

In the banana dance footage discussed earlier, the fact that Baker is playing a character is lost on many of today's viewers. It is simply Baker doing her banana dance. She is seen as the creator of that performance because she is doing that performance, and it can be both inspiring and confusing. Yet Baker's character is a figment of the boss's imagination, even while Baker is actively performing her choreography in the context of her work at the Folies Bergère. That is essentially the conundrum of Baker's prismatic image.

Baker's cinematic prismatic functions less as a resistance strategy and more as a realistic survival tactic of play and experimentation that she tapped into, consciously or not, to present the self in a protective way as she navigates varied audiences. This approach emerges through Baker's films but also in the way she staged her life in the press, where she moves between self, performer, and character. Baker the woman, the living historical reality of an African American woman establishing herself as a huge success, is a phenomenon in and of itself. However, the content of her performance complicates this achievement because of the controversy and accolades her work incited in Europe. As an African American, Baker was celebrated for her success, but she was also criticized for not being progressive enough in her film and stage roles. Add to this another layer where her movie characters are portrayed by the star of the film, yet they are minor characters in plots that use them as entertainment and elicit little emotional investment. However, by moving between self, character, and persona within her cinematic prism, Baker is able to dodge the limitations of all three configurations.

Baker's characters are simplistically drawn stereotypes, to be sure, but in them I also find a theory of Black people's perception of their uneasy place in an integrated world dominated by white-defined desires and standards of beauty. Baker is an Othered figure who is yet familiar, then again foreign—a truly diasporic figure in an African American context. Baker addresses this complexity even if she cannot fully account for the intimacies of Black cinematic pleasure: characters and scenarios that reflect feelings of belonging and being recognized in a diverse society. For African American spectators—for Black women viewers in particular—seeing another Black woman on-screen brings the anxiety of misrepresentation and the threat of a presence worse than not being in the picture at all. Baker's own films are comedies featuring a glamorous Black woman star, but at the same time, they are tales of being left out as she is repeatedly rejected by the lead, an average and not even particularly compelling white male character. In films set outside the United States and, further, through the portrayal of non-American personae, the figure of Baker achieves a level of professional success and recognition that vindicates African American talent—which is ironic unless one understands that her position in a non-US context, an international

context, signifies the African American idealization of a Blackness unbur-
dened by US-based racism.

But there is a sadness, a harsh comedy even, to Baker's role of Zouzou. That
sequence of her running past posters announcing Josephine Baker's own performances collapses the character and the off-screen character, but it also shows
that Baker's stardom is not enough. When I look at this scene, sometimes I
imagine her laughing instead of crying and wonder how that changes the end
of the film. Carpio describes laughter as a "wrested freedom" for African Americans. Black laughter could be threatening on the one hand or, on the other, used
as a sign of Black inferiority. In *Laughing Fit to Kill*, Carpio outlines three main
forms of humor—relief, superiority, and incongruity—and how they apply
to African American comedy when Black people are the conscious tellers of
the joke. Relief humor is understood to provide "a balm" and an escape hatch
for otherwise life-threatening frankness and natural anger at experiences of
injustice.[48] It presumes a context of inhibition and sublimation, one that is
often guarded by violent means. Laughter was a matter of life and death, and
for this reason it was largely oriented to a safe in-group. Novelist Paul Beatty
suggested subtle differences between laughing *at* and laughing *with* when he
distinguished between African Americans being thought of as "having not a
collective consciousness but a collective funny bone" in the eyes of an omnipo-
tent judging white eye with nothing to lose and no skin in the joke.[49] Here
both Carpio and Beatty resonate with W. E. B. Du Bois's foundational notion
of a contemptuous white gaze. Du Bois writes, "It is a peculiar sensation, this
double-consciousness, this sense of always looking at one's self through the eyes
of others, of measuring one's soul by the tape of a world that looks on in amused
contempt and pity. One ever feels his twoness,—an American, a Negro; two
souls, two thoughts, two unreconciled strivings; two warring ideals in one dark
body, whose dogged strength alone keeps it from being torn asunder."[50] Carpio
and Beatty write of the stakes of Black humor and what it means to joke and to
laugh and take up that risky space menaced by the neighbor, the coworker, the
passerby who watches, judges, tracks Black life to the last breath.

Black laughter is on that razor edge of knowing when not to laugh. Black
laughter threatens the status quo. To paraphrase Haggins, a Black person had
to make sure his or her jaw was tight, which might mean either silence or coding commentary for those in authority.[51] Although Carpio used examples
from the slavery era to illustrate the concept of relief humor, it is certainly
the case that during Reconstruction, Jim Crow, and the post–civil rights
era, African Americans navigated white-dominated spaces with care—as
they continue to do—and certain kinds of aggressive, resentful, revelatory,

and self-protective jokes are best shared in private. Black humor was precious underground humor; it was a shelter.

Carpio's second form of humor—superiority—"relishes exposure" and thrives on the pleasure of other people's misfortunes.[52] Applied to African American humor, superiority humor is roasts, toasts, and "yo mama" jokes that are common to Black (often male) jocularity. Interestingly, this humor found spectacular expression through Richard Pryor's integrated comedy clubs and stages rather than Black-only rooms. As historian Mel Watkins wrote of the 1960s comedian, Pryor "began unveiling the satirical barbs concealed beneath the black jester's clownish attire."[53] What were once subtle, indirect, and pro-tected (and protective) strategies now became blunt, especially where white racism and Black urban folklore and storytelling were concerned. What had been a guarded secret during slavery and segregation was now out in the open.

Carpio suggests that the form of humor that has the greatest revelatory power is that of incongruity, the humor of contradictions and oppositions: "This theory sug-gests that we laugh when our expectations are somehow disturbed." It "suspend[s] normativity." It "allows us to see the world inverted, to consider transpositions of time and place and to get us, especially when the humor is hot enough to push our buttons, to question habits of mind that we may fall into as we critique race."[54]

Carpio's analysis goes in a direction that is beyond the scope of this study of Baker in that she is interested in the ways that "racial conflict, and the obsessive ways that it colonizes American minds, can divest everyone, albeit at different registers, of a sense of reality," yet there is much that applies here.[55] Her work looks at how the ideologies that supported slavery continue to support racism today. In particular, Carpio sheds light on a sort of necessary "grief," a recogni-tion of mourning as part of the assessment of both the violence and absurdity that is slavery's legacy—and laughter is part of that sorrow.[56] While Baker's work is not directly about slavery, her mode of performance explores how material that appears lighthearted can have a "piercing tragicomic" dimension, "disassociated from gaiety," that would go unnoticed without a sense of incon-gruity.[57] Baker's film roles unveil moments when Baker and her characters process loss and the haunting of what might have been as we see them caught between narratives of stardom and invisibility, belonging and alienation.

NOTES

1. Atwater, *African American Women's Rhetoric*, 8. Baartman was called the Hottentot Venus, "Hottentot" being a pejorative name given to Khoisan people with cattle by European settlers: "They had acquired cattle by migrating

northwards to Angola and returned to South Africa with them, some 2,000 years before the first European settlement at the Cape in 1652. Prior to this, they were indistinguishable from the Bushmen or San, the first inhabitants of South Africa, who had been in the region for around 100,000 years as hunter-gatherers."

2. See, for example, Hobson, *Venus in the Dark*. Baartman's life and legacy is examined in Crais and Scully, *Sara Baartman and the Hottentot Venus*.

3. "The Hottentot Venus," *Bells Weekly Messenger*, September 23, 1810.

4. Strother, "Display of the Body Hottentot," 8.

5. Ibid., 4.

6. Ibid., 22.

7. Magubane, "Which Bodies Matter?"

8. See Hays, "The Lecturing Empire."

9. *British History Online*, "The Haymarket, West Side." The property at 224–225 Piccadilly, where the *Bells* article says the Hottentot Venus exhibit was located, was leased in 1903 to provide land for the construction of the tube railway station Piccadilly Circus.

10. Ibid.

11. Lindfors, *Africans on Stage*, x. Of racialized freak shows, Lindfors writes, "Players, promoters, and spectators—individually and in concert helped to shape European and American perceptions of Africans in the nineteenth and twentieth centuries. The shows that brought them together tended to replicate and reinforce the dynamics of the unequal relationship that existed between colonizer and colonized, master and slave. Africans were again denigrated, humiliated, dehumanized, and exploited."

12. Willis, *Black Venus 2010*.

13. Alexander, *The Venus Hottentot*, 6.

14. Lindfors, *Africans on Stage*, 22.

15. "Court of King's Bench, Saturday, Nov. 24. The Hottentot Venus," *Times* (London), November 26, 1810, 3.

16. Magubane, "Which Bodies Matter?," 57.

17. "Civil Actions—The Hottentot Venus," *Times* (London), November 29, 1810, 3.

18. Ibid.

19. Ibid.

20. Ibid.

21. Ibid.

22. Daniels, "Exhibit A.," 65. Daniels drew background information from Percival Kirby; see Kirby, "More about the Hottentot Venus."

23. Daniels, "Exhibit A.," 65.

24. Ibid., 66.

25. Holmes, *African Queen*, 73.

26. Index, *Bells Weekly Messenger,* January 1, 1814, 3.

27. Holmes, *African Queen,* 74.

28. Lindfors, *Africans on Stage,* 27; see also 41.

29. Maseko, *Life and Times of Sara Baartman.*

30. Holmes, *African Queen,* 93.

31. Danzik, (News) *Champion* (London), January 7, 1816, 5.

32. Cuvier, "Extrait d'observations faites sur le cadavre d'une femme," 259–74.

33. Today, artists working at the articulation of race and gender have sought to remember Baartman through poetry and visual art. See, for example, Renee Cox, *Hot-en-Tot* (1994), a performative photograph in which the model, standing in profile and looking directly at the camera, wears plastic forms of exaggerated prosthetic breasts and buttocks, referencing accounts of Saartjie Baartman's physicality. Overall gelatin silver print 40 B 60 , Parsons School of Design.

34. Loti, *A Spahi's Love-Story,* xii.

35. Loti, *A Spahi's Love-Story,* 18–19.

36. Ibid., 145.

37. Berrong, *Pierre Loti,* loc 926, Kindle.

38. Ezra, *Colonialist Unconscious,* 6.

39. *Zou Zou* Press Book, African American Contributions to Film Collection, Black Film Center/Archive, Indiana University Bloomington.

40. Holmes, *African Queen,* 3. Baartman's name is spelled variously, but in this book Saartjie (pronounced Saar-Key) Baartman is standard.

41. See Ezra, *The Colonial Unconscious,* 99. Baker's shadow dance, in which a spotlight shines on her, casting her shadow on the walls behind her, brings to mind Aaron Douglas's silhouettes, which combined modern design aesthetics with African and African American design principles. In *Blues Aesthetic,* art historian Richard Powell writes, "Douglas' sparse silhouettes perfectly capture the dreamy mood and ironic perspective of many blues performances. Years later Douglas described his flat and geometric delineation of form as 'suggestive of the uniqueness found in gestures and bodily movements of Negro dance and (in) the sounds and vocal patterns . . . (of) Negro songs.'" Powell, *Blues Aesthetic,* 25.

42. Slavin, *Colonial Cinema and Imperial France,* 19.

43. Young, *Fear of the Dark,* 32.

44. Author's translation.

45. Lott, *Love and Theft,* 39.

46. Johnson, *Black Manhattan,* 93.

47. Jean-Claude Baker, *Josephine: The Hungry Heart,* 135.

48. Carpio, *Laughing Fit to Kill,* 2.

49. Beatty, *Hokum,* 2.

50. Du Bois, "Of Our Spiritual Strivings," 3.

51. Haggins, *Laughing Mad,* 1.

52. Carpio, *Laughing Fit to Kill*, 6.
53. Watkins, *On the Real Side*, 13.
54. Carpio, *Laughing Fit to Kill*, 6.
55. Ibid., 7.
56. Ibid., 9.
57. Ibid., 7.

FOUR

SEEING DOUBLE

Parody and Desire in *Le pompier de Folies Bergère* and *Princesse Tam-Tam*

THE *CHICAGO TRIBUNE* ADVERTISED A screening of Baker's third feature film, *Princesse Tam-Tam*, at the World Playhouse on July 29, 1938, three years after its French première.[1] An August article in the *Chicago Defender* read,

> Starting Saturday the World Playhouse will present the American premiere of the famous star of the Folies Bergere. Josephine Baker, making her first screen appearance in "Princesse Tam-Tam" a lavish, musical which was filmed in Tunis, Africa and in Paris. Dialogue is in French, with English titles. At present Miss Baker is appearing in London where she is the star at one of the most fashionable nightclubs. During the action of the story Miss Baker renders a number of the songs for which she is famous and also does her unforgettable "Conga" dance in one of the most elaborate musical numbers yet to be brought to America.[2]

The film's delayed release in the United States is curious, and it might be explained by a perceived lack of interest in Baker among American audiences following the largely negative reception of her performances at the Ziegfeld Follies in 1936. At that time, she had performed the conga and other dances choreographed by George Balanchine at New York's Winter Garden Theatre in February 1936, with costar Fanny Brice and then up-and-coming comedian Bob Hope. Biographer Stephen Papich described the ordeal as "one of the greatest disappointments of her life." In Papich's account the production standards and technical support were deemed lower than those at the Folies Bergère and the Casino de Paris, and the American show lacked the convivial atmosphere Baker had become accustomed to in Paris. The other stars of the Ziegfeld show ignored her, and the producers dismissed the high-fashion gowns she had

brought from Paris in favor of costumes she found "vulgar and unattractive."
Her ideas were either rejected or entirely ignored. Baker returned to France
"stunned" and "disillusioned."[3] She did not directly address the distribution
of this particular film but rather the lack of regard for her as an artist who had
earned accolades in France and around the world.

It is remarkable, too, that Baker's previous films *La sirène des tropiques* and
Zouzou seem to have been so little known that the *Tribune* and the *Chicago
Defender* advertised *Princesse Tam-Tam* as Baker's first film. Still, that the
screening is mentioned in the *Chicago Defender* at all demonstrates the ongoing interchange between the circulation of Baker's films and changing African
American film culture ten years after *La sirène des tropiques*.[4] Distributed by
Sack Amusement Enterprises, *Princesse Tam-Tam* circulated in Black American
movie theaters during the late 1930s, as shown by its promotion in the Black
press.[5]

Although its US circulation was delayed, *Princesse Tam-Tam* was released
in France almost immediately after *Zouzou*, and it capitalized on Baker's continued success in the music hall as a live performer and her increased bank-
ability, particularly following her international tours of the late 1920s. In terms
of themes, *Princesse Tam-Tam* addresses assimilation, which had also been
significant in *La sirène des tropiques* and *Zouzou*, but it is more explicit and
pronounced here. Baker repeatedly portrayed the so-called primitive figure
in transformation to a supposedly modern one, and this story is layered on to
the backstage musical plot of the unknown talent who is discovered to be a
star singer. In this film, Baker's makeover, a key plot point here and in earlier
films, hinges on the question of where the title character, Princess Tam Tam,
given name Alwina, truly belongs. Baker herself knew where she belonged—in
France and on the stage, where she excelled at her chosen craft—but the location of home was an unsettled point of contention she rehearsed repeatedly in
her films through her characters.

Baker's relationship with filmmaking did not improve over the course of her
three features. In a conversation with biographer Papich, she summarized her
career in film as follows:

> I had made *Tam Tam*, and I didn't like that, and *La Sirène des Tropiques*. Then,
> when I made *Zou Zou*, they advertised that "Baker Talks." They got that from
> MGM and Garbo—"Garbo Talks." Boy, did I talk, and some newspaper took
> the dialogue the way I said it and twisted it just a little and made it sound like
> I was saying obscene things. I just couldn't make it in the cinema, no matter
> how hard I tried. They gave me the best directors too. The best thing I ever

got out of films was meeting Jean Gabin. I like him very much, and still do. He would come to my club in the Montmartre, and we would dance. He was the best dancer I ever worked with. He could take my body and make it do anything. Yes, that was the best thing I ever got out of films. When they do my life story, they won't have to worry too much about putting anything in there about films, cause that was the one place where Josephine fell flat. But that's all right, isn't it? Everybody has a place. Some stars are Broadway stars, and some are film stars, and some are recording stars. I happen to be a stage star. I'm at my best on a stage or in a night club. So, there is nothing wrong with my never making it in films.[6]

Baker considered her films a failure, but she failed in spectacular and instructive ways. I see them as wonderful experiments and serious reflections on her star image. In my eyes, her films sparkle with her presence, and I do consider these films to be hers. Baker was the only African American woman to receive top billing as a big international star. (The film career of gorgeous and gifted Nina Mae McKinney, who played the female lead in 1929's *Hallelujah*, never really took off, sadly.) And she did so in French. Baker arrived in Paris as a nineteen-year-old who did not speak any French; ten years later she was starring in films and speaking French lines. As Baker says, she excelled on the stage, and it was her success on the stage that formed the basis for her films. In and of themselves, Baker's films are sources of knowledge about her—but also about the worlds of symbols and stories; about formations of Blackness in the United States, Europe, and Africa; about dance; and about what it means to be in cinema in the 1930s as a Black woman actor and global entertainer.

In this chapter, I provide close readings of particular sequences in two films made at opposite ends of Baker's film career: a short silent film titled *Le pompier de Folies Bergère* (from roughly the late 1920s) and *Princesse Tam-Tam* (1935). The latter has a film-within-a-film structure similar to that of the earlier short. I demonstrate how Baker's dance was used in both films as a pretext for employing camera tricks that manipulated cinematic perspective, blurring the lines between reality and fantasy, subject and object. Baker played a cameo role in *Le pompier de Folies Bergère* (The fireman of the Folies Bergère), which is also known in France as *Un pompier qui prend feu* (A fireman catches fire) and *Les hallucinations d'un pompier* (The hallucinations of a fireman). Estimated to have circulated sometime around 1928, the film resurfaced in 2000 at the Lobster Films archive in Paris. The film consists of repeated appearances of nude white women and a rupture in which Baker appears as a figment of the fireman's imagination. Baker's appearance occurs in the context of her transformation from subway attendant to dancer—object of service to object of fascination. Baker's cinematic prism here involves the binary contrasts that serve as her backdrop, with a staging common to her music hall shows. The women are nude; Baker is clothed. They are in groups; she is alone. They pose; she is presented theatrically and given her own filmic performance space. The other women characters are still; she moves. The white women's nudity serves as the backdrop for Baker's eclectic, Africanist, and highly energetic dance style. In *Princesse Tam-Tam*, Baker's dancing is combined with songs and narrative in a more elaborated consideration of her character's personal desires to be seen, to travel, and to be in love and how those feelings are exploited by her love interest.

Baker's films continually shed light on how ethnological fantasy marked the encounter between Europeans and Africans. Whereas Baker's live dance was said to present her as a phenomenon of movement and a spectacle of percussion, rhythm, and syncopation, film narratives tended to frame her as a medium of translation or, rather, as a figure in transition, between the imagined Other's culture and its role in the West. The ragtime-turned-jazz aesthetics Baker embodied on stage had a major influence on experimental artists who sought new principles for their art. The film *Le pompier de Folies Bergère* is a reflexive, somewhat ironic tale about Baker's aesthetic influence on French society, from the avant-garde elites to popular appeal among working classes and civil servants, as portrayed in *Le pompier de Folies Bergère*. Black dance as understood through Baker's cinematic inflections inspired some filmmakers' idea of pacing and montage. The dancer's bodily accentuation of the beat creates a visual percussion that contains both visual continuity and a sense of disruption and incongruity. It's ultimately an erotic comedy but in a particularly enigmatic and cinematic prismatic way.

LE POMPIER DE FOLIES BERGÈRE AND ITS CINEMATIC INFLECTIONS OF RACE

The foundational aspect of Baker's cinematic prism in *Le pompier de Folies Bergère* is that it is a star vehicle for Baker; her specific appearance, which cites her well-established exoticism, is central to the story. She appears in a cameo as "herself" and expects to be recognized. The film uses revelation as a trope, as Baker plays a civil servant in a subway station who turns into Baker. A key point is that Baker's American identity manifested in a number of ways, including the uniquely American flapper hairstyle she wore regardless of the role she played. As a performer, and particularly as an urbanized American, Baker had greater access to the various hair-straightening systems that had been available in the northern United States since the late 1800s than did the colonial women she represented in her feature films and stage performances. Baker wore the short, shiny, straightened, and clearly-not-African hairstyle so consistently that it became part of her signature look, remaining constant while she morphed through various ethnic roles. (In *Princesse Tam-Tam* and *Zouzou*, she wore her hair a little longer but still straight.) Together with her relatively conventional Western makeup, tap shoes, brassiere, and hairstyle, Baker Americanized and modernized French colonial Black performances by conflating Americanness and Blackness in a hybrid or nation-culture-race-welded persona, referencing ideas about the United States, Europe, and Africa at once.

Le pompier de Folies Bergère was likely filmed between 1925 and 1928, the years of Baker's first wave of stardom before her departure for a two-year international tour, after which she returned more focused on singing. It was perhaps screened in a public venue as part of a shorts program, or it might have been included in Baker's show at the Folies Bergère. Shot in various Paris locations, the film runs five minutes long and is at this time missing head and tail credits and any intertitles that might have been part of the reel. The director is unknown, and the identities of the actors other than Baker are unknown. Archivists of Lobster Films, whose collection includes early erotica, jazz films, slapstick, and newsreels, identified Baker. The film's narrative places it easily in any of these categories. The actor playing the role of the fireman may well be Dorville, a middle-aged actor who received top billing in what ironically became known as Baker's shows at the Folies Bergère music hall. Dorville's older, short, stocky frame, white skin, and comic stupidity provided a perfect foil for the tall, clever, and elegant Black Venus, and he served also as a surrogate white male audience on-screen.[7]

The film's humor is based on the hallucinations suffered by an inebriated fireman whose drunken subjectivity constitutes the film's point of view and the pretext for the superimpositions, blurring, extreme close-ups, diagonal camera angles, dissolves, and overall sense of fragmentation that all serve to make the viewer aware of the camera's role in shaping the story. The use of these cinematic devices aligns subjective disorientation with the figure of Baker. However, Baker's dance is filmed differently from the rest of the movie, which raises questions as to what precisely is the subtext of her role in the film. The film's humor moves through a number of forms but relies heavily on the incongruous juxtapositions of Baker and the chorus of nudes as well as Baker and the fireman. *Le pompier de Folies Bergère* enhances and explores Baker's iconicity through the metaphors of transportation, an involuntary meeting, and shock. Baker performs the Charleston in an extended sequence.

Le pompier de Folies Bergère begins with a one-second shot of a billboard showing Baker, presumably outside the Folies Bergère, where the fireman appears to be in an argument with a security figure. Had the fireman been thrown out of the music hall? The two figures visible in the shot are tiny compared to the billboard, which fills the frame from top to bottom. For a sense of scale in a succeeding shot, a mail carrier walks in front of the billboard, and only Baker's legs on the sign are visible. Baker's pose in the poster mimics the angularity in her dance, commonly seen in her films, particularly her bent knees in the Charleston. The suggestion is that the fireman was already disoriented from seeing Baker's intoxicating performance. Seeing Baker perform intoxicates people.

In the second sequence, the fireman leaves the exchange with the security guard and stumbles up some stairs into a café. Once inside, he drinks what appears to be wine, and his hallucinations begin. The fireman sees a miniature image of nude white women dancing in a circle on his table. In trying to pick them up, he slaps at them, spilling the contents of his glass. This image is a prelude to Baker, folding her into the body culture of the era and contrasting her with the white female body in general. The fireman serves as both white male audience surrogate and a comic foil for Baker. Further, he represents official order coming undone. He is our host on a trip to the cultural underground, where the racial or colonial unconscious resides. The fireman's disordered mental state is mirrored in his environment. Thus, aboveground and in the daylight, he wanders Paris, whose formidable urban planning and architecture are mocked by his drunken perspective. The fireman hallucinates that buildings sway and turn toward each other, and streets rise up at odd angles and in fragmented shots. As if these events are not strange enough, he sees café patrons and subway commuters turn into nude white women the moment he looks at them.

For the most part, these nudes do not move when they shed their clothes, nor do they address the fireman; they simply sit or stand still, apparently unaware of and unaffected by his fantasies, while he watches in delight. The nudes are analogous to the chorus of dancers that precede Baker's appearances onstage. In the film, Baker appears in a sequence that takes place on a subway platform. When the fireman meets her, a very different dynamic unfolds between fantasizer and fantasized, as the film's experimentations with the film form give way to Baker's experimentations with dance. In other words, the seemingly plotless series of phantasmic transformations in the film's opening sequences in which fully dressed white men and women turn into nude white women lead to Baker's cameo, which forms the film's structural and thematic climactic performance.

Confused and stunned by his visions, the fireman leaves the street and descends to the subway. Underground, the subway tracks tilt and sway in one shot followed by a noncontinuous shot of commuters entering the train, a shot of the fireman clapping at someone or something, and then a shot of Baker wearing what appears to be a uniform and sitting on a chair. The sequence with Baker lasts a little over one minute. It is filmed to mimic a theatrical perspective that is straight on and shows her full body. The subway provides a shallow, improvised stage, but it is somewhat off-center.

Baker's character in the film is itself a cinematic prism, and because of her uniform, the location, and her interaction with the fireman, I have assumed she is a subway attendant. She is seated when the fireman enters the platform, but when he attempts to wait on the train (perhaps without paying), the attendant stands in front of him with her arms out. The sequence then begins not with a cut or other cinematic editing device but through performance. The attendant and the fireman touch each other, bend at the knees, look directly at each other, and freeze.

The stillness interrupts the continuity of the actors' performances. Time stops for a moment, marking a transition into another realm, that of deep colonialist fantasy. Previous sequences were mostly governed by the camera's tricks and represented the fireman's point of view as an inebriated person. When the fireman sways, for example, the buildings appeared to sway, too. The dominant element in this sequence, however, is performance rather than editing or cinematography. Baker's appearance divides the film into two parts, and her freeze highlights the transformation.

The actors then unfreeze and slowly back away from each other while remaining bent at the knees. The attendant, Baker, strikes a pose. In a demi-plié position, she raises her right hand and points down toward her head as if she were about to spin like a top. Cut to the delighted fireman, anticipating the performance and potentially a repeat of the nudity he had enjoyed in earlier scenes. Cut to the attendant, who turns and, through a filmic dissolve, transforms into *La Venus Noire* (the Black Venus). The subway attendant exchanges her uniform for Josephine Baker's costume: grass skirt, brassiere, tap shoes, and flapper hairstyle. As a figment of the fireman's imagination, the Baker figure reveals his subconscious, which is brought to the cinematic surface as a racially charged notion that is capable of exoticizing a woman of color, an African or Caribbean woman, who is merely at work in the subway. He has replaced the uniform of her social role with a costume from colonialist fantasy—another social role, this one involuntary.

That the fireman's movements mirror Baker's suggests a possible level of equality between the two civil servants. However, because certain key details of filmmaking support the fireman's perspective and authority, the rest of the dance sequence does not quite bear this out. He is alone with the attendant, and she is under his sole gaze. The close quarters of the subway and, of course, the underground location might be read as subversive of the colonialist world aboveground, but it is visually the fireman's terrain. He is in control. As with the farmer in the banana dance film, this subway sequence is the viewer's fantasy. The mirroring thus underscores their shared role in the fireman's colonialist fantasy. Not only is the film's trajectory entirely directed from the fireman's point of view, but his gaze appears to create the subway attendant's transformation into Josephine Baker. Baker thus figures in the film as a psychological and visual phenomenon.

Reaction shots of the fireman clapping and looking at her (there are no significant shots of Baker looking at him once the dance has begun) reinforce the idea that the fireman creates this exotic, dancing vision for himself. But Baker is not entirely passive, for her manipulation of stage-dance clichés forges a critical tension here between the fireman's point of view and what he sees. We watch him watching her, as though he were a stand-in for the audience's white, colonialist male gaze; moreover, we watch the force of Baker's famous persona in redefining the conventional colonialist fantasy. The earlier moment of stillness can be interpreted as a low-tech time-travel device that transforms the subway attendant and the fireman from city employees into actors in the narrative of heterosexual colonialist fantasy, where each character returns to a time when European explorers imagined the jungle to be filled with surreal female creatures of nature. The fireman still wears his uniform in his new role of colonialist spectator, showing that in many ways he remains rooted in the present while superimposing on the subway attendant images of native women and of female jazz performers in Paris, such as Josephine Baker. For her part, the attendant reemerges through these layers of stereotypes as a hybrid creature, the jazz Cleopatra, not only a rhetorical figure but also a socially and culturally significant, if numerically small, part of the French domestic scene and a product of colonization.

Baker's iconic performance in *Le pompier de Folies Bergère* sheds light on various elements of her art and her persona, what she meant to the French, and how she fit into the broader phenomenon of African Americans' success in Paris during the 1920s. The advertisements on the curved wall that forms the background of Baker's improvised stage connect a colonialist fantasy with noncolonial references. As though passing out of the frame or, in other words, out of the film's temporal and visual margins, the sign inscribed with the name of the Folies Bergère music hall is only partially visible, while another sign, advertising new radio technology, is centered behind Baker. To begin the dance, Baker taps her feet and does a few slow movements. Then she turns toward the radio ad, examining it closely. Reaching out, Baker appears to manipulate the radio dials, associating herself through a trompe l'oeil with modern technology. Indeed, though she often wore fantastical African-inspired outfits, just as she does in this sequence, Baker and jazz were associated more closely with the United States than with Africa. Yet a notion of Africa served as a rhetorical means of talking about the cultural products of people of African descent. In rapidly edited shots, Baker runs through a combination of movements and postures that include a Russian-style kick, moves that appear Asian or Egyptian in origin, a shoulder shimmy and a rear-end shimmy, a mocking ballerina's twirl, tap, and the Charleston—all while making funny faces of no discernable ethnic or racial origin.

The variety of references points to Baker's elastic ethnic persona and her capacity to embody the spectrum of exotic dances that converged on Paris. As Fatima Tobing Rony writes, "The fascination in ethnographic cinema for the displayed body of the woman of color is rendered carnivalesque in Baker's shows. For Baker was not only the symbol of the 'black woman,' but of all colonized women, and she performed acts which represented her as Inuit, Indochinese, African, Arab, and Caribbean."[8] Baker provocatively combined this plastic sense of ethnicity with her entanglement of sexuality and comedy. In *Le pompier de Folies Bergère*, we see this presence literally superimposed on the civil-service professions of subway attendant and firefighter.

The savage persona beneath the veneer of a woman of color's assimilation is a recurring theme in Baker's films. *Le pompier de Folies Bergère* portrays Baker at the apex of a prismatic convergence of Black renaissance, primitivism, orientalism, and modernism. First, the film has a modernist sensibility. It is created from a totally subjective individualist point of view, and it makes use of techniques associated with the avant-garde, such as fragmented perspective, subjectivity, and camera tricks that subvert the tableau perspective of more conventional films. The film's modernist technique is supported by the setting in the cafés and in the streets and with modes of public transportation that helped make Paris the most modern of cities. Second, Baker's presence in the film and the film's modernist methods support each other; appearing on film allowed her performance to be cut and shaped by the camera's selective and changing angles, editing her performance with a precision that lighting could barely approximate onstage. Baker represented the idea of identity-as-change in her stage performances, and in this film, she changes characters, with her star persona being in some ways reduced to a hybrid costume.

This segment features both representational mirroring, in that Baker and the fireman perform the same movements while watching each other, and funhouse mirroring, where the differences between their bodies are highlighted. The mirroring segment figures Baker and the fireman as spectacle and spectator—the primitive and the modern—while animating these dichotomies into dialectics. Though alcohol was the vehicle for the fireman's hallucinations, the catalyst that causes his private fantasies to find public exhibition before his and our eyes, Baker changed the way he perceived the world around him. In earlier sequences, before seeing Baker, the fireman is merely disoriented by confusing visions. But after seeing her—after contact with this performer whose persona is dominated by the motif of transformation, whether by ever-changing dance moves, costumes, and locations or being associated with various ethnicities and characters who undergo making over as part of their constant search for assimilation—and after all that has taken place with his figment of Baker, the fireman now has a story to tell.

Through drunkenness, the fireman gives free rein to his subconscious wishes, and the peep-show cast of the film permits him and viewers to see through society's taboos to look beneath the smooth surface of the body's skin. In what Elizabeth Ezra calls the "colonialist unconscious," Blackness is embodied in a *sauvage* figure, which is appropriated as the motor of personal liberation. The aesthetic of this supposed transformation and collective efforts coalesced as primitivism.

Baker, who is filmed theatrically, is folded into the film's formal style of superimpositions, blurring, super close-ups, and other camera play, making it clear that her high-speed, disjointed, and angular movements were an inspiration for the film and that the fireman's unexpected encounter with her in the subway is the film's narrative and visual core. Surrealist in texture, Baker's performance here can be understood as a vision of the contact of Africa with Europe on European soil and the shock of modernity. For it was one thing to encounter Black people on the so-called Dark Continent or to imagine a figurative Black Other, but it was quite another to meet actual Black people in Paris. During the 1920s, it must have seemed that the Other, precisely like a return of the repressed colonialist unconscious, was being brought to Paris in ethnographic pieces for display in museums, where they became a living part of the city's bustle.

The most curious and enigmatic doubling or mirroring moment in the subway sequence is the superimposition of two images that show Baker dancing and Baker sweeping the platform. This moment alludes to a small wave of colonial subjects' relocation to the city after the war. The scene seems to exemplify the process by which the colonialist fantasy of playful, sexually available native women became mixed and modernized with a new narrative of colonial women's work in the capital city. Or it might be seen as a satirical reference to the limitations of Baker's performance style and stardom, especially the possibility of her appearing in an American film as a star. The image suggests the contrast between France and the United States on race issues, as French journalists never tired of celebrating themselves for having had the good taste to recognize Baker's gifts while the Americans would have made her a maid either in real life or on the stage. Yet here she is in two types of servitude and fantasy. What I have referred to as Baker's Americanness may point not only to ideas about America but also to the real, contemporary world of work, modernity, and primitivism's troubling politics of race and gender in Paris. In this superimposition of Baker dancing and Baker sweeping, the film displays her double embodiment as spectacle and figure of labor. Baker's performer Self and performer Other are visible as two exposures on the same image.

BAKER'S TALES OF UNREQUITED ROMANCE

Surprisingly, given her undeniable personal success (she lived in a castle!), Baker's films offer a melancholy and pessimistic image of modern Black life with African diasporic characters that were isolated in white-dominated environments. They are acts of comedic grief in that although they picture forms of success, they likewise portray the shadows and limitations of celebrity. Yet the stage, where Baker performed her exuberant dances, could still represent a liberating space of social validation and personal expression in the films, even if only provisionally. Desirous of intimate familial bonds, Baker's character is brought into conflict with her own identity as Creole or Tunisian, a foreigner, within an alienating, all-white French environment.[9] She feels that she has to leave home and become someone else. Her characters, feasting on mere crumbs of attention from the so-called love interest, were willing to bet on the budding of true love against all odds, crossing oceans to grovel at the feet of rather unspecial fellas who did not want her. Her "lovers" were never suitors. They never tried to gain her trust and affection. Rather, she pleaded for their attention. The storyline of each of Baker's romantic-comedy musicals is essentially the protagonist's quest for belonging to a community through being loved and accepted by her white male partner, yet this proved an empty fantasy. In such scenarios, Baker strategically burlesqued her delicate position as a celebrated foreigner in France and a newcomer making the transition from live music hall performance to the cinema.

As mentioned in this book's introduction, Baker's lead roles were paradoxical. Her films were vehicles created specifically to showcase her celebrity, yet the romantic plots maneuvered around her rather than toward her, threatening to undermine her status. Baker's characters competed against white female supporting characters who were idealized for their whiteness. As an attraction, Baker's role is a lead role. But as a character, Baker is, incongruously, merely the Black best friend, an alternate, a minor player without a fully developed story or emotional trajectory. No one in the stories truly cares about her. She is instrumental to the plots of other characters despite her ambition. Lacking romantic plot framings of affection and desire, Baker plays the Black woman on her own in a world defined by others, where the emotional centers lie elsewhere, beyond her reach. And she works and works. Baker's characterizations exemplify the way that the cinema, particularly its inherent vicissitudes of representation, was a pivotal yet broken medium in expressing her unique formations of celebrity in the 1920s and 1930s. The instability of images and the political volatility around Black visibility led to Baker's dichotomous legacy across multiple spheres. By rejecting the possibility of Baker as a romantic lead, the filmmakers rejected the possibility of making a Black star that fulfills the desires of representation the term *star* suggests. Yet as an artifact, the film's structures can teach us the limits of Black stardom within an industry organized by whiteness.

Baker's performance in *Princesse Tam-Tam* was heavily marked by the genre of colonial cinema and framed by racialized unrequited romance. The musical's exceptional capacity to integrate story and song, and the conflict between insiders and outsiders, makes it a unique vehicle for exploring French anxieties around assimilation. In this experimentation with film, Baker emerged from music hall revues, nightclubs, and parties as a particularly effective conduit of "'jazz' as a state of being, a precarious holding ground between two cultures, neither Black nor white, but something fantastic and modern; a place of spontaneity and improvisation, of energetic lively music; a place of violent bodily motions, erotic gestures and sexual freedoms."[10] The songs in *Princess Tam-Tam*, and similarly in *Zouzou*, speak to Alwina's interior life and personal longings, while the story alternately highlights (in order to exploit) or suppresses those feelings.

As noted throughout this book, Baker's appearances on-screen and live in nightclubs and music halls blurred the lines between realism and myth, making her a potent symbol of primitivism. Baker's personal story, recast as it was in colonialist desires and fears, has the double effect of showcasing her perceived evolution as a performer and her assimilation to French culture, thus symbolizing the potential of colonial people to both assimilate French values and

Fig. 4.1. Josephine Baker as Alwina and Jean Galland as the Maharaja of Datane in *Princesse Tam-Tam* (1934). Photo by Michael Ochs Archives/Getty Images.

integrate with French people in metropolitan France. *Zouzou* and *Princesse Tam-Tam* figure Baker as an emblem of France's *mission civilisatrice* ("civilizing mission") and in so doing register the country's ambivalence toward the presence of colonial people in France.[11] France's image of the Other was always a combination that included references to Africa and Asia.[12] Baker as Princess Tam Tam, together with the Maharaja character, embodies this symbolism.

BAKER'S COLONIAL CINEMA, AN ACT OF RE-GENRE

Princesse Tam-Tam is a prime example of colonial cinema, which has centuries of precursors in orientalist paintings, tourist postcards, stamps, travelogues, ethnomuseums, dioramas, and even wax museums, such as the Musée Grévin's display of colonial scenes, colonial novels, and illustrated magazines. The postcards are particularly interesting because the two kinds, *scenes* and *types*, depict daily life and ethnic types of people in the featured territory and stills from colonial films, which often showed costumed European actors surrounded by purported "natives" of the country. The native is pictured both as a type and as nothing but potential, raw material. In addition to these forms, colonial cinema was influenced by Black dance films and musical revues via Baker's music hall spectacles. Baker's films similarly presented ethnic types, and *Princesse Tam-Tam*, filmed on location, attempted to depict the scenes from which the types derived—and I would argue that there is a form of ethnographic gaze on the French in this film as well. The evocations of colonialist imagery in *Princesse Tam-Tam* recall, re-present, and re-genre that of the banana dance, the tropical sets designed for *La sirène des tropiques*, and the Saartjie Baartman precedents in *Zouzou*. When Baker's character, the North African shepherdess Alwina, replaces salt with sand, and we view the snobby French tourists through Alwina's eyes, we get a glimpse of the turned tables of assimilation as they make her feel like an outsider in her own home.

Baker's live persona in film brought these colonial legacies into cinema, particularly in her role in *Princesse Tam-Tam* as well as in the production itself. The director of *Princesse Tam-Tam*, Edmond Gréville, had been a journalist for *Comoedia* and a novelist before becoming a filmmaker. Gréville was part of the second generation of filmmakers identified with poetic realism in French cinema. This group included Jean Renoir, Julien Duvivier, and Marc Allégret. In *Princesse Tam-Tam*, Gréville became involved in colonial cinema, or what film scholar David Henry Slavin has called "the other first wave." According to Slavin, colonial cinema was a genre of filmmaking popular in the 1930s, during Baker's film era, but it had been established in the 1920s, during her dominance of the music hall. Colonial films combined melodrama and action in a spectacular, usually North African, setting, as *Princesse Tam-Tam* did. Thus, Baker drew on widely available models of filmmaking for her own work.

Although colonial films are usually set in Africa, they are ultimately and inevitably about whiteness. "Even the poetic realist films of the Popular Front era, with their celebration of the common man, legitimated racial double standards when they took up colonial themes. Applying the inconsistent logic of the white blind spot, as well as willful ignorance, they presented women of color as self-sacrificing saviors of white men, and contrasted European women as agents of their destruction."[13] Conquering *le cafard* (homesickness) and resisting "miscegenation" with colonial people are the principle motivations for the action in colonial films. There is a fear of losing contact with Europe, since perhaps by living in the colonized territory, the European will inevitably become like the colonials.

Because these films were shot on location, what was intended to come out of them, despite the fantasies they indulged in, was a sense of reality. The films' claims to providing unique access to the "real" helped sustain the French film industry. Like the nineteenth-century racial burlesques, colonial films combined verisimilitude and fantasy. *Princesse Tam-Tam* exploited colonial film's generic markers, such as being filmed on location and exploring the relationship between Europeans and "natives" in Tunisia.

Princesse Tam-Tam's aesthetic lineage is part of its narrative. In the story, a writer, Max de Méricourt (played by Albert Préjean), seeks an escape from his snobby wife and a cure for his writer's block by taking a trip to Tunisia. In North Africa, Max meets a shepherdess named Alwina (Baker) and begins to construct a novel out of his interviews with her. (The plot of his novel is the basis for a sequence later in the film.) When Max learns that his wife, left alone in Paris, has been keeping company with an exotic maharaja, he initiates a plan to transform Alwina into Princess Tam Tam, whom he plans to take to Paris to make his wife jealous. Once in the French capital, the fake princess has trouble sustaining her role, and her undoing serves as the vehicle for the film's climactic musical production. Ultimately, the film is a dense network of reflections, all tied to the conceit of imitation. The film's inner workings are perhaps best observed in the film's formal devices rather than in the dialogue, so I will focus on dissolves and the gaze employed in the musical numbers. Lasting twenty minutes, the grand musical number is the culmination of the film's themes while not quite resolving the issues it raises.

Let us begin to unpack this film by looking at the ending. The film builds to the excitement of an elaborate party where the featured entertainment is a music-hall-style revue that includes a dance troupe and musicians with Afro-Latin rhythms, providing the pattern for a visual percussion that contains both visual continuity and a sense of disruption. The stage is filled with a variety of rhythms, images, and sounds, creating a dreamlike confluence of effects. The turban-wearing master of ceremonies is an uncanny figure who marks the transitions between sequences. The transitions often show a dissolve between live dancers and dolls. This device is a reference to the Hollywood musical's common transformation of women into dolls with uniform features and movements. But it is also an internal reference to the film's plot. In Alwina's transformation from a shepherdess to a princess, she is like a doll under Max's control.

When the party scene opens, the princess is seated at a table alone until the best friend of Max's wife sits beside her, offers her several drinks, and encourages her to take to the stage. As she drinks the wine, Alwina/Princess Tam Tam becomes as intoxicated by the music as she is by the alcohol (reminiscent of the fireman in the short film *Le pompier de Folies Bergère*). The two sources of Alwina's intoxication, the music and the wine, are represented by cuts back and forth between the stage and Baker. As Alwina's excitement builds, the shots become tighter, and an insert of a shirtless, dark-skinned man drumming on a tom-tom clarifies Baker's connection to the music. It also serves as a reference back to the drummers in *la danse des bananes*. He represents the princess's supposed internal jungle essence, and his drumming is her heartbeat. The royal pretense is coming undone, as close-ups show her swaying to the music with her eyes closed. As the tension builds, the eye-line matches between Méricourt, his wife, and her best friend make them appear to look at one another, leaving Alwina/Princess Tam Tam altogether on the outside. She is now on the verge of leaving her princess persona behind.

In the next sequence, Alwina/Princess Tam Tam jumps up from the table and tears off her sleek lamé gown, revealing a floor-length black slip. She appears to run to the wings and enters the stage kicking off her shoes. Finally, she takes center stage; the primitive dancer is unleashed. The dance is difficult to inventory because Baker moves so quickly. She mixes African and Latin dances, including the rumba, occasionally dancing flirtatiously with one of the musicians onstage. Her gestures communicate a sense of abandon and do not appear to follow any particular routine or dance format. She throws her head back with her arms outstretched. She beats her abdomen as if it were a drum. And she uses as much of the stage as possible, beginning upstage, running downstage, and then traversing the stage from one end to the other. The audience's reactions are registered through Max, who shows initial shock and then pleasure as other spectators applaud the performance.

I draw several meanings from the film's ending. First, Alwina's African essence proved ungovernable in a Parisian setting. She was treated as ethnographic subject through her interviews with Max and then was made into a colonial subject through the transformation he dreamed up. Max longed to civilize her. Fascinated with the possibility of taming her—like the fireman in the short film *Le pompier de Folies Bergère*—Max re-creates her in his fantasies, presenting her not as an average foreigner but as an elite creature that is meant to be unreachable even by high society. A self-conscious reference to the tropes of colonial film, Max gives Alwina a new identity and dresses her as glamorous but also as exotic. Creole hoop earrings, flashing colors, and sharply cut suits and dresses define Tam Tam's costuming in contrast to that of Max's French wife. It is also important to remember that this film was a vehicle for Baker, and in it she wore the sorts of gowns she would wear onstage or in a nightclub. Baker also habitually represented her personal story of progress in her stage and screen performances, and *Princesse Tam-Tam* puts a new spin on it.

Baker's career and its complications enable us to envision the ways in which her managers, scriptwriters, choreographers, and promoters were unable to fully control her, a living "object" onstage. Although Baker's image was manufactured and carefully maintained by her and by her managers through the various stories they spun about her personal life, Baker's capacity for improvisation and spontaneity complicated any attempt to control her. And yet the intensity with which Baker enjoyed, approved, resisted, or detested her life-in-pictures, I find, is managed and expressed via her cinematic prism.

In *Princesse Tam-Tam*, then, Baker as a Tunisian woman is drawn into a Frenchman's ethnographic and exoticist gaze. Through their shared fantasizing—and it is shared since she *wants* to go to Paris—she is transformed into a civilized *sauvage*. Alwina becomes Princess Tam Tam through elocution, posture, and math lessons. An extended montage of instructional scenes depicts her transformation. In Paris, she becomes something quite different from either persona before returning to Alwina.

The novel-within-a-film narrative places Max's transformation of Alwina into Princess Tam Tam on the level of fantasy. Max's masquerade of the shepherd girl acting like a princess is complicated because of the civilizing process it presumes. Like a dream structure, this sequence in the film is a summary of Max's novel, which conveniently precludes the possibility that the trajectory of the story will find its way into the reality space of the film.

The in-between character Baker creates in this prism represents the performance potential and the supposed ethnic essence of the native on foreign soil. Onstage and in costume, this potential and essence is transformed into the primitive or primitivist persona. She also dances a combination of African, American, and improvised movements, further complicating her connection to a specific ethnicity. In one sense, this film was progressive in how it posited multiplicity and fluid identities, but in another sense, the fantastic elements of the construction make it difficult to see the film through a political framework.

Baker's cinematic prism in this film sheds light on a dialogue about this very question. Drawing a parallel between the primitive and themselves, Baker and Black jazz performers benefited from confusion between what it meant to be Black and what it meant to be American. As Blacks, they shared the supposedly positive aspects of the primitive such as spontaneity, rhythm, and sensuality. As Americans, they were at the vanguard of modernity, representing ancient and new worlds. Baker galvanized the colonialist modes she found in Paris for her own purpose, but it is also evident that she modernized them by combining American forms and either real or imagined African forms. That Baker wore Africanist outfits onstage only underscored the distance between her ultra-modern, supremely glamorous offstage—and increasingly Parisian—persona and the culture that the costumes caricature. In Max's novel, which the film portrays, both the North African Alwina and the Parisian Princess Tam Tam play the role of cinema's beloved Black musical entertainer.

DREAM UN-STRUCTURES AND RACE TYPES

Baker's movies are antimusicals, because in the end, she is cut out of the musical's society. Such exclusion goes against generic convention. The character Princess Tam Tam cannot remain in civilized society in the film's logic; the convention would be that she belongs in her newly adopted country. But of course, she is a charade, even within this fiction. Indeed, as the ultimate Other, Baker's character is the opposite of the white male character she entertains, and she contrasts with the wife she is meant to make jealous. Max brings Alwina to Paris not as his girlfriend but as a princess, as a competing feminine ideal. Inassimilable and shamed out of the possibility of having both romantic bliss and celebrity, Alwina returns to Tunisia.

The film's use of dissolves between shots mirrors the way that narrative and dialogue in musicals melt into singing and dancing spectacles. The musical numbers and events and themes in the narrative are divided by a blur. An example of this device would be the recurring theme in *Princesse Tam-Tam* of women turning into dolls and back again. But there is another sense in which the film oscillates between parallel storylines. Max pairs himself with Alwina in an apparent competition with his wife and the Maharaja. But such a characterization overlooks the fact that the film is Max's story. In Max's fantasy, he imagines himself as both the Maharaja and Dar, the Tunisian servant who is in love with Alwina. The two men of color resemble each other in that they both appear to be white actors in blackface, perhaps due to the shading of the film stock or the video transfer. Metaphorically, Max plays all the parts and is all the men in the film and is partner to both his wife and to Alwina. The couples appear to be parallel, but they are, in a sense, the same couple with the gender and racial roles reversed. The dissolves between Max's world and Alwina's world in the middle of the film show a gradual blending of their worlds as opposed to the cross-cutting in the beginning of the film and the dualistic contrast that this style typically suggests. Dissolves are like dreams, the gradual blending of worlds, or fantasized connections.

When examined closely, these dissolves can yield interesting images of their own. For example, at the end of the sequence of Alwina's transformation into Princess Tam Tam, there is a telling superimposition in a dissolve between a shot of Baker's character receiving praise from an instructor and one of her opening a door. On the door is a decorative monkey. In the dissolve, there is a moment when the monkey, a symbol of the signifying trickster, appears to be inside Baker's head. This image, easily lost in a casual viewing of the film, illustrates Baker's cinematic prism as a kind of cultural negotiation, a third place where multiple representations are joined. Baker's role as a third is more than an uncomplicated blending of two oppositions. Tensions arise when two images are laid one over the other as an epigram of contradiction, and the original contexts of the actions depicted remain.

This image is suggestive of Baker's hybridity, or what cultural theorist Homi Bhabha calls "the split screen of the self and its doubling."[14] However, the split here is not a neat one. The simultaneous overlay creates a confusing blur between the two images. The fantastical nature of Baker's persona was a product of perception. The layered image illustrates that the story of Baker's persona lies not only in the content of her films—its themes and contexts—but also in film's formal language. In her rather conventional narrative films, Baker's exoticist presence and role as a dancer served as motivation for a kind of technical enchantment or experimentation that manifested as dissolves or as the shadow dance in *Zouzou*.

Baker's prismatic image pushes beyond a simplistic positive/negative, success/tragedy schema and into a much more unwieldy and complicated terrain. Bhabha's concept of stereotypes helps illuminate the multiple and interconnected instances of double-sidedness, of Baker's ambivalent images, on which the prismatic concept is built. Bhabha argues that while stereotypes are predictable and easily recognizable in many ways, they are nevertheless multisided and unstable—hence, the necessity of repetition and reiteration of their authority over our perception.[15] Yet stereotypes also exert very certain and traceable power over how groups view one another by relying on imagistic patterns. Sociologist Patricia Hill Collins's concept of "controlling images" specifically frames the way that stereotypes function as instruments of power meant to dominate Black women.[16] Collins writes, "Portraying African-American women as stereotypical mammies, matriarchs, welfare recipients, and hot mommas has been essential to the political economy of domination fostering Black women's oppression. Challenging these controlling images has long been a core theme in Black feminist thought. As part of a generalized ideology of domination, these controlling images of Black Womanhood take on special meaning because the authority to define these symbols is a major instrument of power."[17] The effect of such images, she continues, is to "normalize" racial oppression and to obscure reality by giving consumers of media the impression that they already know all there is to know about Black women. Later, Collins turns her attention to the development of Afrocentric notions of beauty and humanity to counter Eurocentric notions of what is sexually desirable to elite white men.

Bhabha defines stereotypes as unsuccessful efforts at control and asserts that both the object and the wielder of the stereotype see their own doubles reflected there in a form that each one wants and does not want. He argues further that stereotypes' instability is the basis for their adaptability: "It is the force of ambivalence that gives the colonial stereotype its currency [and] ensures its repeatability in changing historical and discursive conjunctures."[18] Such instability and ambivalence constitute the flexible arena where Baker's discourse of paradox does its work. Where the term *stereotype* is used to dismiss inaccurate, undignified Black on-screen portrayals—comparing images to other images, not necessarily real people—what I see as Baker's wielding of stereotypes of herself opens the gateway to complex and critical viewing and surprising characterizations. Baker plays a controlling image in her films but does so in ways that foreground the contradiction of her off-screen celebrity and her on-screen marginalization. The person who is in a sense inside the prism, the performer, has to believe that the stereotype's back-and-forth can be flipped in their favor, doesn't she?

Stereotypes are unstable in this regard because the subject of the stereotype is not at all unaware; the subject, the person within the image, is always watching and ultimately more expansive and more agile than the narrow and clumsy formations of demeaning stereotypes. Baker exemplifies this dynamic when she embodies a push and pull with her own images. She might be most creative when in contradiction. If stereotypes rely on a kind of obviousness for their credibility or shock value, Baker reveals they can be more deeply fractured when characters embody them within colonial fantasy, which is itself contradictory and incoherent. Fractured and multisided like a prism, their refractions contain oppositions, particularly when individuals appear to embrace rather than resist them. Watch *Princesse Tam-Tam* without the sound, and Baker's perfected made-up face and elegant presence dominates—when it is not undercut or made awkward by the comical gestures that she employs in order to blend in with the child actors who surround her in many of the film's early scenes. No wonder she did not enjoy her time in the movies; she was never cultivated into scenes that truly suited her gifts. Baker wears all these incongruities, creating pleasure despite taking on filmic ideas meant to belittle and shaking them up. As her skirt of bananas mixes up the possibilities of individuality and mimicry, taking control within a controlling image, so too does her portrayal in *Princesse Tam-Tam* show a performer of rare talent stuck in a film too small for her—yet being amazing in it.

The very stereotypes and images that shame many viewers delight others. In fact, stereotypes are resilient because they are enormously complicated, unstable, and reverberant with changing realities and unrealities. Drawing from Bhabha's concept of doubling, I find that stereotypes endure because they can change to fit the moment, and there is always an appeal to a segment of viewers who enjoy, and can make use of, their properties of doubling and misrepresentation. Stereotypes are always partially not true and always in dispute. Baker's prism reflects the ways in which identity incorporates the stereotype, becoming what Stuart Hall called a "moveable feast," full of negations and change.[19] Baker's mediated persona and film characters reflect this dynamic not despite being stereotypes but because of them. Baker's hybridity is a form of partiality inherent to the structure of stereotypes. Thus, while it is tempting to look at Baker's films as if they reflect a stable representation, it is important to recognize that ideologies of race and gender operate in unpredictable ways and that Baker's own creativity contributes to the perceptual effects of her film performances. Furthermore, Baker is an audience herself, providing an oppositional gaze on her double-sided images.

Baker's performances are less portrayal than palimpsest. If we pause Baker's paradoxes and examine their poetics, we can more directly trace how Baker authored and played with these contradictions blurring into one another in her coverage by the American press—especially the African American press—and, most profoundly, in her film performances. Baker's dances are actions that she took through the prismatic lens of film. Baker was not merely a puppet, symptomatic of colonialism. She was self-animated. Baker's own writing about her experiences with film enables us to explore issues of representation, agency, and desire with her creativity at the core of such readings of her work. I have reflected on Baker's prismatic image, at times shot by shot, aiming at a sustained engagement with the performer's ideas and, to the greatest extent possible, relying on Baker's own words. While a film-based analysis might appear one-dimensional, film studies' concern with issues of sound, image, genre, authorship, performance, technique, history, context, and more allows us to see Baker's riches by contemplating many dimensions of her work. By viewing Baker's world through her eyes, elaborate digressions into detailed historical context are minimized in favor of close analysis of her films and their afterlives.

Although Baker was a living historical figure, it is impossible to find a pristine original against which to measure Baker's copies. Baker *is* meta—a cluttered meta with odd and mismatching pieces. Because of her film roles and her life-in-pictures, the figure of Baker always already refers to another construction, stereotype, or imitation in process, incomplete and liminal even if it is to

Baker's own constructed persona or one of her characters. Both in her own time and ours, Baker was a complex figure, not entirely free nor merely trapped. The woman who would spy for the French Resistance and address the March on Washington was there in the young woman who found herself riding a huge cultural wave. We can see the playful exuberant woman barely twenty with a relentless work ethic flickering in the eyes of the courageous woman who devoted herself to humanitarianism and the advancement of civil rights in the United States.

None of these dynamics necessarily reduces Baker to a flat stereotype, because although working within a narrow bandwidth of possibilities, the effects of Baker's repetitions are creative, and when taken together, they form a cinematic prismatic whole—fractured but coherent and vital. Baker, as a celebrity whose fame was based on her own life, was part of a larger machine of which she was aware, a machine that she generated with her stories. Baker was famous for being a successful African American performer. She fashioned a specific public image *as* an image—through films, newspaper photos, and public appearances. The result and the process of Baker's image making, improvised and canted as it was, is what I call the cinematic prism.

Baker's dialogic films are alive with complex signifying and double-talk between the actor and her character. Between them resides Baker's internal dialogue about her own conflicting desires, her own sense of what her ambitions cost her. She never completely became her characters because they were already part of her. Rather, the characters were a vessel for the already-known Baker's performance style. Her image was a free-floating sign that would take on varied meanings according to its context, but by repeating a version of her personal story, Baker remained recognizable. Yet by plotting her transformation in the narratives of her films, paradoxically, Baker's capacity for continual alteration and invention became as much a part of her performance as her visual and narrative predictability. Baker's burlesque was burlesque for the modern age. Precisely because of the ways in which Baker's authorship was fractured by the participation of screenwriters, directors, and coauthors, my imperative in this book is close analysis of Baker's signification through the concept of burlesque as an articulated concept of oppositionality that accounts for Baker's paradoxes without flattening them.

IN NONCONCLUSION: THE SIGNIFYING BAKER

The signifying trickster character of Black folklore provides a principal framework for theorizing Baker's image as a prismatic image, consisting of her images arranged at angles to each other, some of them oppositional to each other while also being oppositional to the Black Venus narrative when we take her onstage and offstage work into account. Like Esu-Elegbara, the divine trickster of Yoruba mythology, the figure of Baker remains a sign of signs. Baker was adaptable yet unchanging, an illusion yet authentic, free-floating yet fixed. She is always recognizable. Not a sign of her times but a sign of her own self, Baker was a discourse about her own career. Baker, ever in the literary present of her own film story, is a trickster figure, a "signifying monkey."[20]

At the core of signifying is self-reflexivity. It is a discourse that contains its own criticism, a metaprismatic criticism. Holding closure at bay, signifying calls for a new and necessary analysis of Baker and film that is as open-ended and multifaceted as the subject itself. Baker signifies and is a signifier in the sense that she is an unmoored motion image but also in the sense that she repeats and revises performance codes from France and the United States. Baker contains a diversity of influences. That awareness of concurrent cross-narratives within Baker is the only resolution I can truly offer.

Like the fireman character in the short film *Le pompier de Folies Bergère*, Max finds his voice through Alwina's story and doubling hers as the Princess Tam Tam. Having found the primitive within himself, the authentic voice he was looking for, he is ready to write his novel through the imagined transformation of Alwina. In her musical number, Alwina returns to North Africa by passing through a blend of her primitive shepherd persona and the modern princess role. This blend is the primitivist modern Black woman music hall star.

Baker's films center on exotic Black woman characters, but the way they are surrounded by white average characters exaggerates her minor differences in skin color. Those who are white form a community, and she is the one who does not belong. She is tolerated when she is of service or making a sacrifice, a tolerance that is also conventional in colonial film.[21] Despite the framework of sacrifice, Baker's film characters were independent and ambitious. Baker's films and race films all revolved around modern Black characters who found themselves in a quandary of identity and belonging. Other examples of this type of character include Sylvia Landry (Evelyn Preer in *Within Our Gates*, 1920) and Louise Howard (Lucia Lynn Moses in *Scar of Shame*, 1927).[22] The characters were quite different from one another, but they shared a sense of disorientation within their respective circumstances. Similarly, Baker's films explored characters with fractured identities in geographical locations new to them. Despite the subtitles and foreign language, they resonated with African Americans' complex experiences of modernity. But Baker played a Black woman in specifically white-defined imaginaries, where she sought the attention of a white man who used her. It is a picture of what Black women have faced and continue to face in the unequal economy of love and sexuality in a white normative world. It also exemplifies Baker's fragile position in the industry as a Black woman entertainer.

Baker's authority over her characters in these filmic experiments was incomplete and intermittent but not entirely absent. When she noticed that her films ended with her alone, she protested, suggesting that maybe the producers thought audiences would object to an on-screen romance between her, an African American, and a white French costar. Her manager, Pepito Abatino, dismissed her concerns, saying, "Zouzou is a star. She lives for her work. Like you." But Baker did not let this stand: "There were times when I wondered whether being a star was enough." The way Baker seemed to fully dedicate herself to playing a rejected woman, sometimes even overplaying these scenarios of unrequited love, suggests that Abatino's justification was not satisfactory to her. As Alwina, Papitou, or Zouzou, Baker embodied vacillation between aspirations to be the special star and desires to fit comfortably in a white-dominated society.[23]

Despite Baker's hard-to-pin-down role as an author and her feelings of disappointment about her experiences in the movies, she embodied the desire (her own and her critics') for a Black female cinematic stardom. In contrast to Baker, I find that Baker deserves credit as her films' true author, as the engine of her films' meaning. She is their central authority, and she is great in her films. Expressing ownership of her work and her early optimism, Baker said, "I'll shoot movies written for me."[24] And so she did. The stories of her films were based on her stage performances and her glamorous Parisian persona. Structured as a makeover within a colonialist musical with a romance plot, each of Baker's three main feature films—*La sirène des tropiques, Zouzou,* and *Princesse Tam-Tam*—drew on Baker's life and career, sometimes directly referencing her fame with posters advertising her shows or novelty items based on her music hall shows. Baker represented her own transformation. As Baker said, "Who doesn't have his vanity? I admit mine. In all the shows I've done, films included, I've insisted that the different stages of my life be represented. Each time . . . there is just a hint of a reminder of the past, for the sake of contrast."[25]

As the artist, it was up to her how to bring the bones of her characters to life, and she did this by drawing on her own life's story. Issues of film production and issues of Baker's life reflected each other. Baker's multiple forms of collaborative autobiography limited Baker but also created a prismatic authorship where she asserted her agency in expressing her thoughts. Baker had to be the most important aesthetic agent on set, animating, embodying, and putting flesh on the scripts written for her voice, body, and persona. Baker was the whole reason these films existed at all. It behooves us now to imagine how she might have used these contradictory and potentially demeaning roles to her advantage. As films that were based on her persona, they are by definition about her process, and they are reflexive. I argue that this doubling makes space for Baker's reflections as it does for us to see her work as double talk, as signifying her own desires and the obstacles to their fulfillment.

Baker's cinema linked aesthetics of space and time, visual and verbal, recorded and live performance through her burlesque of the exotic within her cinematic prism. Baker's style, particularly her screen roles, contrasted with the aesthetic of precision of a chorus line. Baker achieved a sort of vernacular glamour through constantly shifting her offstage identity and appearing to be spontaneous and natural in her presentation. Such a blend influenced Baker's dual role in *Princesse Tam-Tam* as both the primitive and the civilized. The history of the film industry, the intertextual history of colonialism, and changing ideas about Blacks intersected in the phenomenon of Baker's success.

In my analysis of *Princesse Tam-Tam* and the short film *Le pompier de Folies Bergère*, I am interested in themes of doubling and dualities. I consider these films together because Baker's characters in both films were dreamed up by the white male character she played opposite. Fatou of the banana dance performance at the Folies Bergère was a fantasy character, and the whole scenario was framed by the lounging plantation boss. He imagined that a bunch of bananas tumbled out of the sky and turned into Josephine Baker. Similarly, *Princesse Tam-Tam* and *Le pompier de Folies Bergère* involved nested fantasies in which Baker played a character playing another character in the mind of a white male character. On the one hand, the way Baker inhabited her character makes it easy to forget the premise of the film. And Baker's cultural significance is what makes these films relevant at all for discussion today. The performances by the other actors and the plot as well are easily forgettable. But it is still productive, crucial even, to remember that Baker played characters that, although constructed from stereotypes, became the prism of her pioneering cinematic presence. In both films, Baker was the fantasy figure of a white male character, and the cinematic prism explores the tension between the autonomous and the dependent in Baker's work.

Baker's screen performances constantly referenced her live performances, but her manufactured image took over and eventually replaced her presence. Her image was complicated by the multiple dilemmas she was entangled in, including her discomfort with the medium. In Paris, Baker found herself the star (part agent and part doll) of a preexisting colonialist narrative of fantasies about Black female sexuality, complete with representational objects and behavior (bananas, feathers, nudity, frenetic dancing, jungle backdrops) and costumes (raffia skirt, beads, *les créoles* hoop earrings, and so forth). Baker galvanized and modernized such "found objects," improvising combinations of movements from a variety of folk dance traditions. Baker's live stage and early film performances occurred in the context of the history of Black entertainment in Paris and broadly accepted mythologies of Africa that also relied on ethnological images, primarily of women. Baker was a facilitating bridge between older ethnological images and newer commercial images where no specific ethnic type is cited; the character is just Black. Thus, at the same time that Baker's performance became Africanized in Paris, what was seen as Blackness (of Africa and the Caribbean) was transformed in part by Baker; it was being commercialized, modernized, and, to some extent, Americanized via Baker's exotic, American, and glamorous persona. Americanness and Africanness presented two different kinds of exoticism, but together they fulfilled audiences' dual fascination with the United States and with Africa.

The French films and Baker's Parisian stardom signified new and alternate futures for African American creativity in the cinema and established Baker's place on the leading edge of Black popular culture in the interwar period. Baker's forays into filmmaking were as outlandish and avant-garde as the tales of her promenades with her pet cheetah, Chiquita, or dancing in a costume of bananas. From the mid-1920s through the 1930s, the African American press eagerly reported and reviewed all the Baker news and films. The *Chicago Defender* covered Baker and other Parisian "race acts" in a column called "Across the Pond." Praise such as "Josephine Baker of *Shuffle Along* fame is the talk of Gay Paree. Her services are at a premium. She is considered the best in Paris" indicates the admiring tone of much of Baker's press coverage.[26]

Baker's racial identity did come into question, even if she was framed as essentially Black most of the time. One article comments on Baker's press in other publications, noting that "London papers are trying to change the nationality of Josephine Baker. Of course, some influence is being brought to bear by the multitudes of southern Americans who are in London. Any way Miss Baker won't stand for it."[27] Such metacommentary sought to claim Baker and what she meant as a successful African American abroad. This is important because it is an example of the importance of Baker's Black identity for African Americans in the United States. Michel Fabre, the late French scholar of African American literature and culture, describes the desire of African Americans at home to share in the international achievement of the expatriates through the concept of *lieux de memoire*, or sites of memory and recognition. As a "beacon of recognition," Baker's success in Paris, Fabre argued, proved to both Black Americans and white Americans that when given the chance, African American dance, music, and other artistic endeavors would thrive within the mainstream rather than within niche Black audiences alone. Her success, it was hoped, would help vindicate an entire group of people. More than this, she evoked "a feeling of racial pride and 'togetherness' on a worldwide scale."[28]

I would argue that Baker's American communities truly needed her, not as a beacon of abstract ideas like liberty or even memory but rather as a model, *un lieu de l'avenir*, or a portal to the future, and a suitable screen onto which their desires and anxieties could be projected and worked through.[29] Fabre was on point when he wrote, "What made Baker's success exceptional was, on the one hand the magnitude of its economic rewards (of which Blacks had traditionally been deprived); and, on the other hand, the legitimization of her dancing as a highbrow aesthetic contribution (not only entertainment) in Europe very much the way that jazz was considered there."[30] Baker's public recognition was expected to mean something. The logic of the expectations placed on her crossover appeal meant that if Europeans accepted African American performers, such benevolence would extend toward recognizing the humanity of African Americans as a whole going into a brighter, more equitable, and more humane future.

When Baker left the United States, she became an influential figure not only in French society but in American society, as part of a phenomenon of Black performance in Paris by expatriate Americans. The *Chicago Defender*'s "Across the Pond" column described the pressure on Black entertainers to perform Black success on the social battlegrounds where Black worthiness was constantly tested. The *Oakland Tribune* mentioned Baker in an article on the controversial opening of *La revue nègre* and a larger comparative assessment of the Parisian nightlife. The article, titled "Paris Eclipsed by N.Y. in Its Nightly Revels," plays on competition between Paris and New York for the label of having the most exciting nighttime entertainment and being the edgiest cultural capital, noting Baker's controversial performances in *La revue nègre* at the Champs-Elysées music hall in particular. William Ivy wrote, in the *Oakland Tribune*, "This entertainment given entirely by American negroes led zy [*sic*] Josephine Baker, attracted the attention of the police on the opening night, and a ukase [a citation] from the prefecture caused a considerable modification in the costumes before the show was allowed to proceed."[31] Published in the fall of 1925, the article anticipates the new energy Baker would bring to Parisian entertainment, particularly the Folies Bergère in 1926.

From a distance, Baker's success appeared to be transcendent, if spicy and scandalous. But it was not without risks, which Baker managed ingeniously through the possibilities of her cinematic prism. The prism of Josephine Baker switches between alternative interpretations. The sublime slides into the ridiculous and the inspirational into the commercial and back again as Baker illuminates the inherent structural ambiguity of perception and performance—an ambiguity especially common to the reception of comedic Black physicality. A beautiful paradox, Baker appears at once liberated and undignified as her combined passion and powerlessness challenge the academic will to define objects of study with exactitude. Readings of her image oscillate between pronouncements of agentive self-commodification and exploitative stereotyping, between pioneering film roles and unsurprising racist and sexist tropes.

If Baker's performances were "far superior to the pictures they were in,"[32] the French films maintain historical and conceptual importance, and the fact that she appeared in starring roles makes her a Black film pioneer. The films placed the St. Louis–born dancer in a transnational and cross-genre film historical context. Baker's successful and exotic persona was the basis for her film stardom and the early imagination of what Black film could mean. For today's audiences, Baker's films open a lens on the lone Black figure negotiating white social worlds. Through her cinematic prism, Baker reflexively recycled material from her own life and implicitly pointed to a diasporic framing of African American cinema.

Through her film performances, Baker became a self-referential image, a sophisticated and modernist persona through a meta-element of commentary she brought to her films that I call her cinematic prism. I mean to highlight Baker's choreography of moving between self, performer, and character as she built a cinematic prismatic persona. Viewing Baker through the speculative lens of the cinematic prism unlocks the possibility of seeing her reflect on aspects of her own experience as she navigated both the entertainment industry and Parisian society. Cinematic prism names the means by which Baker the performer projected a broader, metalevel celebrity identity that I call La Bakaire, an offstage and off-screen version of her Parisian self that mediated the at times conflicting operations of her transatlantic and multiplatform fame. The cinematic prism obtains where Baker's exoticist cinema portrays the outsider woman's fraught search for coherent personal identity within plotlines that map onto the social politics of race and ethnicity.

The cinema performed a unique mediation on Baker, owing to its characteristics as a multisensory and collaborative medium whose product circulates to a variety of audiences and thus takes on diverse meanings. On the stage as a live performer, Baker was the star she wanted to be. Cinema updated Baker imperfectly yet transformed her from a live performer to a mediated image. But even on the level of story, her films showed what she had done to update herself. Each film included a makeover segment in which Baker's character receives new clothes and the glamorous treatment. This mode of representation gave her a modern context, lending her status as modernity's medium of entertainment but also giving her access to its lexical structures of communication and spectacle. Baker's stage performances leading up to her first film anticipate the elements of film in that they involve visuality, episodic scenarios, and characters derived from the colonial imaginary.

Baker's characters, her Parisian public persona, and the idea of her private self all interacted as part of her overall star structure. Indeed, Baker's stages included the film screen, the music hall, and the pages of the international news. The press generated the fantastical Baker in much the same way as the fireman and Max de Méricourt did in the films discussed earlier. As La Bakaïre, Baker held a kind of authority over a series of multifaceted comedic, exotic, and erotic performance-art pieces, both on film and in celebrity news coverage of her stage shows. Baker's screen characters were derived from her career and her already-famous public persona. These portrayals enabled her to layer her film characters on her off-screen personas and vice versa; they reflected each other from all available perspectives. In promotional interviews for the films and for her music hall performances, Baker played with her image and celebrity bio as she told and revised her personal stories in the media. By combining fact, query, and sensation, Baker coauthored her story with reporters, publicists, and gossip columnists. Baker corroborated many details of her biography while revising others. Baker's authorship is one of manipulation.

BAKER'S CINEMATIC PRISM AND THE
AFRICAN AMERICAN PRESS

Baker's capacity to manipulate the press was illustrated most vividly by media coverage of her purported marriage to her manager, Pepito Abatino, an Italian count. Journalists tracked Baker's career as it unfolded, providing details of the broader context in which her films were received but also shedding light on the continuity between her off-screen and on-screen images. Indeed, in many ways, journalists' stories reflected the continuity that Baker was creating between her on-screen and off-screen images by feeding stories to the press. In 1927, media in the United States, France, and the Black diaspora whipped up a frenzy around Baker's marriage to Abatino. Some welcomed the union as "a first," an achievement for African Americans, while others expressed incredulity about the possibility of "the first negro countess."[33] An article in the *Indiana Evening Gazette* conveyed a sense of pride but also of wonder: "Josephine Baker, a colored beauty, and Harlem's own dancing darling, who is now filling theatrical and cabaret engagements in Paris has been married to a real Count, an Italian nobleman."[34] Journalist Sam Love's article came under the elaborate headline, "Harlem Hopes to Welcome First Negro Countess and Her Lucky Rabbit Foot: Josephine Baker, Slim and Dusky, Idol of Paris Cafes Adds Title to Her Ming Bricabrac and Diamonds."[35] Love's compliments were, however, decidedly backhanded, as he described "little Josephine Baker, skin the color of Coca Cola, eyes bigger than peeled grapes, hair straighter than your eyesight. And dance? Man kind!" In some ways, this statement conveys typical tongue-in-cheek hype about celebrities, but the phrase "little Josephine Baker" diminishes and infantilizes Baker while the comparisons to food underscore her status as a consumable commodity in the entertainment marketplace.

Meanwhile, writing in the *Baltimore Afro-American*, William Jones's "Day by Day" column began, "And now Josephine Baker, queen of the 'Black Bottoms' ... has a large bank account, and has acquired for herself a foreign count." The rhyme of *count* and *account* adds derisive humor to the story. The count is further compared to "a parasite."[36] The story of Baker's reported marriage was spectacular as a substitute for a sentimental entertaining scene in an ongoing romance revue that had been playing out in her films and in the press. But was it real? When a correspondent from Paris sent in a tidbit to the *Baltimore Afro-American* saying that no proof had been found of Baker's marriage to Count Abatino, the newspaper concluded that Baker was playing the role of a countess in a film and speculated that the film would be called *The Count*.[37] On July 9, the newspaper published an article titled "Josephine Baker Is 'Countess' in Film." The brief story said, "The French press here, finding no substantiation of the story of Josephine Baker's marriage to an Italian count, expresses a belief that the whole affair was prearranged publicity for exploiting of the photoplay in which the theatrical idol will be starred in August."[38]

Baker's announcement of marriage to Abatino was controversial but also elaborately constructed. In the Caribbean, the Jamaica *Gleaner* reported Baker's wedding story through its "Daily Express Paris Correspondent" column. On July 15, the column declared, "Josephine Baker, the coloured dancer and star of the Folies Bergere in Paris, is now Countess di Abatino, wife of the Italian Count Pepito di Abatino of Palermo."[39] The supposed wedding took place on her birthday, with only "the count's relatives and a few friends of the dancer" in attendance. Describing the count as a "delicate-looking man," the article went on to quote Baker's reasons for keeping the wedding a secret: "Oh, because I am only twenty-one and this is the first time I have ever been married and I didn't know what the etiquette was." A *Gleaner* reporter, however, claimed to have uncovered the truth: "When my search for the marriage record failed at the town hall of the arrondissement where Miss Baker stated she had been married I immediately called on the dancer at her apartments and she confessed that she was not a countess [and] that no marriage had taken place." In "The Sequel" section of the same article, Baker's deception is placed in context: "The craze among stage artists for hoaxing the public has spread to Paris. I ascertained this afternoon that . . . the 'marriage' of Josephine Baker, the coloured star of the Folies Bergere, in Paris, to the Italian Count Pepito di Abatino the announcement of which caused a tremendous sensation in America is also a myth."[40]

For her part, however, Baker maintained that she was married and eventually, inevitably, linked her life to an upcoming film: "We have been engaged for some months ever since we were selected to make a film together. He is to play the part of an Italian count, and I am to be a young Spanish washerwoman who is a princess without knowing it."[41] Baker further mixed fact and fiction, a strategy of self-representation she had used before, by adding, "We're going to have a real wedding in the picture. . . . The real wedding and the film wedding will be identical."[42]

Although Abatino did appear in *La sirène des tropiques* in a minor role, the film described here was never made and had no formal title. Two years later, when Baker was still being asked about the circumstances of her marriage announcement, she told the *New York Amsterdam News*, "That was just a good joke, honey. I just never married the prince. Ain't that funny? Nope, old dear, Pepito is just my manager."[43] Baker did exploit the press in the process of creating her star image and associating herself with cinema. The hoopla surrounding the wedding ultimately served to enhance Baker's celebrity by aligning her with African Americans' overall political advancement. To the extent, then, that her cinematic prismatic image circulated in the media, Baker remained its most powerful engine in that she was the authority over her image if not its sole author.

Viewing the marriage story through Baker's cinematic prism, it becomes a performance. La Bakaire, the celebrity and Parisian alter ego, did marry Abatino in a sense, even if the actual person of Josephine Baker had not. La Bakaire was Baker's expatriate Parisian meta- or alter ego: daring, glamorous, and cosmopolitan. Of course, since Baker was her married name from an earlier marriage in the United States to Willie Baker and since she chose to use her middle name instead of her given first name, Freda, Josephine Baker was already a constructed entity.[44] But her success in Paris and the circulation of her image and life's story through newswires like the Associated Press as well as her coverage by the African American press made that city and its mythologies constitutive parts of her celebrity image, which in turn became part of the interpretive framing through which her contemporary audiences received her work. The reported attention of a man that could be seen as white, such as Abatino, validated Baker's appeal and cast a positive spotlight on Black women generally: "The news of her wedding to the Italian count caused much excitement in Harlem. . . . According to returning visitors from Paris, Josephine could have picked a count if she had wanted to, whether she has a real one now for a husband or not."[45] Thus, the social equality implied by an African American woman marrying a European man, together with the social mobility that his supposed title of count seemed to offer Baker gained through her tale of social advancement, actually made the matter of whether the marriage was a hoax a secondary concern.

In the Baker archive, the status of the first person remains a question. We might normally look to Baker's memoirs for the performer's self-representation, yet hers were coauthored, and her former husband, Jo Bouillon, completed her autobiography after her death, which he then arranged to publish. Aside from her films and newsreel footage, Baker's archive includes coauthored autobiographies (*Les mémoires de Josephine Baker*, with Marcel Sauvage and *Josephine*, with Jo Bouillon and Mariana Fitzpatrick), several biographies (*The Hungry Heart*, by Jean-Claude Baker; *Josephine Baker and La revue nègre: Paul Colin's Lithographs of Le tumulte noir in Paris, 1927*, by Paul Colin, Karen C. C. Dalton, and Henry Louis Gates; and *Jazz Cleopatra: Josephine Baker in Her Time*, by Phyllis Rose), and a single novel (*My Blood in Your Veins*, with Felix de la Camara and Pepito Abatino). Most of these books both feed the reader's fascination with Baker's celebrity and offer some measure of its deconstruction. In lieu of offering another biography, this book attempts to understand Baker's cinematic surface and her effects as a performer and to consider Baker's conundrum of authorship in terms of African American literary practices, where mystery or contradiction is a mode of protection, like a mask.

Despite her literary collaborations, Baker was not primarily a writer. Rather, it was in the ways she created and maintained her image that she authored herself. And, as she lent her likeness to imprint a number of products, including films and musical recordings, she showcased her own aesthetic. The *Manitowoc Herald* (WI) reported, "The Folies Bergères claimed Josephine at a huge salary. She's been packing the house ever since. Her form has been done by French sculptors. Her face has been painted by French artists. She has opened a cabaret of her own. Her vogue goes on undiminished."[46]

Baker authorized her enterprise to whatever degree she could. That Baker was covered so widely in the American press speaks to the novelty and reach of her success in Paris. Her fame indicated an alternative, flipped universe in which this Black woman was well compensated and where she was seen as beautiful and worthy of being sculpted and painted—an improvement in many ways over being seen as the opposite of womanhood, as she would have been in American popular culture. Even her complexion was an item of Parisian fashion: "Nowadays, if a woman wants a certain shade of creamy brown silk stockings, she doesn't describe it as such. Not at all. . . . If she is in Paris, she says to the salesgirl: 'Let me see that new Josephine Baker shade.' . . . Now that's real fame."[47] Baker's face and recognizable image is the equivalent of a signature written by her body. She is a performative and semiotic phenomenon to which we have limited and refracted access through her films, photographs, and quotations in the press today, but she was always a constructed object.

I am not saying Baker was compromised. I am not saying that she was resistant. I am saying that she was reflexive and paradoxical, and the insight I am offering is to trace it and respect it and learn from it. I see Baker as an exemplary trickster—another way of thinking about her oppositionality within the cinematic prism. Like Esu-Elegbara, the liminal and wily trickster figure of African folktales, Baker presides over crossroads, where she is both exploited and liberated, subject and object. The women Baker portrayed in her films were each in a subordinate social position typical of trickster figures. Her characters would vie for the affections of basic and unspecial white men who had social advantage over her. They want to be wives, assimilated into the fundamental and intimate rituals of society, but the male characters can only seem to spectacularize her racial and gendered difference instead. They want to look at her, not live with her.

Though I would not claim that they are great films of world cinema, and neither would Baker, I appreciate them as conceits, as metaplatforms that, through repetition, examine difference, agency, and the workings of Baker's persona. Baker's films do cultural and theoretical work in showing her process. I have addressed the ways that Baker employed her film characters in her signifying and how she turned her multiplicity to her advantage. The coolness with which Baker described her experiences in making films only enhanced this sense of reflexive remove. The contrast between her physical comedy prism and her glamorous persona prism emphasized the superficiality of the performance, but for today's audiences, the interpretive context has changed, and we are in a better position to understand what she was up to. This process extends to her characters, which were masks she wore as pretexts for her revelation within the films. Her film characters were like masks in the sense that they were images she crafted.

Baker was a trickster, a structure as much as an achiever. Out of necessity and creativity, Baker was adaptable yet unchanging, a spectacular illusion yet authentic, free-floating yet fixed. Baker's image is always already layered, because as a recording, it is lifted from the live and original action to the level of staging. Baker is a prism of her pictures, films, and written assessments of her performance. But Baker the icon and persona are also creations of language—the languages of film and dance, primarily, as well as the texts of her coauthored autobiographies and the many works of art and scholarship she has provoked, unmoored from her biography but tied still to history.

Rather than seeking the true person behind Baker's image or displacing the significance of her banana days by considering her days as an activist, this book attends to Baker's dense surface through her first images in the 1920s and 1930s in film.[48] What is significant about dichotomous readings of Baker is that they are dichotomous. Baker is a densely constructed figure embodying cultural forms, media, and movie genres, formed within a highly complex political and aesthetic context. Baker serves as subject and source, problem and methodology. Unpacking Baker yields a methodology, the cinematic prism, for theorizing the relationship between cinema and Black female visibility. This approach involves historical analysis, archival research, and close readings informed by critical theory to address the riddle of Baker.

Baker's agency or authorship is understood here in terms of her presence, her experimentations with film, and her authority. Her sheer capacity to make herself important is witnessed in both her longevity onstage and the continual, perhaps ritualized interest in her career among both among scholars and fans. As she shimmied and thrust her feathers and bananas, Baker was not a mere object; through practice, she cultivated her authorship, producing an internal composure and independence that allowed her to be comfortable in her skin, whether on- or offstage, clothed or not so clothed. Her vulnerability and look-at-me-ness, her willingness to stand up onstage, was a form of power. Baker's agency lies in having done what she did, and the beauty is we are still discussing her work.

NOTES

1. "'Princess Tam,'" advertisement in the *Chicago Tribune*, July 29, 1938, 14.
2. "Josephine Baker Stars in Film," *Chicago Defender*, August 6, 1938, 18.
3. Papich, *Remembering Josephine*, 106–7.

4. "Josephine Baker Stars in Film," *Chicago Defender*, August 6, 1938, 18.

5. "*Princess Tam Tam* Features Jo Baker," *Pittsburgh Courier*, October 15, 1938, 21.

6. Papich, *Remembering Josephine*, 112.

7. Hammond and O'Connor, *Josephine Baker*, 77–82.

8. Rony, *The Third Eye*, 199.

9. The term *Creole* is still often applied to white women in *béké* (colonial families) in the Caribbean.

10. Archer-Straw, *Negrophilia*, 105.

11. For a survey of colonial films and a study of their place in French cinema, see Slavin, *Colonial Cinema and Imperial France*, 34. According to Slavin, Jacques Feyder's *L'Atlantide* (1921) is considered "a primal text" of colonial film. It was based on a 1918 novel of the same title by Pierre Benoît and has been adapted four times, in 1921, 1928, 1932, and again in the 1980s. The film tells the story of a young officer who, under the influence of drugs, the desert, and a mysterious woman, murders his superior. It set a paradigm for colonial films that followed, especially in its evocation of "the Arab woman [as] the moukère, 'manless,' instantly available and giving herself entirely, sacrificing even her life for the colonizer. This myth supplanted myths of 'empty lands.'" Like the films it later influenced, *L'Atlantide* draws on myths of the Dark Continent in a North African setting and features the dress and cultural practices of Muslims. Orientalism and Africanism are combined in the colonialist films of North Africa.

12. Nenno, "Femininity, the Primitive, and Modern Urban Space," 145–61.

13. Slavin, *Colonial Cinema and Imperial France*, 16.

14. Bhabha, *The Location of Culture*, 113.

15. Ibid., 66.

16. Collins, "Mammies, Matriarchs," 67. Black women have been the target of negative images as punishment for their resistance to race and gender oppression, argues Collins.

17. Ibid., 90.

18. Bhabha, *The Location of Culture*, 64.

19. Hall, "The Question of Cultural Identity," 277.

20. See Gates, *The Signifying Monkey*, 6, and Thompson, *Flash of the Spirit*. The figure of Esu-Elegbara, a divine trickster figure of Yoruba mythology, as explicated by Henry Louis Gates Jr., perfectly captures Baker's indeterminacy and multiplicity. Both Gates and Thompson describe the trickster as a liminal figure that presides over crossroads. Seen through their formulations, Baker's doubleness may be a duality in which she inhabited seeming contradictions such as male and female while she reinforced doubly layered identities such as American and French, Black and European.

21. Slavin, *Colonial Cinema and Imperial France*, 19.

22. *Within Our Gates* and *Scar of Shame* are both examples of silent-era race films or early narrative films produced for segregated Black audiences.

23. Baker and Bouillon, *Josephine*, 94.

24. Josephine Baker, *Les mémoires*, 142. "Je tournerai des films ecrits pour moi."

25. Josephine Baker, as cited in Rose, *Jazz Cleopatra*, 165.

26. "Across the Pond," *Chicago Defender*, July 31, 1926, 7.

27. Ibid.

28. Fabre, "International Beacons of African-American Memory," 122.

29. Ibid.

30. Ibid., 128.

31. Ivy, "Paris Eclipsed by N.Y.," 25.

32. Tinée, "French Movie Has Josephine Baker," 9.

33. Love, "Harlem Hopes to Welcome."

34. "Colored Dancer Weds Real Count," *Indiana Evening Gazette*, June 21, 1927, 2.

35. Love, "Harlem Hopes to Welcome."

36. Jones, "Day by Day," A6.

37. "Josephine Baker Is 'Countess' in Film," *Baltimore Afro-American*, July 9, 1927, 7.

38. Ibid.

39. "Hoax Wedding by Coloured Paris Dancer; Supposed Secret Marriage of Josephine Baker to an Italian Count; and the Sequel," *Gleaner* (Jamaica), July 15, 1927, 8.

40. Ibid.

41. Ibid.

42. Ibid.

43. "Josephine Says P. Abatino Is Not Her Husband," *New York Amsterdam News*, January 2, 1929.

44. In Philadelphia, Baker married Billy Baker, a former jockey then working as a Pullman porter. Rose, *Jazz Cleopatra*, 50.

45. Anderson, "Former Harlem Negro Dancer," 16.

46. Bronner, "Two American Negresses," 13. The article describes Florence Mills and Josephine Baker.

47. Ibid.

48. Jules-Rosette, *Josephine Baker in Art and Life*, 1–9. This recent study is most illuminating in the chapters that concern Baker's post–World War II efforts to establish a school for multicultural study and an international family of adopted children at her home. Jules-Rosette addresses "a need to remove Baker from reductive stereotypes and to humanize her legacy" through focusing on the performer's humanitarian work and the narratives of family and self-sacrifice in which she eschewed the primal savage role for the Madonna role.

EPILOGUE

Long Live Josephine Baker!

"JOSEPHINE BAKER SAYS IT'S ALRIGHT," sings a rousing rock chorus in *Passing Strange* (2009), a musical by singer, songwriter, and playwright Stew Rodewald (known as Stew) based on his personal experiences in Europe. Adapted to film by Spike Lee, *Passing Strange*'s overarching theme is the relationship between location and identity. In this song, Baker—perhaps the most famous of Parisian expats—serves as a metaphor for transatlantic travels and transformations of identity in tension with longings for home and nostalgia for an essential irreducible and unchanging self. Josephine Baker says it's all right to work and live in the vicissitudes of performance, stereotypes, and creativity.

In the play, Stew relocates from Los Angeles to Berlin and Amsterdam—new locations that open up conceptual space for him to pursue dimensions of his music, spirituality, sexuality, and worldview that he had felt were beyond his reach as long as he remained at home, where he was both sustained and constrained by its comforts. However, *Passing Strange*'s literary and historical references to Baker and other figures of transnational Blackness invite broader interpretations.

The project of *Passing Strange* rests on the notion of a collective memory of the Black traveler in Europe seen through the misperceptions of both American Black culture and African culture. For example, in the play, Stew ponders the ways in which he was viewed and interpreted through a "ghetto" persona that was nothing like the comfortable, middle-class existence he had had in Los Angeles. Black images from rap music, the movies, and the news were projected onto him, and he ended up performing them, regardless of how ill-fitting they might have been. In this strange kind of passing, in which he ends up conforming to what Blackness is being understood to mean in this European

166

Fig. E.1. The *Chicago Defender* reported that Baker piloted her
own plane, 1935. Photo by Roger Viollet/Getty Images.

environment, he found himself refracted in a complex perceptual context that
he did not author and thus could not entirely control. The dynamic that Stew
describes echoes Baker's Parisian adventure.

In an interview, Stew was asked about the way he appears onstage, more
or less as himself, while another actor plays a version of him—his younger
self traveling in Europe. The interviewer comments on the show's reflexivity:
"There's a real meta element to the show. You're on stage, speaking to a character who might be you. And now, you're watching you, speak to that character
that might be you, on film. Is it strange?" Stew replies,

> Well, no, because I still don't think of it as myself. That guy is a composite. I
> could go through point by point, everything in this film, and this play, that
> didn't happen to me. These things are based on things that happened to
> everyone from Josephine Baker to James Baldwin to friends of mine. I went
> to Europe with two black artists and one Jewish artist, and we experienced
> all manner of everything from objectification—girls wanting to sleep with us
> 'cause we were either black or Jewish all the way to like, you know, good stuff.
> What I am saying is: there's stuff in that movie that's from my Jewish friends'
> experience, there's stuff in there that's from Dexter Gordon's experience,

there's stuff there from Josephine Baker, from me, and just shit that just happened. So I mean, I don't see that as "Stew" at all, I see that as a young man who has a lot in common with me, but probably has a lot in common with you.[1]

Not only does Stew stand onstage, narrating the story, but he also takes an active role, engaging the younger version of the composite him in humorous and thoughtful exchanges. Thus, Baker and the character Stew both represent fragmentation and change. The artist Stew resists narrow and concrete interpretations of the play and its references. When he is asked to comment on how it feels to watch himself as a character in the film, he takes the opportunity to construct a more expansive way to think about subjectivity and persona in the play. The idea of a composite persona is central both to Stew's autobiographical work and to this book. Baker here serves as a rich reference point for a mythical type or figure in Black culture: the European sojourner. Stew's story—like Baker's, Baldwin's, and many others'—reveals the complications of identity captured in the phrase "passing strange."

The song "Josephine Baker Says It's Alright" evokes Josephine Baker in order to name aspects of Stew's experiences but also to extend his own character across time, space, and gender to speak to hers. His story does not take place in Paris, where Baker based her career. Nonetheless, the figure of Baker serves as a geographical, psychological, and cultural linchpin for Stew's story. Baker is herself a composite figure, impressive for her complexity, drive, and self-awareness. As an African American actor, Baker played characters that referenced the tropics and the French colonial world, but when Black American filmmaker Spike Lee evokes her decades later in his film, he raises the question of what Baker has meant to Black film.

Evocations of Baker such as Stew's are not mere cameos or offhand references to a famous figure of the era; they bring Baker's body language and the imaginative space she authored into the film as an aesthetic palimpsest and influence—with the codes of race, gender, and power she brings with her as well as the American and French performance histories and theoretical issues in which she was entangled. Filmmakers seeking to reference or transfer into their art her concern with fragmentation and multifaceted views in form, movement, and perspective seized upon her signification.

Baker's films already burlesque her recognizability, and in so doing they make her available for a wide range of interpretations by varying audiences while remaining essential and legible. Through sampling, Baker's iconicity becomes complete. Despite not being present and visible, she figures in a film

Fig. E.2. Josephine Baker highlights her offstage
elegance with this suit accented by bracelets.
© Hulton-Deutsch Collection/CORBIS.

narrative as a psychological, visual, and aural force, metabolizing the longings, delusions, and wishes of characters, audiences, and other performers and art-ists.[2] Baker citations by generations of artists demonstrate her iconicity, her self-versioning, and her audiences' multiple and changing public perceptions of her. In turn, Baker's syncretic dance practice, emphasizing change, disjuncture, and the use of multiple embodiments, makes her citable.

The 1930s films fall within a specific colonialist imaginary that was promi-nent at the time. Baker's postexotic work, *The French Way* (or *Fausse Alerte*; Jacques de Baroncelli, 1945), finds her playing a maternal facilitator of romance between two characters, and her performance focuses on singing. This reads as a citation of her earlier unrequited love scenarios. As Jean-François Staszak writes of Baker, "She wanted—and succeeded—to be acknowledged as an artist, and not only a Black artist. From the time of the Casino de Paris' revue (1930–1931), she recorded her first songs in French and began to wear sophisticated gowns on stage."[3] This film proves that Baker was able to move beyond her exoticist dance performance and present a new definition of glamorous Blackness.

In *The French Way*, Baker also finally achieved her underlying goal of creating a persona similar to that of Ethel Waters, the woman who had turned down an invitation to perform in *La revue nègre*, leaving the way open for Baker to seize the opportunity. The press coverage of Waters (described in chap. 1) established her status as "queen of the blues singers" and "famous phonograph star."[4] In the early 1920s, Baker was a young up-and-comer when Waters was a star—the star that Baker aspired to be. Baker's cinema persona of the glamorous singer echoes Waters's image, but it was in her live performances of the 1950s—onstage, where she was most comfortable—that she accomplished what she sought. *The French Way* reveals an entertainer, unhappy with her film efforts, who stopped trying to be the center of that particular kind of attention. She is the star of the film, certainly, but her role is quite different from those she performed in her earlier films. Typically, Baker's film characters are self-gazing objects to be seen simultaneously by others. She is bananas fallen from above and chased by her landlord in *La sirène des tropiques*. In *Zouzou*, she is a little girl seated at a vanity table, and in *Princesse Tam-Tam*, we first see her as a face among cacti for contrast. In contrast, in *The French Way*, she is the woman of the house, seeking someone to do repairs for her. She is Zazu, a cabaret owner. No longer bothered with the petty love plots of her silly earlier films, Zazu actively decides to help others along. Her performance onstage is complicated and not easily dismissed as decoration, because she performs in her own club.

Baker as a cultural figure was controversial at every stage of her career, and she continues to be so today. She was both celebrated and criticized for dancing within a colonialist idiom. She portrayed a range of stereotypical characters that she revised in her own way. Strong reactions that tend to either exalt or condemn her became part of her construction as a star. Two contemporary artists, Jean-Ulrick Désert of Haiti and Carrie Mae Weems of the United States, rework Baker's star image through foregrounding her postwar incarnation as a grande dame, a mature and highly stylized singer and stage performer. Examining Désert's and Weems's work side by side provides a comparative scene that illustrates the split in Baker's star image as goddess and accomplice.

Though Désert and Weems both approach and appropriate the image of the postwar grande dame, each artist presents a quite different (ever-contingent) provocation: Josephine Baker as goddess and Josephine Baker as accomplice, leaving viewers to decide a goddess to whom and an accomplice to what. Désert's *The Goddess Project* (2009–) consists of various artworks that use Baker as their central leitmotif. I focus here on *Shrine of the Divine Negress No.1* (2009) and *Divine Negress Butterfly Fans* (2009). Weems's *From Here I Saw What Happened and I Cried* (1995–96) is an anthology of thirty-three toned prints, the eighteenth of which frames Baker in multiple senses of the word, with accompanying text as well as among a series of images of African Americans related to the intimate relationships between Blacks and whites during and after slavery.

Produced in the early 2000s and the late 1990s, respectively, Désert's and Weems's works draw on Baker's continued cultural relevance and allow us to envision the most salient aspects of Baker's dialectics. The project *Shrine of the Divine Negress No.1* replicates Baker's image in a work that is reminiscent of stained-glass religious iconography. Here Baker is a secular deity containing the mystery, dimension, and power not of divinity but of celebrity. This multimedia star is at once revered and ironized through ecclesiastical associations to omnipresence and the divine come to earth in human form, as Jesus Christ is said to have done. Désert's work evokes as well the stories of the Greek gods and goddesses, who magnified humans' quotidian and ordinary desires of ambition, jealousy, fantasy, and desire to epic proportions through intergenerational conflict and translocational drama.

Yet the same image on the objects Désert distributed as *Divine Negress Butterfly Fans* (handheld fans constructed of die-cut four-color offset printed cardboard and wood) emphasizes contrasting traits of accessibility, functionality, and ephemerality—or to be even more precise, disposability. Similar to a rendering in stained glass, Baker's meanings in this work are fractured, yet they make up a diverse whole. Her skin appears somewhat darker brown here than is suggested in typical black-and-white studio portraits, emphasizing Baker's African heritage. And while there are religious connotations, the multiple colors and the butterfly imagery give the work a sense of play. Reaching into Désert's biography, Baker's image evokes Erzulie, the Haitian goddess of love, beauty, sensuality, and sweetness. This aspect of Désert's *Divine Negress Butterfly Fans* recontextualizes Baker's bananas as an exuberant celebration of life. The artist reworks Baker's dominant 1920s image through deploying and foregrounding the postwar era, when she was known as both a social activist and a glamorous stage and film presence.

Black celebrity underpins how Baker's star image is formed. Baker is an entertainer with particular meanings within the African American community, which evokes a sense of intimacy but also takes away the protections that more distant forms of fame might afford. Weems's use of Baker's image in *From Here I Saw What Happened and I Cried* draws on the politics of identity that characterized African American art and cultural criticism of the 1990s. And as a Black star both in Baker's time and today in Weems's time, Baker is expected to represent Black people and to help negotiate their place in American society. The use of text across the images connects Weems's piece to Black feminist writings and historiography, while the historical range of Weems's work narrates what Toni Morrison called "the unspeakable" realities of African American women's bodily experiences and memories of slavery. The order of the prints suggests narration, a certainty of meaning and direction. And the gaps between photographs, which are normally meaningless, here evoke absences and silences that remain. Baker's image is framed with the words "YOU BECAME AN ACCOMPLICE." The text shouts in all caps, and its stark whiteness stands out emphatically from the prints. The phrase is resounding, accusatory, and shaming. Though wearing a headpiece that suggests a crown, Baker sits with her head down. Like Désert's *Shrine of the Divine Negress No.1* and *Divine Negress Butterfly Fans*, Weems's red-tinted photograph depicts a very different Baker than the youthful bananas dancer. "YOU BECAME AN ACCOMPLICE" calls on the grande dame postwar image of Baker but from a deeply critical standpoint. Yet the framing seems to suggest that Baker has been captured and framed for a crime she did not commit.

What is she an accomplice to? Who is the speaker in the narrative? Baker was awarded the French Légion d'Honneur for her work as a spy on behalf of the French Resistance. From this perspective, Baker's capacity for duplicity was deemed heroic by her adopted country. Weems's reddened frame suggests shame, but its obvious artifice makes it easily removable and lessens its condemnatory power. What is Baker being accused of here? Is she a traitor? An accomplice implies someone with an ulterior motive, an agenda secreted away within one's private motivations. Where Baker has been accused of performing stereotypes, the accomplice suggests deviance, intention, and interiority. As an accomplice, Baker's costume becomes a device in service to a larger agenda. Weems's project implies a sense of ownership and interpretive dominance that perhaps speaks to a Black community's wider sense of owning its celebrities, who serve as their proxies in the mainstream.

Désert's and Weems's pieces enable us to envision Baker's dialectics through the contrasting images of the goddess and the accomplice within the worlds of entertainment and politics. The pieces are works of appropriation in which the artist extracts and reuses an artifact, effectively relaunching it in a new narrative, now with both original and second-generation meanings layered. Reworked in this way, Baker's image contains its alternatives within itself. Baker holds together oppositions: both goddess and accomplice, mainstream and Black, accessible and famous, intimate and epic. The kaleidoscopic design in Désert's *Shrine* makes this point especially explicit. Désert and Weems move us beyond Baker's banana days, yet the stillness and focus on the face in each work underscores its opposite—the much more popular head-to-toe image of an animated Baker dancing. Désert and Weems invent as they engage Baker's legendary confluence of ideas about race, history, humor, eroticism, and liberation. The image of Baker's bananas choreography watermarks Baker scholarship and her evocations in contemporary art. Together, Désert's and Weems's works reexamine Baker's status as an ethical figure and return us to the question of whether Baker is an example of racist and sexist exploitation or a symbol of Black female liberation. A query that seems to limit Baker is actually a gateway to understanding how Baker used her paradoxes as a dialectic for her own amusement and reflection.

It may seem a curious choice to begin this book with Baker's banana dance and its citations, emphasize the interplay of her exotic personas across her feature films, and then land here with two artists who manipulate and engage with Baker's postwar persona. However, Baker's grande dame persona was always somewhat of a reaction against that earlier dancer persona; Baker herself remained engaged with her banana days and reflected on them with pleasure. The primitivist-modern duality Baker uniquely displayed as she parodied and created her film roles can be seen as a destabilizing joke on the insistent gaze of her audiences, directors, and managers. The prism is a distorting lens. One way to see Baker is as a split between two opposites, but the cinematic prism encompasses Baker's movements drawn from many types of Otherness, whether Arab, Asian, African, or American. Baker could be feminine or masculine as well as androgynous. Baker played all the parts in order to become invisible and then visible in multiples. The grande dame who is explored in the works of Désert and Weems is just one reflecting angle of the long afterlife of Baker's cinematic prism.[5]

The American-born Parisian entertainer made a career of being a spectacle, particularly in the 1920s, when she performed at the Folies Bergère in a skirt of bananas. Yet how often have we considered Baker as a thinking spectator? For my own visual interpretations of Baker's legacy, I created a video in which I use the multiscreen format to place the younger Baker of the 1920s in direct

Fig. E.3. Josephine Baker bends gender norms in top
hat and tuxedo. Photo by Popperfoto/Getty Images.

dialogue with the older Baker of the mid- to late twentieth century. In *José-phine Baker Watches Herself*, I use editing techniques such as slow-motion and freeze-frame, epigraphs, subtitles, music, and, most importantly, found audio. Excerpts of Baker discussing her banana dance in an interview with NBC late-night television host Johnny Carson and from a Canadian Broadcasting Corporation interview program are deployed to ground the banana dance in her authorship and personality. I disrupt the image and sound sync to gesture beyond the explanatory value of the very material I call on as a primary source of Baker's thoughts about herself. Although Parisian sensation Josephine Baker is commonly associated with traditional media and live performance, we experience her work in digital formats today.

The title *Joséphine Baker Watches Herself* captures my argument and visual strategy of the video essay in that the material is arranged in a way that implies that the older Baker of the 1970s watches the younger Baker of the 1920s. In the video, Baker becomes her own authoritative audience, watching and analyzing her work, debunking any notion of her as an unthinking puppet. But I explore Baker's voice as affect as well. The sound of her voice and her calm, amused demeanor as she discusses her career tells us that if she was used as an ethnological object, she never absorbed it but remained a creative subject. After years of reading interpretations of her work and hearing my own voice in my head, it was startling to hear Baker's voice speaking for herself. I found her demeanor reassuring. Her warmth, clarity, and thoughtfulness come through in her pauses and in her laugh. She speaks with humor and gentleness about her banana days, describing the way the public embraced her and emphasizing that she focused on her work and her own goals. Her apparent peace of mind about all elements of her work conveys the sense that she enjoyed her career but never wanted to get carried away by the hype of it. Her comments focus on her work ethic and her authorship. *Joséphine Baker Watches Herself* reframes Baker as both spectacle and spectator, the final authority on her work.

In another short video essay, this time focused on *Zouzou*, I explore the possibilities of new media remediations through the heuristic of videographic criticism, framed and informed by the evocations of "sass" as put forth by Anna Everett in her transformative 2009 book, *Digital Diaspora: A Race for Cyberspace*. Everett documents and examines the idea of Black consciousness, particularly a pan-African consciousness, as Black "netizens" found one another through the tools of cyberspace in the mid- to late 1990s. Emphasizing "people's participatory expressions," likewise the heart of videographic criticism, Everett defines the early Black web as a critical bypass around the limits of mainstream media and mainstream narratives. Moving with sass, fortitude, and ingenuity, Black women in particular seized cybertools to look back at misrepresentations and assert their presence in the public sphere, even bridging gaps between those who had computers and those who did not. These women recast a diaspora of exiles as a network of members.

As a form of sass, videographic criticism allowed me to reexamine the narrative system of desire in *Zouzou*. I created a sixty-second video essay consisting of ten video clips from *Zouzou*, each lasting precisely six seconds, assembled with straight cuts. The audio is one continuous sequence from the film in which two characters discuss Zouzou's crush on Jean. There are no explanatory titles. I edited together moments when the characters Jean (played by Jean Gabin), Claire (Yvette Lebon), and Zouzou are in a scene together and moments when

Baker was alone. As the desiring male in the film, Jean's gaze is like a spotlight that, when directed at a character, brings the audience with him. Since Baker was the star of the film, as indicated in the opening titles, one expects the desiring gaze to shine in her direction. But something sadder, yet not unexpected, happens instead, as the ghost of Baker's incongruous stardom emerges from the frame. Each clip in the film shows Jean looking away from Zouzou, while she chatters on cheerfully oblivious to being ignored. When she is shown on her own, she is in the rain, crying and otherwise isolated. Although I had theorized the way Baker's films undermined her in words, it was not until I held *Zouzou* under the editing lens that I found the true visual system of Baker's exclusions from her own film. The films present her and then look away. Perhaps this is why, as discussed in earlier chapters, Baker did not enjoy filmmaking but rather found it cold and tedious. Nonetheless, her achievement as the first global Black woman film star stands as a monument to her capacity to shine regardless of whether the spotlight found her and the unique space that she occupied between race films, colonial cinema, and Hollywood, perfectly designed for her particular magnificence.

Baker should have been recognized as an African American film pioneer long ago. Unfortunately, in addition to the geographic conventions of Black film, which tend to revolve around either the United States or the African continent, disciplinary boundaries between film studies, African American studies, and performance studies, together with the fact that Baker's films were relatively few and were French productions, has discouraged her necessary inclusion in the canonical history of early twentieth-century Black American performers, directors, and films. Baker is discussed in all these fields but usually as a passing reference or as one example of a larger phenomenon. She is seen as more a cultural figure than a film historical figure. Rather than exploring one or another aspect of Baker's representation or viewing her as symptomatic of a larger phenomenon, I have treated Baker as a phenomenon that contains a variety of characters. More than a notable cultural figure, Baker is a film pioneer through her cinematic prismatic of comedy dancing and reworking existing types.

Baker's agency is difficult to pin down by conventional means. Baker authorized her story many times on film as well as in books such as *Les mémoires de Joséphine Baker avec Marcel Sauvage; Avec 30 dessins inédits de Paul Colin* (1927), *Voyages et aventures de Joséphine Baker* (1931), and a novel called *Mon sang dans tes veines: roman d'après une idée de Joséphine Baker* (1931), edited by La Camara and Pépito Abatino. But Baker wrote with her life. She directly put herself into the film by including autobiographical representations of her public life in her films. Sometimes the element from her life might be a bit of footage documenting a pastime or public appearance, as when a journalist for the *New York Amsterdam News* noted, "Whenever she placed a bet on a horse it was almost sure to win at the big Arc de Triomphe Prix of Longchamps." *Princesse Tam-Tam* depicts just such a scenario in a montage of scenes of Baker's public life recast as her film character's Parisian experience. There was ever that doubling between Baker characters. Baker's films might include posters promoting the real Baker's shows at the Folies Bergère or footage from newsreels as at the conclusion of *Zouzou*.

Baker had a strong, irrepressible desire to express herself, a desire that marks any artist. She once wrote a short story that one of Baker's biographers, Stephen Papich, registered in her name with the Writers Guild of America, titled "The Fairytale of Wisdom." In parentheses, Baker (or Papich) wrote, "Written by Josephine Baker in Beverly Hills, California during the quiet, peaceful hours in the middle of the night on September 20, 1973."[6] The story explores the theme of uniting across difference, which Baker had explored in her activism and her public statements about her diverse adoptive family. Taking up the theme of social conflict, the story is about an epic standoff between the Sweet People and the Monster who oppressed them. Did Baker intend to make this into a movie? Or do her earlier films feed this "fairy tale"? Perhaps this story, or one like it, and the desire to narrate, to author a story, fueled her creativity in a variety of domains. Josephine Baker authored Josephine Baker.

Yet there is no concrete evidence to date that Baker actually wrote screenplays. Her input is thus difficult to discover by traditional means, and her collaborations were many: Maurice Dekobra, a well-known French writer at the time, penned the screenplay for *La sirène des tropiques*. Baker's manager Pepito Abatino wrote a novel on which *Zouzou* was based. Abatino has screenwriting credit, while Yves Mirande has dialogue credit for *Princesse Tam-Tam*. And Michel Duran wrote Baker's fourth and last feature, *The French Way*. Making movies necessitates collaboration, of course, and Baker's partnering with journalists further mediated her authorship, as did her use of a translator. But her voice is not lost completely. And what her name is on is not the point. Baker is the authoritative presence in her work, full stop, and that presence is the engine of all the theories and speculation and attention to her performances over the years.

It was a risky approach, but Baker spoke in a fractured mode. Yet she connects with audiences, even now, decades after her death, through her powerfully kaleidoscopic authorial voice. Rather than being undermined by the ambiguity of cinematic reflexivity accorded to her mediated image, she was emboldened and enriched by it. She was the intellectual and spiritual author of the work in which she appeared. If not a tactical intention, it is a tactically relevant effect, and this book is concerned with her effects. Baker fragmented her authorship and retained authority to protect and retell conflicting versions of her personal life in a strategy to sustain her privacy—all while living in the public eye. Baker's agency must be understood in terms of her presence, her capacity to make herself important and to protect her artistry. Baker's longevity onstage and the continual (perhaps ritual) interest in her career among scholars, artists, and fans alike testify to her humanity. She authored her performance through practice and originality, deriving her prismatic authority paradoxically from the very deauthorizing vulnerabilities that threatened to unmake her.

NOTES

1. "Spike Lee, Stew, and a Rock Musical: 'Passing Strange,'" *BlackBook*, September 14, 2009, https://bbook.com/film/spike-lee-stew-a-rock-musical -passing-strange/.

2. Stew's quotations, evocations, and translations of Baker, like those of Beyoncé and Diana Ross, fit into a history of artists sampling Baker in their work. Baker citations have appeared in several films, including *Touki Bouki* (Djibril Diop Mambéty, 1972), *Alma's Rainbow* (Ayoka Chenzira, 1994), *Madame Sata* (Karim Ainouz, 2002), *Coffee and Cigarettes* (Jim Jarmusch, 2004), *The Triplets of Belleville* (Sylvain Chomet, 2003), *Frida* (Julie Taymor, 2002), and *Tree Shade* (Lisa Collins, 1998).

3. Staszak, "Performing Race and Gender," 633.

4. Advertisement for the Black Swan Troubadours in the *Savannah Tribune*, May 4, 1922, and advertisement for the Lafayette Theater in *New York Age*, May 26, 1923.

5. Baker's afterlife continues with *Perle Noire: Meditations for Josephine Baker*, a tribute to Josephine Baker staged in January 2019 at the Metropolitan Museum of Art by Julia Bullock. *Josephine Baker's Last Dance* by Sherry Jones is a novel published in December 2018.

6. Josephine Baker, "The Fairytale of Wisdom," George P. Johnson Negro Film Collection (Collection 1042), UCLA Library Special Collections, Charles E. Young Research Library, University of California, Los Angeles, 1.

BIBLIOGRAPHY

Alexander, Elizabeth. *The Venus Hottentot*. Minneapolis: Graywolf, 1990.

Allen, Robert C. *Horrible Prettiness: Burlesque and American Culture*. Chapel Hill: University of North Carolina Press, 1991.

Allred, Kevin. "'Schoolin' Life': Teaching Beyoncé and Engaging Youth." *Feminist Wire*, February 22, 2012.

Anderson, Harvey. "Former Harlem Negro Dancer Has All Paris at Her Feet." *Port Arthur News* (TX), June 26, 1927.

Archer-Straw, Petrine. *Negrophilia: Avant-Garde Paris and Black Culture in the 1920s*. New York: Thames and Hudson, 2000.

Atwater, Deborah F. *African American Women's Rhetoric: The Search for Dignity, Personhood, and Honor*. Lanham, MD: Lexington Books, 2009.

Baker, Jean-Claude. *Josephine: The Hungry Heart*. New York: Random House, 1993.

Baker, Josephine. "The Fairytale of Wisdom." George P. Johnson Negro Film Collection (Collection 1042), UCLA Library Special Collections, Charles E. Young Research Library, University of California, Los Angeles.

———. *Les mémoires de Joséphine Baker*. Collected and adapted by Marcel Sauvage. Paris: Dilecta, 2006.

———. *Les mémoires de Joséphine Baker avec Marcel Sauvage; Avec 30 dessins inédits be Paul Colin*. Paris: Kra, 1927.

———. *Voyages et aventures de Joséphine Baker*. Paris: M. Seheur, 1931.

Baker, Josephine, and Jo Bouillon. *Josephine*. Translated by Marianna Fitzpatrick. New York: Harper and Row, 1977.

Baldwin, Michelle. *Burlesque and the New Bump-n-Grind*. Golden, CO: Fulcrum, 2004.

Beatty, Paul, ed. *Hokum: An Anthology of African-American Humor*. New York: Bloomsbury, 2006.

179

Bellour, Raymond. "The Unattainable Text." In *The Analysis of Film*, edited by Constance Penley, 21–27. Bloomington: Indiana University Press, 2001.

Berlin, Edward A. "Ragtime." In *Grove Music Online*, edited by Deane Root. Accessed March 10, 2015. http://www.oxfordmusiconline.com/subscriber /article/grove/music/22825.

Berrong, Ricard. *Pierre Loti*. London: Reaktion Books, 2018. Kindle.

Bhabha, Homi. *The Location of Culture*. New York: Routledge, 1994.

Blanchard, Pascal, and Nicolas Bancel. *"Le Zoo Humain," de l'indigène à l'immigré*. Paris: Gallimard, 1998.

Blanchard, Pascal, Sandrine Lemaire, Nicolas Bancel, and Dominic Thomas, eds. *Colonial Culture in France since the Revolution*. Bloomington: Indiana University Press, 2013.

———. "The Creation of a Colonial Culture in France, from the Colonial Era to the 'Memory Wars.'" Introduction to *Colonial Culture in France since the Revolution*, edited by Pascal Blanchard, Sandrine Lemaire, Nicolas Bancel, and Dominic Thomas, 1–50. Bloomington: Indiana University Press, 2013.

Booth, Michael R. "Burlesque." In *The Oxford Encyclopedia of Theatre and Performance*, edited by Dennis Kennedy. Oxford: Oxford University Press, 2005. E-reference ed. http://doi.org/10.1093/acref/9780198601746.001.0001.

Borshuk, Michael. "An Intelligence of the Body: Disruptive Parody through Dance in the Early Performances of Josephine Baker." In *EmBODYing Liberation: The Black Body in American Dance*, edited by Dorothea Fischer-Hornung and Alison D. Goeller, 41–57. Hamburg, Germany: LIT, 2001.

Braddock, Jeremy, and Jonathan P. Eburne, eds. *Paris, Capital of the Black Atlantic: Literature, Modernity, Diaspora*. Baltimore: Johns Hopkins University Press, 2013.

British History Online. "The Haymarket, West Side." In *Survey of London: Volumes 29 and 30: St James Westminster, Part 1*. Accessed August 8, 2010. http://www .british-history.ac.uk/survey-london/vols29-30/pt1/pp210-214. First published 1960 by London County Council.

Bronner, Milton. "Two American Negresses Take London and Paris by Storm." *Manitowoc Herald* (WI), July 1, 1927, 13.

Brooks, Daphne Ann. "'All That You Can't Leave Behind': Black Female Soul Singing and the Politics of Surrogation in the Age of Catastrophe." *Meridians* 8, no. 1 (2008): 180–204.

———. "Suga Mama, Politicized." *Nation*, December 18, 2007.

Burke, Luke. "Lynn Whitfield Celebrates the 20th Anniversary of 'The Josephine Baker Story.'" *BET*, February 28, 2011. http://www.bet.com/news/celebrities /2011/02/27/lynn-whitfield-celebrates-the-20th-anniversary-of-the-josephine -baker-story-.html.

Burt, Ramsay. "'Savage' Dancer: Tout Paris Goes to See Josephine Baker." In *Alien Bodies: Representations of Modernity, "Race" and Nation in Modern Dance*, 49–71. London: Routledge, 1998.

Butler, Bennie. "The Theatre." *Inter-State Tattler* (New York), September 6, 1929.

Caddoo, Cara. *Envisioning Freedom: Cinema and the Building of Modern Black Life*. Cambridge, MA: Harvard University Press, 2014.

Carby, Hazel. "Women, Migration and the Formation of a Blues Culture." In *Cultures in Babylon: Black Britain and African America*, 7–66. New York: Verso Books, 1999.

Carpio, Glenda. *Laughing Fit to Kill: Black Humor in the Fictions of Slavery*. New York: Oxford University Press, 2008.

Cheng, Anne Anlin. *Second Skin: Josephine Baker and the Modern Surface*. Oxford: Oxford University Press, 2011.

Coffman, Elizabeth. "Uncanny Performance in Colonial Narratives: Josephine Baker in *Princesse Tam-Tam*." *Para-doxa: Studies in World Literary Genres* 3 (1997): 379–94.

Colin, Paul. *Josephine Baker and La revue nègre: Paul Colin's Lithographs of Le tumulte noir in Paris, 1927*. Introduction by Henry Louis Gates Jr. and Karen C. C. Dalton. New York: H. N. Abrams, 1998.

Collins, Patricia Hill. "Mammies, Matriarchs, and Other Controlling Images." In *Black Feminist Thought: Knowledge Consciousness and the Politics of Empowerment*, 67–90. New York: Routledge, 2008.

Crais, Clifton, and Pamela Scully. *Sara Baartman and the Hottentot Venus: A Ghost Story and a Biography*. Princeton, NJ: Princeton University Press, 2010.

Cuvier, George. "Extrait d'observations faites sur le cadavre d'une femme connue à Paris et à Londres sous le nom de Vénus Hottentote." *Mémoires de Musée de l'Histoire naturelle* 3 (1817): 259–74.

Daniels, J. Yolande. "Exhibit A: Private Life without a Narrative." In *Black Venus 2010: They Called Her "Hottentot,"* edited by Deborah Willis, 62–67. Philadelphia: Temple University Press, 2010.

Davis, Andrew. *Baggy Pants Comedy: Burlesque and the Oral Tradition*. New York: Palgrave Macmillan, 2011.

Davis, Angela. *Blues Legacies and Black Feminism: Gertrude "Ma" Rainey, Bessie Smith and Billie Holiday*. New York: Vintage Books, 1998.

Dayal, Samir. "Blackness as Symptom: Josephine Baker and European Identity." In *Blackening Europe*, edited by Heike Raphael-Hernandez, 35–52. London: Routledge, 2004.

Du Bois, W. E. B. "Of Our Spiritual Strivings." In *The Souls of Black Folk*, 2–7. New York: Oxford University Press, 2007.

Durham, Aisha. "Check on It: Beyoncé, Southern Booty, and Black Femininities in Music Video." *Feminist Media Studies* 12, no. 1 (March 1, 2012): 35–49.

Dyer, Richard, and Paul McDonald. *Stars*. London: British Film Institute, 1998.

Edwards, Brent Hayes. *The Practice of Diaspora: Literature, Translation, and the Rise of Black Internationalism*. Cambridge: Harvard University Press, 2003.

Everett, Anna. *Returning the Gaze: A Genealogy of Black Film Criticism, 1909–1949*. Durham, NC: Duke University Press, 2001.

Ezra, Elizabeth. *The Colonial Unconscious: Race and Culture in Interwar France*. Ithaca, NY: Cornell University Press, 2000.

Fabre, Michel. *From Harlem to Paris: Black American Writers in France, 1840–1980*. Urbana-Champaign: University of Illinois Press, 1991.

———. "International Beacons of African-American Memory: Alexandre Dumas Père, Henry O. Tanner, and Josephine Baker as Examples of Recognition." In *History and Memory in African-American Culture*, edited by Geneviève Fabre and Robert O'Meally, 122–29. New York: Oxford University Press, 1994.

Farès, El-Dahdah, and Stephen Atkinson. "The Josephine Baker House: For Loos's Pleasure." *Assemblage*, no. 26 (1995): 73–87. http://doi.org/10.2307/3171418.

Field, Allyson N. *Uplift Cinema: The Emergence of African American Film and the Possibility of Black Modernity*. Durham, NC: Duke University Press, 2015.

Fleming, Crystal M. *How to Be Less Stupid about Race: On Racism, White Supremacy, and the Racial Divide*. Boston: Beacon, 2018.

Francis, Terri. "Sighting the 'Real' Josephine Baker: Methods and Issues of Black Star Studies." In *Black Venus 2010: They Called Her "Hottentot,"* edited by Deborah Willis, 199–209. Philadelphia: Temple University Press, 2011.

———. "What Does Beyoncé See in Josephine Baker? A Brief Film History of Sampling La Diva, La Bakaire." In "Josephine Baker: A Century in the Spotlight," edited by Kaiama Glover, special issue, *Scholar and Feminist Online* 6, nos. 1–2 (Fall 2007–Spring 2008). sfonline.barnard.edu/baker/francis_01.htm.

Gates, Henry Louis Jr. *The Signifying Monkey: A Theory of African American Literary Criticism*. New York: Oxford University Press, 1988.

Gibson, Brian, dir. *The Josephine Baker Story*. Screenplay by Ron Hutchinson. Aired March 16, 1991, on HBO.

Glenn, Cerise L. "Stepping In and Stepping Out: Examining the Way Anticipatory Career Socialization Impacts Identity Negotiation of African American Women in Academia." In *Presumed Incompetent: The Intersections of Race and Class for Women in Academia*, edited by Carmen G. Gonzalez, Yolanda Flores Niemann, Angela P. Harris, and Gabriella Gutiérrez y Muhs, 133–41. Logan: Utah State University Press, 2012.

Glissant, Édouard. *L'intention poétique (Poétique II)*. Paris: Gallimard, 1997. First published 1967. Published in English as *Poetic Intention*. Translated by Nathalie Stephens. Callicoon, NY: Nightboat Books, 2010.

Glover, Kaiama L., ed. "Josephine Baker: A Century in the Spotlight." Special double issue, *Scholar and Feminist Online* 6, nos. 1–2 (Fall 2007–Spring 2008). http://sfonline.barnard.edu/baker/.

Gottschild, Brenda Dixon. *The Dancing Body*. New York: Palgrave, 2003.

Griffin, Farah J., and Cheryl J. Fish, eds. *A Stranger in the Village: Two Centuries of African-American Travel Writing*. Boston: Beacon, 1998.

Groo, Katherine. "Shadow Lives: Josephine Baker and the Body of Cinema." *Framework: The Journal of Cinema and Media* 54, no. 1 (2013): 7–39.

Guild, Leo. *Josephine Baker*. Los Angeles: Holloway, 1976.

Guterl, Matthew Pratt. *Josephine Baker and the Rainbow Tribe*. Cambridge, MA: Belknap Press of Harvard University Press, 2014.

———. "Josephine Baker's Colonial Pastiche." *Black Camera: An International Film Journal* 1, no. 2 (2010): 25–37.

Haggins, Bambi. *Laughing Mad: The Black Comic Persona in Post-Soul America*. New Brunswick, NJ: Rutgers University Press, 2007.

Hall, Stuart. "The Question of Cultural Identity." In *Modernity and Its Futures*, edited by Stuart Hall, David Held, and Tony McGrew, 273–326. Cambridge, UK: Polity, 1992.

Hammond, Patrick, and Bryan O'Connor. *Josephine Baker*. Boston: Little, Brown, 1988.

Haney, Lynne. *Naked at the Feast: The Biography of Josephine Baker*. London: Robson Books, 1981.

Harris-Perry, Melissa V. *Sister Citizen: Shame, Stereotypes, and Black Women in America*. Princeton, NJ: Princeton University Press, 2011.

Hartman, Saidiya. *Wayward Lives, Beautiful Experiments: Intimate Histories of Social Upheaval*. New York: Norton, 2019.

Hays, J. N. "The Lecturing Empire, 1800–50." In *Metropolis and Province: Science in British Culture, 1780–1850*, edited by Ian Inkster and Jack Morrell, 1–119. Philadelphia: University of Pennsylvania Press, 1983.

Henderson, Mae Gwendolyn. "Colonial, Postcolonial, and Diasporic Readings of Josephine Baker as Dancer and Performance Artist." In "Josephine Baker: A Century in the Spotlight," ed. Kaiama Glover, special double issue, *Scholar and Feminist Online* 6, no. 1/2 (Fall 2007–Spring 2008).

Henderson, Mae G., and Charlene B. Regester. *The Josephine Baker Critical Reader: Selected Writings on the Entertainer and Activist*. Jefferson, NC: McFarland, 2017.

Hobson, Janell. *Venus in the Dark: Blackness and Beauty in Popular Culture*. New York: Routledge, 2005.

Holmes, Rachael. *African Queen: The Real Life of the Hottentot Venus*. New York: Random House, 2007.

hooks, bell. "The Oppositional Gaze." In *Black American Cinema*, edited by Manthia Diawara, 288–302. New York: Routledge, 1993.

———. "Selling Hot Pussy: Representations of Black Women's Sexuality in the Cultural Marketplace." In *Black Looks: Race and Representation*, 61–77. Brooklyn, NY: South End, 1992.

Hotchner, Aaron E. *Papa Hemingway: The Ecstasy and Sorrow*. New York: Morrow, 1983.

Hoy, Don R. "The Banana Industry of Guadeloupe, French West Indies." *Social and Economic Studies* 11, no. 3 (1962): 260–66. https://www.jstor.org/stable /27853684.

Hughes, Langston. "When the Negro Was in Vogue." In *The Big Sea*, 223–32. New York: Hill and Wang, 1993.

Ivy, William. "Paris Eclipsed by N.Y. in Its Nightly Revels." *Oakland Tribune*, November 13, 1925, 25.

Jacobson, Matthew. *Whiteness of a Different Color: European Immigrants and the Alchemy of Race*. Cambridge: Harvard, 1998.

Jackson, Jeffrey. *Making Jazz French: Music and Modern Life in Interwar Paris*. Durham, NC: Duke University Press, 2003.

Johnson, James Weldon. *The Autobiography of an Ex-Colored Man*. New York: Vintage, 1989.

———. *Black Manhattan*. New York: Knopf, 1930.

Jones, William. "Day by Day: Josephine Baker Marries a Count." *Baltimore Afro-American*, June 25, 1927, A6.

Jules-Rosette, Bennetta. *Josephine Baker in Art and Life: The Icon and the Image*. Urbana-Champaign: University of Illinois Press, 2007.

———. "Josephine Baker: Inventing the Image and Preserving the Icon." In *Josephine Baker: Image and Icon*, edited by Olivia Lahs-Gonzales, 3–28. St. Louis: Reedy Press and Sheldon Art Galleries, 2006.

Julien, Eileen. "Now You See It, Now You Don't: Josephine Baker's Films of the 1930s and the Question of Color." In *Black Europe and the African Diaspora*, edited by Darlene Clarke Hine, Trica Danielle Keaton, and Stephen Small, 48–62. Urbana-Champaign: University of Illinois Press, 2009.

Karp, Ivan, and Steven D. Lavine, eds. *Exhibiting Cultures: The Poetics and Politics of Museum Display*. Washington, DC: Smithsonian Institution, 1991.

Kennedy-Karpat, Colleen. *Rogues, Romance, and Exoticism in French Cinema of the 1930s*. Madison, MD: Fairleigh Dickinson University Press.

King, Bobbi, Eileen Southern, and Eubie Blake. "A Legend in His Own Lifetime." *The Black Perspective in Music* 1, no. 2 (1973): 151–56.

King, Don Roy. "Wayne's World." *SNL Transcripts Tonight*. Accessed March 16, 2015. http://snltranscripts.jt.org/90/90swayne.phtml.

Kirby, Percival. "More about the Hottentot Venus." *Africana Notes and News* (Johannesburg, South Africa) 10, no. 4 (1953): 126–33.

Kraut, Anthea. "Whose Choreography? Josephine Baker and the Question of (Dance) Authorship." In "Josephine Baker: A Century in the Spotlight," ed. Kaiama Glover, special double issue, *Scholar and Feminist Online* 6, no. 1/2 (Fall 2007–Spring 2008).

Levinson, André. *La danse d'aujourd'hui: Etudes, notes, portraits.* Paris: Duchartre and Van Buggenhoudt, 1929.

Lewis, Theophilus. "Theatres." *Inter-State Tattler* (New York), August 26, 1927.

Liepe-Levinson, Katherine. *Strip Show: Performances of Gender and Desire.* New York: Routledge, 2003.

Likosky, Stephan. *With a Weapon and a Grin: Postcard Images of France's Black African Colonial Troops in WWI.* Atglen, PA: Schiffer Military History, 2017.

Lindfors, Bernth, ed. *Africans on Stage: Studies in Ethnological Show Business.* Bloomington: Indiana University Press, 1999.

Lofgren, Charles A. *The Plessy Case: A Legal-Historical Interpretation.* New York: Oxford University Press, 1987.

Lorde, Audre. "Uses of the Erotic: The Erotic as Power." In *Sister Outsider: Essays and Speeches,* 53–59. Freedom, CA: Crossing Press, 1984.

Loti, Pierre. *The Sahara.* Translated by Marjorie Laurie. New York: Brentano's, 1921. Project Gutenberg e-book. http://www.gutenberg.org/files/59077/59077-h/59077-h.htm.

Lott, Eric. *Love and Theft: Blackface Minstrelsy and the American Working Class.* New York: Oxford University Press, 1993.

Love, Sam. "Harlem Hopes to Welcome First Negro Countess and Her Lucky Rabbit Foot: Josephine Baker, Slim and Dusky, Idol of Paris Cafes Adds Title to Her Ming Bricabrac and Diamonds." *Syracuse Herald,* June 21, 1927.

Magubane, Zine. "Which Bodies Matter? Feminism, Post-Structuralism, Race and the Curious Theoretical Odyssey of the 'Hottentot Venus.'" In *Black Venus 2010: They Called Her "Hottentot,"* edited by Deborah Willis, 47–67. Philadelphia: Temple University Press, 2010.

Malone, Jacqui. *Steppin' on the Blues: The Visible Rhythms of African American Dance.* Urbana-Champaign: University Illinois Press, 1996.

Maseko, Zola, dir. *The Life and Times of Sara Baartman: The Hottentot Venus.* Brooklyn, NY: First Run/Icarus Films, 1998.

McIntyre, O. O. "New York Day by Day," *Olean (NY) Evening Times,* June 27, 1928, 2.

Miller-Young, Mireille. "Putting Hypersexuality to Work: Black Women and Illicit Eroticism in Pornography." *Sexualities* 13, no. 2 (April 2010): 219–35.

Mintz, Sidney. *Tasting Food, Tasting Freedom: Excursions into Eating, Culture, and the Past.* Boston: Beacon, 1996.

Morais, Audley. "Around the Movies: Miss Baker." *Gleaner* (Jamaica), January 4, 1930.

Mulvey, Laura. "Visual Pleasure and Narrative Cinema." *Screen* 16, no. 3 (Autumn 1975): 6–18.

Nenno, Nancy Pauline. "Femininity, the Primitive, and Modern Urban Space: Josephine Baker in Germany." In *Women in the Metropolis: Gender and*

Modernity in Weimar Culture, edited by Katharina von Ankum, 145–61. Berkeley: University of California Press, 1997.

Njami, Simon. Foreword to *Josephine Baker in Art and Life: The Icon and the Image*, by Bennetta Jules-Rosette. Urbana-Champaign: University of Illinois Press, 2007.

Papich, Stephen. *Remembering Josephine: A Biography of Josephine Baker*. New York: Bobbs Merrill Company, 1976.

Perron, Wendy. "Dance in the Harlem Renaissance: Sowing Seeds." In *EmBODYing Liberation: The Black Body in American Dance*, edited by Dorothea Fischer-Hornung and Alison D. Goeller, 23–39. Hamburg, Germany: LIT, 2001.

Pickens, Josie. "The Scandalous Joy of Rihanna and Josephine Baker." *Ebony*, June 4, 2014. http://www.ebony.com/entertainment-culture/the-scandalous-joy -of-rihanna-and-josephine-baker-999#axzz3TzoEGzl1.

Powell, Richard. *Blues Aesthetic: Black Culture and Modernism*. Washington, DC: Washington Project for the Arts, 1989.

Powrie, Phil, and Éric Rebillard. "Josephine Baker and Pierre Batcheff in La Sirène Des Tropiques." *Studies in French Cinema* 8, no. 3 (2008): 245–64.

Regester, Charlene B. *African American Actresses: The Struggle for Visibility, 1900–1960*. Bloomington: Indiana University Press, 2010.

Régnier, Pierre de. "La revue nègre." *Candide*, November 12, 1925, 6.

Robinson, Alonford James. "East St. Louis Riot of 1917." In *Africana: The Encyclopedia of the African and African American Experience*, 2nd ed., edited by Kwame Anthony Appiah and Henry Louis Gates Jr. Oxford: Oxford African American Studies Center. Accessed June 24, 2017. http://www.oxfordaasc.com /article/opr/t0002/e1327.

Rochambeau, Maurice. "How Josephine Baker Captured Paris and Berlin." *Baltimore Afro-American*, December 28, 1929.

———. "Josephine Baker." *Baltimore Afro-American*, December 7, 1929, A8.

———. "Seeking New Thrill, Jo Baker Gets Biggest One in Movies." *Baltimore Afro-American*, January 11, 1930.

Rogers, J. A. "News European Writer Tells of Josephine Baker's Picture; Speaks Well of Former Chorus Girl's Work in New Picture." *New York Amsterdam News*, February 15, 1928.

———. "Sexiest Spot in Paris." *New York Amsterdam News*, July 27, 1927, 15.

Rony, Fatimah Tobing. *The Third Eye: Race, Cinema, and Ethnographic Spectacle*. Durham, NC: Duke University Press, 1996.

Rose, Phyllis. *Jazz Cleopatra: Josephine Baker in Her Time*. New York: Doubleday, 1989.

Rosemond, A. "News of Paris." *New York Amsterdam News*, March 21, 1928.

———. "News of Paris." *New York Amsterdam News*, May 23, 1928.

Rudwick, Elliott M. *Race Riot at East St. Louis, July 2, 1917*. Urbana-Champaign: University of Illinois Press, 1982.

Rye, Howard. "Smith, Clara." *Grove Music Online*. Accessed October 4, 2020. https://doi.org/10.1093/gmo/9781561592630.article.J415300.

Schteir, Rachel. *Striptease: The Untold History of the Girlie Show*. New York: Oxford University Press, 2004.

Shapira, Elana. "Dressing a Celebrity: Adolf Loos's House for Josephine Baker." *Studies in the Decorative Arts* 11, no. 2 (Spring/Summer 2004): 2–24.

Sharpley-Whiting, Tracey Denean. *Black Venus: Sexualized Savages, Primal Fears, and Primitive Narratives in French*. Durham, NC: Duke University Press, 1999.

Shaw, Andrea Elizabeth. *The Embodiment of Disobedience: Fat Black Women's Unruly Political Bodies*. Lanham, MD: Lexington Books, 2006.

Slavin, David Henry. *Colonial Cinema and Imperial France, 1919–1939: White Blind Spots, Male Fantasies, Settler Myths*. Baltimore: Johns Hopkins University Press, 2001.

Slessor, Catherine. "Loos and Baker: A House for Josephine." *Architectural Review*, March 5, 2018. https://www.architectural-review.com/essays/loos-and-baker-a -house-for-josephine/10028604.article.

Smith, Lauren. "Rihanna Responds to Sheer Dress Drama with Funny Tweet." *Glamour*, June 6, 2014. http://www.glamourmagazine.co.uk/article/rihanna -bares-all-at-the-cfda-awards-in-new-york-city-wearing-sequin-see-through-dress.

Smith, Shawn Michelle. "Photographing the 'American Negro': Nation, Race and Photography at the Paris Exposition of 1900." In *American Archives: Gender, Race, and Class in Visual Culture*, 159–86. Princeton, NJ: Princeton University Press, 1999.

Snelson, Floyd G. "Harlem—'Negro Capital of the Nation.'" *New York Age*, July 30, 1938.

Soloski, Alexis. "Cush Jumbo Summons the Spirit of Josephine Baker at Joe's Pub." *New York Times*, February 12, 2015. http://nyti.ms/1J3SbCk.

Soluri, John. *Banana Cultures: Agriculture, Consumption, and Environmental Change in Honduras and the United States*. Austin: University of Texas Press, 2005. EPUB.

Sowinska, Alicja. "Dialectics of the Banana Skirt: The Ambiguities of Josephine Baker's Self-Representation." In "Bodies: Physical and Abstract." Special issue, *Michigan Feminist Studies* 19 (Fall 2005–Spring 2006). http://hdl.handle.net /2027/spo.ark5583.0019.003.

Staszak, Jean-François. "Performing Race and Gender: The Exoticization of Josephine Baker and Anna May Wong." *Gender, Place and Culture* 22, no. 5 (2015): 626–43.

Stearns, Marshall, and Jean Stearns. *Jazz Dance: The Story of American Vernacular Dance*. Boston: Da Capo, 1994.

Stewart, Jacqueline N. *Migrating to the Movies: Cinema and Black Urban Modernity*. Berkeley: University of California Press, 2005.

Stovall, Tyler. *Paris Noir: African Americans in the City of Light*. Boston: Houghton Mifflin, 1996.

Strother, Z. S. "Display of the Body Hottentot." In *Africans on Stage: Studies in Ethnological Show Business*, edited by Bernth Lindfors, 1–61. Bloomington: Indiana University Press, 1999.

Thompson, Kristin, and David Bordwell. *Film History: An Introduction*. New York: McGraw-Hill, 1994.

Thompson, Robert Farris. *Flash of the Spirit: African and Afro-American Art and Philosophy*. New York: Random House, 1983.

———. *African Art in Motion: Icon and Act*. Oakland: University of California Press, 1979.

Tinée, Mae. "French Movie Has Josephine Baker as Star." *Chicago Tribune*, August 4, 1938, 9.

Valenti, Jessica. "Beyonce's 'Run the World' (Not So Much)." *Feministing* video. May 23, 2011. http://feministing.com/2011/05/23/beyonces-run-the-world-not-so-much/.

Valentino, Bianca. "Hero Status: Josephine Baker." *Rookie* 17 (January 7, 2013). http://www.rookiemag.com/2013/01/hero-status-josephine-baker/.

Van Lier, Mario, and Debels George. "Josephine Baker visits Volendam— outtakes." August 24, 1928. Fox News Story. C8059, Moving Image Research Collections, Digital Video Repository, University of South Carolina Columbia, South Carolina. https://mirc.sc.edu/islandora/object/usc%3A1750.

Waldo, Terry. *This Is Ragtime*. New York: Da Capo, 1976.

Watkins, Mel. *On the Real Side: A History of African American Comedy*. Chicago: Chicago Review Press, 1999.

Wells, Ida B. *Southern Horrors: Lynch Law in All Its Phases*. New York Public Library digital ed. Schomburg Center for Research in Black Culture, Manuscripts, Archives and Rare Books Division, New York Public Library Digital Collections. Accessed October 2, 2020. http://digitalcollections.nypl.org/items/868f8db7-fa74-d451-e040-e00a180630a7.

Whalan, Mark. "'The Only Real White Democracy' and the Language of Liberation: The Great War, France, and African American Culture in the 1920s." In *Paris, Capital of the Black Atlantic: Literature, Modernity, and Diaspora*, edited by Jeremy Braddock and Jonathan P. Eburne, 52–77. Baltimore: Johns Hopkins University Press, 2013.

Wilkerson, Isabel. *The Warmth of Other Suns: The Epic Story of America's Great Migration*. New York: Random House, 2010.

Willis, Deborah, ed. *Black Venus 2010: They Called Her "Hottentot."* Philadelphia: Temple University Press, 2010.

Willoughby, Vanessa. "Applauding the Bootylicious Feminism of Beyonce and Josephine Baker." *Bitch Media*, March 10, 2014. https://www.bitchmedia.org/post/the-bootylicious-feminism-of-beyonce-and-josephine-baker.

Wood, Ean. *The Josephine Baker Story*. London: Sanctuary, 2000.

Young, Lola. *Fear of the Dark: "Race," Gender, and Sexuality in the Cinema*. London: Routledge, 1996.

Yursik, Patrice Grell. "28 Moments in Black Beauty History: Josephine Baker's ZouZou." *Afrobella*, February 1, 2013. http://www.afrobella.com/2013/02/01/28-moments-in-black-beauty-history-josephine-baker-zouzou/.

INDEX

189

TERRI SIMONE FRANCIS is Associate Professor and Director of the Black Film Center/Archive at Indiana University. Francis is a scholar of Black film and critical race theory whose work involves archival research, cultural history, and visual analysis, framed within the vicissitudes of performance and representation. She published her research on Jamaican nontheatrical films as "Sounding the Nation: Martin Rennalls and the Jamaica Film Unit, 1951–1961" in *Film History* in 2011, and she was guest editor for a close-up on Afrosurrealism for *Black Camera* in 2013. Her essays appear in *Transition* and *Another Gaze*.

Printed and bound by CPI Group (UK) Ltd, Croydon, CR0 4YY

24/06/2024

14519388-0001